THE WHITE HOUSE CHEF COOKBOOK

RENÉ VERDON

THE White House Chef COOKBOOK

1968

DOUBLEDAY & COMPANY, INC.

GARDEN CITY, NEW YORK

Library of Congress Catalog Card Number 68–10570

Printed in the United States of America
First Edition

Respectfully dedicated
to our late President
John Fitzgerald Kennedy
and to
Mrs. Kennedy, Caroline and John
with gratitude for giving
me the happiest years of
my life

ACKNOWLEDGMENTS

THIS BOOK has been a true labor of love for me and I am delighted to have "on the record" the recipes I think most homemakers would enjoy.

I should like to express my thanks to you, my readers, because in a very real sense it was you who practically ordered me to write this book when I lectured on food preparation throughout the United States.

Since I am a relatively new American, and English is not my native language, I called upon my good friend, Dr. Lewis Benton, well-known author, personnel executive and gourmet, to assist me. I am grateful to him for the many hours he gave me and for his unvarying cheerful patience in helping with the preparation and checking of the manuscript. I also wish to express warm appreciation to his lovely wife, Fran Benton, whose delicious cooking played a part in this book. I shall always remember with pleasure the many delightful weekends I spent at the Benton home in Long Island, as we tested recipes.

I am especially grateful to Mrs. Betty Sullivan for her many helpful suggestions and comments.

My dear friends, Jean Vergnes, Raymond Richez and Raymond Vaudard, all of whom are chefs of the first rank, assisted me greatly by testing my recipes, as did Mrs. Grayce Dicker and Mrs. Roberta Block, who also lent their fine cooking skills to testing my creations.

My thanks go to Mrs. Joy Brown for assisting with the typing of the recipes.

Finally, a kiss on the cheek to Miss Clara Claasen, my editor at Doubleday, for true devotion to this task beyond the call of duty.

CONTENTS

Recipes followed by an asterisk may be located by referring to the Index.

COLOR PHOTOGRAPHS

Pâté de Faisan Truffe en Crout
(Pâté of Pheasant in Crust with Truffles)

Turbotin à la Duglère (Halibut Duglère)

Old-fashioned Boiled Chicken Dinner

Purée Favorite. Rack of Lamb Jacqueline with Mint Sauce
Pommes Dauphine (Dauphine Potatoes)

Asparagus with a Variety of Sauces: Maltaise,
Hollandaise, Vinaigrette, and Melted Butter

Mousse of Ham and Maître Jean's Caesar Salad

Floating Island and Madeleines

Gâteau d'Abricot à l'Orange (Orange-flavored Cheesecake with Apricots)
and Parfait aux Framboises Noyau (Champagne Parfait with Raspberries)

INTRODUCTION

AS I travel about your beautiful country these days, talking about food in my new role as a culinary consultant, people often ask me, "How did you become a chef?"

Possibly they think I do not look like a chef when I appear without the tall white cap which is my badge of office, and without a tasting spoon in my hand. To them I may look like a businessman, and in a way they are right. A chef's business is food, and in his kitchen he is running a small business of which he is the boss, as far as the staff is concerned.

Yet it is a good question. How *did* I become a chef? What was the road that led me from my native village in the south of France to the White House kitchen, where I have had the privilege of cooking for two Presidents of the United States?

It was, I believe, the superb aroma of freshly baked bread from the ovens of my father's bakery that first gave me the idea that preparing food might also be for me a life's work. Of a certainty, I was far enough from the White House at the time, living in my native Pouzauges, a town of about six thousand people lying forty-five miles south of Nantes. I was born there in 1924, and grew up in a pleasant, uneventful way, blessed with kind parents who were lovers of good food. We always ate well. My father was fond of quoting Epicurus, especially his dictum that "the fountain and root of every good is the pleasure of the stomach." Father was a competent cook, but he was happy to defer to my mother in the kitchen, since he had to admit that she was more proficient, and in any case he was too busy in his bakery.

My twin brothers must have smelled father's bread and come to the same conclusion that I did. One also became a baker, and the other a fine pastry cook. Our sister, the youngest child, was content to devote her cooking talents to the pleasure of her husband, a well-known veterinarian in France. I am the only one of the family to leave the homeland. Sometimes they write to me jokingly as "the French national hero."

My own hero as I grew up was Escoffier, perhaps the best chef of them all. I knew he had begun his apprenticeship at thirteen, and when I was that old it seemed natural to me to follow his footsteps. It was not a difficult choice. The possibility of a career in gastronomy was already far more attractive to me than anything suggested by my schoolbooks.

There was no opposition at home. Indeed, my parents were very pleased, and encouraged me in every way. Father had only one word of advice to me about jobs: "If you don't like it, quit." He had the conviction that a man must like his work in order to be productive and creative. I remembered his words years later when it came time for me to think about leaving the White House.

I was fortunate enough to begin my three-year apprenticeship in a splendid provincial restaurant, the Restaurant Laperouse, of Nantes. I applied in the company of several other boys, but I was chosen because I was so plainly eager to become a chef. No one could have been more enthusiastic about the prospect than I.

It was hard and very demanding work, but I loved it. The chef and his staff at Laperouse taught me how to hold a knife, the proper method of washing and peeling vegetables, and how to keep the kitchen neat and orderly. Three mornings a week I tumbled out of bed before daylight to go with the boss to market at 4 A.M., learning how he bought vegetables, meat, fish and chicken. My contribution to the expedition was to carry two heavily laden baskets back to the restaurant. The day ended at about 11 P.M., or even later, when everything was put away and the kitchen cleaned up.

Usually there was time to rest in the afternoons, unless I was being punished for making a mistake. For minor offenses I would have to peel mountains of potatoes. Anything more serious, like permitting something to burn, was rewarded by a slap or a kick. But I did not resent these punishments because I was already enough of a chef to think that carelessness in the kitchen was a crime. Occasionally, however, I might conclude that the punishment was unjust, and I would discuss the matter with my father, who always told me I had to decide for myself whether I wanted to continue. There was no thought of quitting on my part. I was learning how to do the work I believed I was born to do, and I was happy.

From being a lowly apprentice to emerging at last as a chef means performing many tasks in a kitchen, and I have done them all in my twenty-eight years of experience in cooking. There is no way to become a real chef without such training. In this classic approach, it is considered almost unheard of to be appointed an Executive Chef before one is thirty-five, yet that was the honor which came to me.

I was employed at the Essex House in New York when my name first was brought to the attention of the Kennedy family, through one of those devious paths by which men are led to change their lives. One of my friends was Chef Roger Fessaguet, of that fine New York restaurant, La Caravelle, and he had often spoken of me to his employers, Robert Meyzen and his partner, Mr. Decre. The Kennedys often dined at La Caravelle, and one night Joseph P. Kennedy asked Mr. Meyzen and Mr. Decre if they could recommend a chef to cook for his son, the President. They recommended me.

That was in February, 1961. Soon after, I was invited to come to the Map Room of the White House, where I was met by Mrs. Kennedy and her secretary, Miss Letitia Baldridge, who interviewed me thoroughly but courteously. I gave Mrs. Kennedy the details of my professional experience, which by this time included such kitchens as Le Castelet, in Chatelaillon, France; Le Ronceray, Le Calvados and Cercle Hausmann, all in Paris; the Normandy Hotel, in Deauville, where King Farouk had often dined; the S. S. Liberté; and most recently in New York, the Carlyle Hotel and the Essex House.

Mrs. Kennedy listened carefully, nodding her approval as she heard these names, and finally told me that my qualifications would be carefully considered, and I would be informed soon about the results.

Then, in a few days, my life was given the exhaustive examination which was necessary for one who would be so close to the President. The Secret Service and the FBI explored my schools, my places of employment, my associations and my friends. Every place I had ever been, both in Europe and the United States, was carefully checked. About a month later, Mrs. Kennedy's social secretary called to offer me the position of White House chef. There could be no question of refusing so great an honor. I accepted with much happiness and pride.

My new career began on March 25, 1961. Moving from the Essex House to the White House was in itself the most tremendous step I had ever taken in my life. It was, I thought, the pinnacle of my life and I could scarcely wait to begin.

For one about to establish himself in so exalted a position, my entry into Washington was somewhat less than triumphal. I arrived by bus, carrying my possessions in two suitcases, and took a cab to the maintenance entrance of the White House. I was gratified to see that when I mentioned my name at the gate, it was obvious I was expected. The guard consulted his list, and my name was on it. A White House usher, Mr. Scouten, came to greet me and shook my hand cordially. This warm welcome made me feel more at home in the somewhat awesome atmosphere of America's presidential residence, where I had never expected to find myself living.

Mr. Scouten led me to the place which would be my home for the next five fascinating years. It was a comfortable room on the top floor of the White House, just above the floor where the Kennedys resided. It contained a television set, a radio, a telephone, a single bed and one chair, a chest of drawers and an adequate clothes closet. There was also a sprinkler system in the ceiling, something I had never before seen in a bedroom.

There were other facilities on the top floor, I discovered. They included a solarium, a terrace, a greenhouse, and a school classroom area for the children, with a bathroom for them. About a year later the floor acquired another tenant, Ferdinand Louvat, a highly skilled pastry chef, who was added to the staff at my request. He was still at the White House as this was written.

There were a number of formalities after I had unpacked my clothing. Mr. Scouten took me to the Secret Service offices in the Executive Office Building, where I was fingerprinted and had a color picture taken for my White House pass, which I had to sign at once.

By the time I had finished, it was too late to eat in the White House that day, so I had dinner in a nearby restaurant. But I did not mind dining alone. I was too occupied in wondering about the next day and what it might bring. I must confess that I felt a certain amount of anxiety about whether I would be able to please the Kennedys. It was well known that they were sophisticated people who were discriminating in their food tastes. I had some confidence, however, because for many years I had cooked for international celebrities. Consequently, I slept well that night and, completely refreshed, went down to the kitchen at 8 A.M. for my first inspection of its facilities.

Miss Baldridge came in about an hour later to see me. Fortunately, she spoke French very well, because my English at that time still suffered from many infirmities. Miss Baldridge was very kind and made me feel at ease. It was not long before I was calling her "Tish," as everyone else did.

She took me to Mrs. Kennedy, who also gave me a cordial welcome in fluent French. We discussed the menus for that day, and my ideas were requested. Later, I gave her my suggested menus every morning when she came to the kitchen. I found her attentive and knowledgeable about food. She was especially interested in the children's menus, always trying to make their food varied, interesting and nutritious. She told me she wanted them to get used to eating every kind of food, and not restrict themselves to a few dishes, as so many children do.

Tish introduced me to other members of the White House staff, including Vice-Admiral George Burkley and Janet Travell, the President's physicians; Pierre Salinger, his Press Secretary; Pamela Turnure, Mrs. Kennedy's personal secretary; Mrs. Walker, who had been housekeeper for eighteen years, and is now retired; Mrs. Evelyn Lincoln, the President's secretary, who was particularly charming; George Thomas, his valet; and Mrs. Providencia Paredes, Mrs. Kennedy's personal maid.

Later in the day, Maud Shaw, the Kennedy children's nursemaid, brought Caroline to the kitchen. She was three at the time—a bright, lovely little pixie. Miss Shaw took me to the nursery and showed me the other member of the family, little John, then only four months old.

I did not have the honor and privilege of meeting the President until the following day, when Mrs. Kennedy brought him to the kitchen. As you may imagine, it was a moment of my life I shall never forget. He shook hands with me, friendly and smiling. I was delighted when he did his best to speak to me in French. Mrs. Kennedy smiled at his efforts.

For him and the family I prepared my first White House meal. This was the menu:

BOULA-BOULA SOUP*

ROAST LEG OF LAMB

ROAST POTATOES

PURÉE CARROTS CORN ON THE COB

MIXED SALAD

CHEESE

CHOCOLATE CHIFFON MOUSSE WITH WHIPPED CREAM

After that meal there followed five happy and eventful years for which I shall always be grateful. Both the Presidents whom I served, and their families, were gracious and considerate, and I count it a high privilege to have served them. Particularly, I recall the heartwarming personal notes, in French, handwritten by Mrs. Kennedy to express her appreciation for some dish I had prepared. President Kennedy was also extremely generous with his appreciative comments. I shared the grief of America when he was so suddenly taken away from us. I had known him as a man full of life and laughter, of wisdom and charm. I had seen him as a kind and loving husband and father. His death struck all of us on the staff as a deep and personal loss.

Not long afterward, when I left the White House, I did not know at once what to do. After five such years, climaxed by so great a tragedy, one did not know where to turn. But I was gratified and flattered to receive offers from many famous hotels and restaurants everywhere in the world. After considering them, I concluded to accept the invitation of the Hamilton Beach Division of the Scovill Manufacturing Company, to act as their Culinary Consultant.

Does this seem an odd turn of affairs for a chef, one who had spent most of his life in *haute cuisine* kitchens? Perhaps, but I have found it most rewarding. My work involves extensive travel everywhere in the country, which I find always fascinating, and my task is to show homemakers that it is not necessary to be a French chef to prepare fine food in their own kitchens. Eventually, a demonstration kitchen will be built in New York to test recipes and illustrate fine table service for the average American home, because it is truly said that real gourmet cooking must be attractive to the eye as well as to the palate.

I have been delighted by the large crowds attending my talks and demonstrations. It is as good for my ego as I hope my advice will be for the palates of my listeners. Thousands of women have asked me when I was going to publish my own cookbook, and it is in answer to these requests that this volume came to be. It is my sincere hope that these pages will convince every woman who reads it that *haute cuisine* is possible for her, that it is not too complicated and expensive and time-consuming, and that even working wives can be chefs in the grand manner. I will remind them here again, as I do often, that if the ingredients are fresh and good and the approach is confident, the best results can be achieved.

In this book I think they will find much to intrigue them in planning their meals. While many of the dishes are classic French preparations, all of them are quite workable in the average American kitchen, and I have been careful to make them so. The recipes, including those I used in the White House kitchen, have been served to world-famous people, and they have also been much enjoyed by my friends, which is perhaps the best test. A lady in the kitchen anywhere will find it practical to prepare these dishes herself. My best wishes to her, for happy cooking and good eating.

THE WHITE HOUSE CHEF COOKBOOK

APPETIZERS & HORS D'OEUVRES

BEFORE I spread out a table of appetizers which I hope will please you, may I begin with some appetizers of my own, so to speak.

I have discovered that people are not only immensely curious about my experiences in cooking for the Kennedys, but they also want to know what it was like to work in the White House kitchen.

It was, of course, in some respects a kitchen unlike any in which I had ever presided. That is to say, the equipment was substantially the same, but the requirements were different. There was, in addition, a staff kitchen with four cooks, to feed the fifty or so people on the White House staff.

The official nature of the President's entertaining called for all kinds of precautions. One always had to be careful, for example, about the use of garlic, since people were going to be breathing in each other's faces all evening. I had to be sparing, too, in the use of cucumber because it is hard to digest, and Mrs. Kennedy was ever watchful of her husband's digestion, not to mention what it might do to distress the guests. For the reasons I have just mentioned, I also had to be sparing with radishes and raw onions.

There were always special dietary problems to be considered in the entertaining of foreign visitors, whose religious faith or other customs might forbid serving some kinds of food. Embassies, of course, were usually careful to give us advance warning by calling the White House social secretary and requesting special dishes.

It was also necessary to be prepared for emergencies. I recall the evening when a guest, for some unexplained reason, did not wish to eat what was served as an entree when it came to the table and asked for a steak instead. Mrs. Kennedy did not lose her composure, but quietly sent down the order to me, which I was able to fill quickly, since steaks were always at hand. I observed that this gentleman was not invited to the White House again.

One curious lady has asked me: "But, Monsieur Verdon, what did *you* eat? Did you have the same menu as the guests?"

Not at all, although if I had liked, it would have been perfectly possible. The staff had its own kitchen, and there I cooked for myself as I would if I had been at home anywhere else, buying in the morning what I fancied for that night.

It may surprise you to know that a French chef does not necessarily eat French cooking when he prepares food for himself. I like the food of every nation—regional and national dishes which naturally could not be prepared for the White House guests at a dinner party because they might not please everyone. It is presumed, and I suppose with truth, that everyone likes French cuisine, and, as a French chef, that is what I had been engaged to produce. My own meals might consist, for example, of couscous, the Middle Eastern dish of which I am extremely fond, or sauerkraut, or samplings from the cuisines of Japan, Mexico or China. On occasion I served myself with such simple, homely fare as corned beef and cabbage—a dish one could not imagine serving at the White House, although the President would surely have liked it if he were eating dinner alone, which he would never do unless he was ill in bed.

Mrs. Kennedy, too, had tastes as cosmopolitan as my own, since she is a traveled, cultured woman, but in the White House one thinks of the guests always, and under my regime the French cuisine prevailed, with some interesting American and other additions, as this book discloses. I might add that Mrs. Kennedy, who enjoyed most the classic cuisine of France, was especially fond of Spinach Soufflé,* Floating Island* dessert and pancakes soufflé. The President's tastes were somewhat heartier, when he was permitted to indulge them.

A word here in answer to questions I have often been asked about the names given to recipes, such as Stuffed Eggs Nanette,* Soufflé Victoire,* Spinach Casserole Suzanne,* Omelette Louis,* Shirred Eggs Albert* and all the others.

The answer, alas, is lost in the minds of the many chefs who created them. Sometimes they are named for friends—for example, Maître

Jean's Caesar Salad,* which you will find in the salad chapter. Maître Jean, former chef at the Colony Restaurant in New York, is my close friend, and this dish, my own version of the classic Caesar salad, is named for him. Others are named for long-forgotten wives or lady friends of the chefs who first prepared them. Occasionally they have a particular significance for the dish, as in the case of breast of pheasant St. Hubert, which refers to the sauce, a purée of chestnuts, served with the game and named appropriately in honor of St. Hubert, the patron saint of hunters.

I have had the honor to name several dishes for Mrs. Kennedy, such as Clams Jacqueline,* which simply salutes her love for clams and her special delight in this version of them.

Still other recipe names are related to the district from which the ingredients come, as in Eggplant Beau Rivage,* meaning that this dish was originally named in honor of that vegetable which came in such succulent quantity from the Beau Rivage region of France.

I must add a word about Quiche Lorraine.* First let me say that although you will sometimes find it made with crab meat and other such substitutes, it is not an authentic dish unless it is made with ham, bacon and cheese. It is an excellent thing to have for buffet dinners or luncheons. Many women who like it do not realize that it can also be made in very small sizes, no larger than tarts. Mr. Kennedy was very fond of the tiny *quiches* for his lunch. They make excellent appetizers at a party, too, and for a buffet they have the virtue that they can be made in advance and heated up just before serving.

So, then, to the first part of my book, the appetizers. I shall never again be able to think of hors d'oeuvres without remembering a conversation with Caroline. The Kennedy children were always a delight, and we saw much of them because they wandered about everywhere. Many important affairs at the White House were less formal because of their gay presence.

I remember that one day we had laid out platters of food and hors d'oeuvres and Caroline, who happened to be passing by, stopped to inspect these appetizers, which were intended for the luncheon delectation of the then Prime Minister of Great Britain, Harold Macmillan. Caroline was especially attracted by the caviar platters.

"What's that?" she inquired, with a child's charming directness.

"That is caviar, my dear," I told her. "It is the tiny eggs of a fish called sturgeon."

"May I have some, please?"

"Well," I cautioned, "most people don't like caviar the first time they taste it."

Caroline considered that formidable danger for a moment.

"Never mind, then," she decided. "I'll taste it the second time."

For more sophisticated palates than Caroline's, I give you the appetizer recipes which follow. Remember that the primary object of serving them is to awaken the appetites of your guests and stimulate the flow of their gastric juices. They should rouse the appetite, but not satisfy the hunger. In the preparation of appetizers, one might add, the chef experiences his greatest freedom to become creative.

For those who believe that the creations are threatened with disaster by drinking before dinner, I can only say it is true that drinking anything but wine dulls the palate, and the true gourmet will not dull his appreciation of a dinner by anesthetizing his senses beforehand. Nevertheless, we must accept as a fact of life that drinking both before and with the appetizers is more than a custom—it is a way of life in our society. We are not all gourmets, the food we eat is certainly far from being *haute cuisine* every day, and alcohol *is* a pleasant, relaxing stimulation at a social affair.

Presidents are no different from other people in the matter of drinking before dinner. President Kennedy, however, had no taste for the omnipresent martini, and also scorned the highball. What he did enjoy was a cold beer, and we always kept a good supply in the refrigerator off the small dining room. Mrs. Kennedy favored the daiquiri, and occasionally the President would ask for one too, but beer was his preference. His predecessors in the White House had different tastes. Mr. Eisenhower was a Scotch drinker, I was told by other staff members, while President Truman drank bourbon, and President Franklin D. Roosevelt was a highball drinker.

Do not worry, then, about your guests who drink before you serve them a splendid dinner. It can scarcely be avoided, and what is lost in gastronomy will be gained in conviviality. Appetizers, if they are really appetizing, will help to mitigate the effect of the alcohol. Here are some of my creations, to be served on a buffet table, or with cocktails, or as a first course.

ANCHOVY BUTTER (18 canapés)

½ cup anchovies (2 2-ounce cans)
½ cup unsalted butter, room temperature

Put all ingredients in blender container, cover and run on high speed until well combined and consistency of smooth paste. Chill until firm. Fill pastry or forcing bag with butter and decorate canapés.

CHEESE CANAPE (30 canapés)

¼ cup milk
1 8-ounce package cream cheese, diced, room temperature
1 3-ounce package blue cheese, crumbled, room temperature
½ teaspoon white pepper
¼ teaspoon salt
½ teaspoon Worcestershire sauce
3 to 4 drops Tabasco sauce
½ cup unsalted butter, room temperature
1 tablespoon chopped chives
3 sprigs of parsley

Put all ingredients into blender container; cover and run on high speed until smooth and well combined. If necessary, stop blender and push ingredients toward blades with rubber spatula. Chill mixture until thick. Fill pastry or forcing bag with mixture and decorate canapés.

CHICKEN CANAPES (5 dozen servings)

1 can (6 ounces) broiled mushrooms
2 cups very finely chopped cooked chicken
½ cup very finely diced celery
⅔ cup sour cream
1 teaspoon grated onion
½ teaspoon curry powder
½ teaspoon salt
*5 dozen small Pastry Shells**
cherry tomatoes

1. Drain and chop mushrooms very fine. Combine with chicken and celery.

2. Mix cream, onion, curry and salt in a 1-cup measure. Spoon over the chicken mixture and toss well.

3. Just before serving, spoon into shells. Use 1 teaspoon of mixture for each shell. Garnish with cherry tomatoes.

CUCUMBER CANAPES (3 to 4 slices per serving)

Cut unpeeled cucumbers into ¼-inch slices. Spread with creamed cottage cheese, top with slices of smoked salmon and garnish with capers.

EGG CANAPES (1 to 2 halves per serving)

Cut hard-cooked eggs in half crosswise. Top each with a spoonful of sour cream mixed with red or black caviar, and place a bit of unmixed caviar on top. Decorate with finely chopped parsley.

CANAPES LORRAINE (4 dozen servings)

1 teaspoon melted butter
1 heaping teaspoon flour
⅓ cup hot milk
1 teaspoon kirschwasser
⅓ pound sharp Cheddar, grated
1 egg, separated
4 dozen 1½-inch rounds thinly sliced white bread
paprika

1. To melted butter add flour, stirring. Gradually add hot milk and cook sauce over low heat, stirring constantly, until it is thick and smooth. Add kirschwasser and cheese and cook the sauce, stirring, until the cheese is melted.
2. Remove the pan from the heat, add egg yolk and mix thoroughly. Cool the mixture.
3. Fold in stiffly beaten egg white.
4. Toast rounds of bread. Mound 1 teaspoon of the cheese mixture on each round. Place rounds on a lightly buttered baking sheet. Dust with paprika. Broil until cheese puffs and is lightly browned.

HOT CREAM CHEESE CANAPES
(Approximately 3 dozen canapés)

1 large package cream cheese, room temperature
1 raw egg yolk
1 teaspoon grated onion
monosodium glutamate

1. Mix all ingredients thoroughly.
2. Spread on salted crackers and broil until puffed and golden.

NORWAY SARDINES MIMOSA (4 servings)

1 teaspoon lemon juice
1 tablespoon sour cream
1 teaspoon prepared mustard
*1 tablespoon Blender Mayonnaise**
1 teaspoon finely chopped onion (or shallot)
pinch freshly ground black pepper
few drops Tabasco
few drops Worcestershire sauce
salt to taste
4 slices toast
2 fresh tomatoes, sliced
2 3¾-ounce cans Norway sardines
1 hard-cooked egg, sieved
8 stuffed olives, sliced

1. Combine the first 9 ingredients and mix thoroughly. Spread the mixture on toast.

2. Top with sliced tomatoes, sardines and sprinkling of egg. Top with olive slices. Cut in triangles to serve.

CRAB MEAT ROYALE (6 servings)

1 pound crab meat
4 tablespoons melted butter
½ cup heavy cream
½ teaspoon dry mustard
1¼ teaspoons salt
¼ teaspoon white pepper
dash cayenne pepper
1 teaspoon Worcestershire sauce
½ cup grated Parmesan cheese
6 crab shells (optional)
3 tablespoons bread crumbs

1. Flake the crab meat, removing any cartilage. Mix with butter, cream, mustard, salt, pepper, cayenne, Worcestershire sauce and 4 tablespoons cheese, and toss lightly.

2. Divide among 6 crab shells or ramekins. Sprinkle with the remaining cheese and bread crumbs. Bake in a 400° F. oven for 10 minutes or until browned.

CRAB ST. GEORGE (3 servings)

1 can crab meat (7¾ ounces)
15 small clam shells or ramekins
2 slices bacon, finely diced
¼ cup chili sauce
*¾ cup Blender Mayonnaise**
2 drops Tabasco sauce
2 drops Worcestershire sauce

1. Flake the crab meat and discard any cartilage. Place in clam

shells or ramekins. Sprinkle with diced bacon. Place shells on a baking sheet. Bake in preheated oven at 450° F. until bacon is crisp and crab meat heated through.

2. Blend chili sauce into Mayonnaise. Add Tabasco and Worcestershire sauces. Spoon mixture over the crab meat, covering it entirely. Broil about 6 inches from source of heat until bubbly and browned lightly.

ROGER'S DEVILED CRAB MEAT (4 servings)

1 cup crab meat
½ tablespoon chopped parsley
½ tablespoon chopped chives
½ teaspoon chopped fresh tarragon, or ¼ teaspoon dried tarragon
Tabasco sauce to taste
salt and pepper to taste
*3 tablespoons Blender Mayonnaise**
1 teaspoon English mustard diluted with 1 teaspoon dry white wine
16 to 18 square or round crackers

1. Mix crab meat, parsley, chives, tarragon, Tabasco, salt and pepper together with Mayonnaise and mustard.

2. Spread on crackers and bake under broiler until brown.

AVOCADO AND CRAB MEAT COCKTAIL (6 servings)

2 small ripe avocados
½ teaspoon grated onion
2 teaspoons lemon juice
¼ teaspoon salt
Tabasco sauce
¾ cup tomato ketchup
2 tablespoons chili sauce
1 tablespoon prepared horseradish
½ teaspoon Worcestershire sauce
¼ teaspoon sugar
lettuce leaves
1 7-ounce can crab flakes or ½ pound fresh crab meat

1. Peel and mash a half of 1 avocado. Mix mashed avocado with the grated onion, 1 teaspoon lemon juice, ¼ teaspoon salt and Tabasco. Set aside in refrigerator.

2. Mix the ketchup, chili sauce, horseradish, Worcestershire sauce, sugar and 1 teaspoon lemon juice. Chill.

3. Line cocktail glasses with lettuce leaves. Peel and cut the re-

maining avocado in ½-inch cubes. Mix the avocado cubes and crab meat, and divide among the cocktail glasses. Pour the cocktail sauce over the crab flake mixture. Top with the avocado paste, prepared in step number 1.

AVOCADO COCKTAIL (1 cup sauce, 16 to 20 avocado balls)

½ cup ketchup
2 tablespoons lemon or lime juice
1 teaspoon Worcestershire sauce
½ teaspoon horseradish
dash of Tabasco sauce
1 teaspoon soy sauce or ¼ teaspoon salt
*1 tablespoon Blender Mayonnaise**
1 large ripe avocado

1. Combine all ingredients except avocado and mix thoroughly.
2. Scoop out small avocado balls and pour sauce over them. Chill thoroughly before serving.

COCKTAIL MUSHROOMS (Approximately 60 mushrooms)

1 clove garlic, minced
¼ cup olive oil
2 tablespoons wine vinegar
2 4-ounce cans whole mushrooms, drained

Combine first 3 ingredients and mix thoroughly. Pour over mushrooms. Store in tightly covered jar in refrigerator for 24 hours. Serve with cocktail picks.

COCKTAIL SKEWERS (20 servings)

2 tablespoons English mustard diluted with 2 tablespoons white wine (dry)
2 tablespoons melted butter
1 package (12 ounces) cocktail franks
20 small mushrooms, washed and drained

1. Combine mustard and butter. Sauté franks and mushrooms in this mixture over medium heat.
2. Thread 20 toothpicks with a frank and a mushroom on each.

RUMAKI (24 servings)
Chicken Livers and Bacon, Hawaiian Style

12 chicken livers
1 apple, pared and cut 1½ inches long and pencil thickness
12 slices bacon, cut in half
salt and pepper

1. Cut livers in half. Wrap liver and apple slices in bacon slices. Salt and pepper to taste.

2. Place on small skewer or wooden picks. Broil until bacon is crisp and livers cooked through.

ECUADOREAN SEVICHE (4 servings)
Cold Fish Cocktail

½ pound fresh halibut or whitefish
½ cup lemon juice
1½ teaspoons Worcestershire sauce
¼ teaspoon Tabasco sauce
1½ teaspoons salt
½ teaspoon coarse black pepper
⅛ cup tomato juice
3 fresh scallions, chopped
1 tomato, peeled, seeded and diced
Boston lettuce

1. Cut fish into ¼-inch cubes. Put lemon juice, Worcestershire sauce, Tabasco sauce, salt and pepper in bowl and mix with fish. Cool overnight in refrigerator.

2. One hour before serving, add tomato juice, scallions and tomato and mix thoroughly with macerated fish. Serve in sherbet glasses, on bed of Boston lettuce.

BLUE CHEESE AND WALNUT HAM ROLL
(Approximately 25 ham rolls)

½ pound blue cheese, room temperature
½ pound unsalted butter, room temperature
¼ cup coarsely chopped walnuts
2 tablespoons kirschwasser
2 pounds boiled ham, sliced thin

Beat cheese and butter until creamy. Beat in walnuts and kirschwasser; chill. Spread on ham slices and roll lengthwise. Cut into 3- or 4-inch lengths, according to slice of ham. Secure with a toothpick.

MUSHROOM ROLLS (12 to 14 rolls)

12 to 14 thin slices white bread
softened butter
½ pound fresh mushrooms, finely chopped
2 tablespoons melted butter
½ teaspoon curry powder
1 tablespoon lemon juice
½ teaspoon salt
dash of freshly ground black pepper
dash of cayenne pepper
additional melted butter

1. Remove the crusts from the bread slices and roll the slices to ⅛-inch thickness with a rolling pin. Spread the surface of each slice thinly with softened butter and set them aside.

2. Sauté the mushrooms until tender in 2 tablespoons melted butter with the curry powder and lemon juice. Add the salt, pepper and cayenne.

3. Spread about 1 tablespoon of this mixture over each slice of buttered bread. Roll like a jelly roll and fasten the ends with food picks. Place on baking sheets. Brush lightly with melted butter and bake in preheated oven (425° F.) until lightly brown, about 15 minutes.

ROQUEFORT ROLL (Approximately 5 dozen slices)

1 pound Roquefort cheese, room temperature
¼ pound butter, room temperature
½ pound cream cheese, room temperature
1 jigger cognac
2 tablespoons finely minced chives
chopped toasted almonds
round unsalted crackers

1. Mash Roquefort cheese, butter and cream cheese. Add cognac and chives and mix thoroughly. Chill slightly.

2. Form into a cylinder 1½ inches in diameter. Roll in almonds. Chill. Slice and serve on round unsalted crackers.

SAUMON EN BIERE (12 servings)
Salmon in Beer

3 pounds fresh salmon
½ cup chopped green pepper
½ cup chopped pimiento
1 cup lime juice
1½ cups beer
½ cup imported soy sauce
1 tablespoon fresh ginger, or
½ teaspoon ground ginger
1 clove garlic, mashed
2 tablespoons grated onion

1. Have salmon skinned and the bones removed. Slice salmon into thin strips, 3 to 4 inches long, cutting at an angle diagonally across the grain.

2. Spread salmon, green pepper and pimiento in a thin layer in a shallow pan. Combine lime juice and 1 cup beer and pour over the fish, completely covering all the slices. Marinate for several hours in the refrigerator. The fish should be opaque and pink.

3. Drain the salmon and rinse with cold water. Drain again.

4. Lay pieces of fish flat and place a little of the marinated pepper and pimiento on the end of each piece. Roll each piece and fasten with toothpicks.

5. Combine soy sauce, remaining ½ cup of beer, ginger, garlic and onion. Serve as a dip for salmon rolls.

CELERY STUFFED WITH CAVIAR
(Approximately 4 dozen pieces)

2 bunches celery
½ pound cream cheese, room temperature
1 tablespoon grated onion
⅓ cup chopped parsley
⅓ cup red caviar
salt and pepper

1. Use only inner stalks of celery. Wash thoroughly and dry.

2. Mix cream cheese with onion, parsley and caviar. Season to taste with salt and pepper. Stuff celery stalks with mixture, cut into 2-inch pieces and refrigerate.

CURRIED OLIVES (Approximately 18 servings)

1 can (9 ounces) ripe olives
½ teaspoon curry powder
1 teaspoon Worcestershire sauce

1. Pour liquid from can of olives into a small saucepan. Add curry powder and Worcestershire. Heat to boiling.

2. Pour over olives. Cover tightly and refrigerate for 24 hours.

GREEN PEPPERS WITH ANCHOVY SAUCE (6 to 8 servings)

6 tablespoons butter
½ cup olive oil
3 cloves garlic, finely chopped
2 2-ounce cans anchovies
2 tablespoons wine vinegar
6 large green peppers, cored, seeded and quartered

1. Heat the butter and oil in a saucepan and add the garlic and anchovies. Cook, stirring, for about 10 minutes. Stir in the vinegar.

2. Drop the peppers into boiling water to cover. Simmer, covered, for about 15 minutes. The peppers should remain firm. Drain.

3. Arrange the quartered peppers skin side down on a platter, and spoon the hot sauce into the center of each. Serve hot.

MARINATED MUSHROOMS AND ARTICHOKE HEARTS (16 to 20 servings)

2 packages frozen artichoke hearts
2 pounds small mushrooms
1½ cups water
1 cup cider vinegar
½ cup salad oil
1 clove garlic, halved
1½ tablespoons salt
½ teaspoon peppercorns
½ teaspoon dried thyme
½ teaspoon oregano

1. Cook artichoke hearts until just tender and drain.

2. Slice mushrooms in half through the stems. Combine with artichoke hearts.

3. Combine water with vinegar, oil, garlic, salt, pepper corns and herbs. Add vegetables and toss lightly.

4. Refrigerate, covered. Stir occasionally. Leave overnight. Drain before serving.

SESAME ARTICHOKES (Approximately 20 rounds)

1 can artichoke hearts
Melba rye or white rounds
¼ pound butter, melted
salt and freshly ground pepper to taste
garlic powder to taste (about ¼ teaspoon)
sesame seeds

1. Drain artichokes and cut each in half. Place each half, cut side up, on a Melba round. Arrange on an ovenproof dish.

2. To melted butter add salt, pepper and garlic powder and spoon generously into artichoke crevices, allowing some to run over the rounds.

3. Bake in preheated oven at 350° F. for 5 minutes. Just before serving, top with sesame seeds and brown under hot broiler for about 3 minutes.

MOUSSE ROUGE (4 to 6 servings)

1 tablespoon unflavored gelatin
2 tablespoons cold water
½ cup boiling water
1 tablespoon lemon juice
1 teaspoon Worcestershire sauce
*2 tablespoons Blender Mayonnaise**
1 pint sour cream
¼ teaspoon dry mustard
1 4½-ounce jar red caviar

1. Soften the gelatin in cold water, then dissolve it in boiling water. Add the lemon juice and Worcestershire and blend well.

2. In another bowl, blend the Mayonnaise and sour cream and quickly stir in the gelatin. Add the mustard and stir in the caviar. Pour the mixture into a 4-cup mold and chill until set. Unmold and serve with cocktail breads.

CHICKEN LIVER PATE (8 to 10 servings)

½ pound butter
1 pound chicken livers
½ clove garlic, finely minced
¼ small onion
⅛ teaspoon basil
2 tablespoons cognac
salt and pepper to taste

1. Melt ¼ pound of butter in a skillet. Sauté the livers quickly until brown on the outside but still pink in the middle (about 5 minutes).

2. Cool until butter just starts to set. Partly cover pan and turn livers several times to prevent darkening.

3. Place livers in blender. Add remaining butter, softened to room temperature, and remaining ingredients. Blend until smooth, pushing down with a spatula.

4. Adjust seasoning and put in a well-buttered 1-quart mold. Cover and refrigerate overnight.

PATE DE CAMPAGNE (20 servings)
Farmer's Pâté

3 pounds shoulder of pork
1 pound pork liver
1 medium onion, chopped
3 cloves garlic, chopped
1 tablespoon Parisienne spices (4 spices Marie), or 1 teaspoon sage combined with ½ teaspoon allspice, salt and freshly ground pepper to taste
2 tablespoons cornstarch
4 whole eggs
1 tablespoon salt
1 cup jellied consommé

1. Grind the meats, using the coarse blade of the meat grinder.

2. Combine the ground meats with all the remaining ingredients except the consommé, and mix thoroughly. Turn the mixture into a tureen or other earthenware jar and cover with aluminum foil.

3. Place in a pan of boiling water and bake for about 2½ hours in preheated oven at 350° F. Cool.

4. Place jellied consommé on top of pâté. Serve with unsalted crackers.

PATE DE FAISAN TRUFFE EN CROUT (25 servings) PLATE I

Pâté of Pheasant in Crust with Truffles

DOUGH FOR PÂTÉ

*2 pounds flour (8 cups)**
1 teaspoon salt
6 whole eggs
1 pound butter, room temperature
1½ cups water

* If there is dough left over, it can be frozen for future use.

Pour the flour on waxed paper and make an indentation in the center. Add salt, eggs, butter and water. Work with the hands until of rolling consistency.

PÂTÉ

2 pheasants, 2½ pounds each, boned
3 ounces cognac
1 teaspoon salt
¼ teaspoon white pepper
1 teaspoon Parisienne spices (4 spices Marie), or 1 teaspoon sage combined with ½ teaspoon allspice, salt and freshly ground black pepper to taste
2 pounds shoulder pork
4 whole eggs
2 dozen truffles

1. Cut the breast of pheasant in slices the size of French fried potatoes. Marinate overnight in the cognac with only a pinch of the salt, pepper and spice.

2. Grind the pork and the legs of the pheasants (bones removed), using the finest knife of a food grinder. Add the eggs, the remaining spices and the marinade to the pork.

3. Line the bottom and sides of a mold, 14 inches long, 4 inches wide and 4 inches high, with ¼ inch of dough. Make layers of the pork and pheasant to halfway mark of the mold. In the center make a row of the truffles. Continue with the layers of pork and pheasant to top, finishing with the pork. Cover with the dough and decorate with dough leaves (using pastry trimmings, cut out leaves with dough cutter in leaf shape). Make 2 holes approximately ¾

inch square and deep on top to let the steam out. Put the mold in a pan in order to avoid drippings in the oven, and bake in pre-heated oven at 350° F. for 3 hours.

Fill the holes with jellied consommé, cool, unmold and serve on a bed of lettuce leaves. May be spread on cocktail bread slices.

TURKEY PATE (8 to 10 servings)

2 cups ground cooked turkey
1 small onion, minced
2 hard-cooked eggs, minced
½ cup ground almonds
salt and pepper to taste
generous dash hot pepper sauce
2 tablespoons cognac
Blender Mayonnaise to bind*
truffles or olives for garnish

1. Combine all ingredients but Mayonnaise. Bind with mayonnaise until a stiff pâté is formed.

2. Place in a bowl and decorate with truffles or olives. Chill.

CHEESE AND KIRSCHWASSER SPREAD (1¼ cups)

4 ounces cream cheese, room temperature
¼ bar butter (2 tablespoons), room temperature
½ cup blue cheese, room temperature
2 teaspoons kirschwasser
salt and pepper to taste
celery
paprika

1. Combine cream cheese, butter, blue cheese, kirschwasser, salt and pepper. Stir well with a whisk until well blended.

2. Stuff celery with mixture and sprinkle with paprika.

CHEESE-BEER SPREAD (Approximately 1½ cups)

1 small Gouda or Edam cheese, room temperature
¼ pound unsalted butter, room temperature, cubed
¾ cup beer
½ teaspoon Worcestershire sauce
½ teaspoon dry mustard
1 tablespoon grated onion
rye bread rounds

1. Cut a 2-inch circle from the top of the cheese and reserve. Scoop out inside of cheese, leaving a shell ¼ inch thick.

2. Combine the cheese and the butter in a blender and blend on high speed until smooth.

3. Gradually add the beer, adding just enough to make a spreadable mixture. Mix in Worcestershire, mustard and onion. Stuff the cheese shell with the mixture. Cover with reserved top of cheese. Chill. Serve with rounds of rye bread.

COLD EGGPLANT APPETIZER (Approximately 1 pint)

1 small eggplant
½ cup chopped celery
⅓ cup chopped pimiento
1 clove garlic, minced
2 tablespoons chopped capers
2 tablespoons chopped parsley
⅛ teaspoon powdered dill
¼ teaspoon oregano
½ teaspoon salt
⅛ teaspoon pepper
⅓ cup salad oil
⅓ cup vinegar

1. Cook eggplant in boiling salted water about 20 minutes or until tender. Drain and cool. Peel and cut in 2-inch lengths.

2. Add remaining ingredients and mix thoroughly. Cover tightly and refrigerate.

EGGPLANT BEAU RIVAGE (12 servings)

2 large eggplants
2 teaspoons lemon juice
olive oil
salt and black pepper to taste
sour cream for garnish
rye bread slices

1. Cut eggplants in half lengthwise. Cut the pulp out of the shells of only 2 halves and brush hollow shells with lemon juice. Peel the other 2 halves. Cut all eggplant pulp into 1-inch-thick slices and broil until soft. Cut broiled eggplant into ½-inch cubes and measure the pulp.

2. Place eggplant and olive oil alternately in blender, using ½ cup olive oil for each 2 cups of eggplant. Blend for 10 seconds. Empty blender after each 2 cups of eggplant. Season with salt and pepper.

3. Chill very well. Pile into hollow shells. Garnish with sour cream. Serve with thin slices of rye bread cut into wedges.

EGGPLANT SPREAD, ATHENS STYLE (Approximately 3 cups)

2 eggplants, about 1½ pounds each
4 tablespoons olive oil
¾ cup sliced onions
1 cup sliced green peppers
2 cloves garlic, minced
1½ teaspoons salt
½ teaspoon freshly ground black pepper
½ cup yoghurt
black bread wedges

Peel the eggplants dice and sauté in the olive oil with the onions, green pepper and garlic until soft but not brown. Stir in the salt and pepper. Cool; mix in the yoghurt. Serve very cold on wedges of black bread.

HUNGARIAN CHEESE SPREAD (12 to 16 rounds)

1 3-ounce package cream cheese, room temperature
1 tablespoon capers
2 tablespoons caraway seeds
2 tablespoons sour cream
½ clove garlic, finely minced, or 1 teaspoon finely minced onion
rye bread rounds

Combine all ingredients except bread and beat well with a fork or electric mixer until well blended. Serve on rounds of rye bread.

NORMANDY ROQUEFORT SPREAD (1 cup)

½ cup Roquefort cheese, crumbled
½ cup butter, room temperature
2 tablespoons Calvados (French applejack)
Melba rounds

Combine all ingredients and mix thoroughly. Serve with Melba rounds.

POLYNESIAN CRAB SPREAD (1 quart)

2 cups sour cream
2 teaspoons curry powder
1 teaspoon onion powder
⅛ teaspoon black pepper
½ teaspoon salt
1 cup shredded coconut, chopped (optional)
½ pound crab meat, flaked

Combine all ingredients. Chill. Serve on crackers or Melba toast.

ROQUEFORT ARIADNE (1 cup)

¼ pound Roquefort cheese, room temperature
¼ pound cream cheese, room temperature
3 pickled walnuts, mashed
pumpernickel

Mash cheese together and add mashed walnuts. Mix thoroughly until it reaches spreading consistency. Serve with pumpernickel wedges.

SARDINE BUTTER NICOISE (1 cup)

1 6½-ounce can spiced truffled sardines
½ cup (1 stick) butter, room temperature
2 tablespoons lemon juice
½ teaspoon salt
dash of cayenne
pumpernickel

1. Mash the sardines with the oil in the can.
2. Blend with remaining ingredients. Serve with pumpernickel wedges.

SARDINE SPREAD (Approximately 1½ cups)

1 8-ounce package cream cheese, room temperature
1½ tablespoons lemon juice
1 can sardines, mashed
salt and freshly ground black pepper
¼ teaspoon onion juice
rye bread rounds

Mash the cream cheese. Beat in lemon juice and sardines. Season with salt, pepper and onion juice. Chill thoroughly. Serve with rounds of rye bread.

CAPER DIP (1 pint)

1 pint sour cream
1½ teaspoons prepared mustard
1½ teaspoons caraway seeds
1½ teaspoons paprika
1 tablespoon grated onion
2 tablespoons parsley
¼ teaspoon sugar
3 tablespoons capers
salt and pepper
unsalted crackers

Place all ingredients except last 2 in a blender container, cover and run on high speed until smooth. Chill. Add salt and pepper to taste. Serve with unsalted crackers.

CLAM DIP (Approximately 20 servings)

1 small can chopped clams
*4 tablespoons Blender Mayonnaise**
1 tablespoon lemon juice
salt to taste
Tabasco sauce
2 3-ounce packages cream cheese, room temperature
1 tablespoon chopped chives
1 tablespoon chopped olives
unsalted crackers

1. Drain the clams.
2. Mix the Mayonnaise and lemon juice; season with salt and Tabasco.
3. Mash cheese with a fork, then mix thoroughly with Mayonnaise.
4. Add the chives, olives and clams to the Mayonnaise and cheese and beat until well blended.
5. Chill and serve with unsalted crackers.

CRAB MEAT DIP (2 cups)

1 clove garlic, cut in half
⅓ cup cream
1 8-ounce package cream cheese, room temperature
1 cup crab meat
2 teaspoons lemon juice
1½ teaspoons Worcestershire sauce
dash salt and freshly ground pepper
unsalted crackers

1. Rub a bowl with cut garlic.
2. Gradually add the cream to the cream cheese in the bowl. Blend until smooth. Add remaining ingredients except crackers. Mix well and chill. Serve with unsalted crackers.

CREAM CHEESE AND AVOCADO DIP (1⅓ cups)

1 medium avocado
1 tablespoon lemon juice
2 3-ounce packages cream cheese, room temperature
¼ teaspoon minced onion
approximately 2 tablespoons milk
salt and pepper to taste

1. Peel avocado, remove pit, then cut into cubes. Sprinkle with lemon juice, then mash well with a fork.

2. With spoon, beat cream cheese until smooth and fluffy. Stir in onion, then avocado, blending well.

3. To avocado mixture add enough milk to make a good dipping consistency; add seasoning. Refrigerate.

SMOKED SALMON DIP (Approximately ¾ cup)

4 ounces smoked salmon, shredded
⅓ cup heavy cream
⅛ teaspoon freshly grated pepper
½ teaspoon capers

1. Place all ingredients in a blender and blend on high speed until smooth.

2. Grind extra pepper over top of dip. Serve with raw vegetables and crackers.

BAKED CLAMS HYANNISPORT (4 servings)

Named in honor of the town I visited many times with the Kennedy family.

24 clams
1 teaspoon shallots or green onions, chopped
1 tablespoon dry white wine
1 teaspoon chopped parsley
2 cloves garlic, chopped
½ bar (¼ cup) butter, room temperature
salt to taste
¼ teaspoon black pepper
1 tablespoon fresh bread crumbs
1 tablespoon grated Swiss cheese (imported)

1. Preheat oven to 400° F.

2. Open clams in half shell, arranging them in a large baking pan.

3. Simmer shallots with wine until ¾ evaporates. Combine parsley, garlic, butter, salt, pepper, bread crumbs and cheese. Mix with spatula to make a paste. Spread mixture on clams. Bake for about 10 minutes.

CLAMS JACQUELINE (8 servings)

48 clams
1 tablespoon chopped watercress
1 tablespoon chopped fresh spinach
1 teaspoon chopped parsley
1 teaspoon lemon juice
1 teaspoon Pernod or Richard Aperitif
1 bar (½ cup) butter, melted
salt to taste
black pepper to taste
dry bread crumbs

1. Open clams on half shell and arrange them in a large baking dish.

2. Mix water cress, spinach, parsley, lemon juice, Pernod, butter, salt and pepper. Spoon the mixture on every clam and sprinkle with bread crumbs. Bake in preheated oven (400° F.) for about 10 minutes.

QUICHE LORRAINE (6 servings per 9-inch pie shell)

CRUST (for 3 pastry shells)

4 cups flour
1¼ cups butter
1 teaspoon salt
2 eggs
½ cup cold water

1. Place flour, butter and salt into large bowl and work together with hands until smooth. Add eggs and water and work with hands until of rolling consistency.

2. Divide dough into 3 equal portions and refrigerate 2 portions for future use. Roll remaining pastry out on floured pastry board to about ¼ to ⅛ inch thick. Place pastry in a 9-inch pie tin and crimp edges. Refrigerate for 1 hour.

FILLING

8 strips bacon
½ cup diced Swiss cheese
¼ cup diced ham
1½ cups light cream
½ teaspoon salt
¼ teaspoon nutmeg
¼ teaspoon white pepper
4 eggs

1. Fry bacon until crisp, and drain. Crush bacon over the bottom of the pie shell.

2. Sprinkle Swiss cheese and ham over bacon in pie shell.

3. Place cream, spices and eggs in blender container; cover and run

on high speed until thoroughly mixed. Pour over bacon, cheese and ham in pie shell. Bake in preheated oven at 350° F. for about 30 minutes or until top is golden brown and mixture is set. Serve warm.

QUICHE OF SEA FOOD NEWBURG (4 to 6 servings)

1 tablespoon butter
1 cup crab meat
1 teaspoon paprika
2 tablespoons sherry wine
2 eggs
1 cup heavy cream
dash of Tabasco sauce
salt and pepper to taste
1 9-inch Pâté Brisée pie shell*

1. Preheat oven to 350° F.

2. In saucepan melt the butter. Sprinkle the crab meat with paprika and sauté in the butter. Add the sherry.

3. Beat the eggs well and add the cream. Pour over the crab meat. Season to taste with Tabasco, salt and pepper.

4. Pour mixture in a pie shell (Pâté Brisée 9-inch pie tin) and bake for about 20 minutes.

QUICHE PIPERADE BISCAYNE (4 to 6 servings)

2 tablespoons olive oil
1 small onion, sliced
1 green pepper, diced
2 cups tomatoes, skinned, seeded and diced
1 clove garlic, minced
1 tablespoon diced pimientos
½ cup diced smoked Virginia ham
salt and pepper to taste
3 eggs, well beaten
1 tablespoon chopped parsley
1 9-inch Pâté Brisée pie shell*

1. Preheat oven to 350° F.

2. In saucepan heat oil and add onion and green peppers. Sauté for 2 minutes. Add tomatoes, garlic, pimientos, ham, salt and pepper. Cook for 10 minutes.

3. Cool and add eggs and parsley.

4. Pour mixture into a pie shell and bake for 25 minutes.

CHEESE LOG (About 2 cups)

½ pound (2 cups) sharp American cheese, shredded
⅓ cup crumbled Roquefort cheese
½ clove garlic, very finely minced
¼ cup sour cream, approximately
⅛ teaspoon Tabasco sauce
¼ cup finely chopped ripe olives
½ cup finely minced parsley

1. Combine the cheeses, garlic and enough sour cream to bind them together. Add the Tabasco and olives.

2. Chill until firm enough to form into a long roll. Roll in parsley. Refrigerate. Slice and serve on rye bread rounds.

PALE GOLD CHEESE PASTRIES (64 pastries)

2 cups flour
1 teaspoon salt
1 cup cream of wheat
1 cup (2 sticks) butter, melted and cooled
6 tablespoons cold water
2 eggs
1 cup grated Cashkavall[1] cheese, packed
¼ teaspoon baking powder
sesame seeds

1. Combine flour, salt, cream of wheat, butter and water. Blend well with fork and let stand for 30 minutes.

2. Filling: Lightly beat 1 egg. Add to cheese and baking powder. Blend well. Let stand for 15 minutes.

3. Roll out dough ⅛ inch thick. Cut with a glass into 2½-inch circles.

4. Place ⅓ teaspoon cheese on ½ circle of dough, fold over and crimp with a fork.

5. Lightly beat other egg and brush over tops of cheese-filled pastry. Sprinkle with sesame seeds. Place on ungreased cookie sheets.

6. Bake for 20 minutes in preheated oven at 350° F. until pale gold.

[1] A hard yellow sheep or goat cheese with tangy flavor from Yugoslavia or Greece, also known as Cacioavallo in Italy. White Cheddar cheese may be substituted, but must be grated frozen.

BARBECUED MEAT BALLS (Sauce for 30 tiny meat balls)

½ cup chopped onion
½ cup chopped celery
½ cup chopped green pepper
¼ cup salad oil
½ cup ketchup
1 tablespoon brown sugar
1 teaspoon dry mustard
1 teaspoon A-1 steak sauce
½ cup beef broth
3 whole cloves
dash chili powder
salt and pepper to taste
*Meat Balls**

1. Sauté onion, celery and green pepper in oil until tender.
2. Add remaining ingredients except Meat Balls and simmer for 20 minutes.
3. Add tiny Meat Balls and simmer for 20 minutes.

CHEESE MEAT BALLS (Approximately 5 dozen balls)

1 pound ground lean chuck or round steak
½ cup fresh bread crumbs
⅓ cup crumbled Roquefort cheese
2 tablespoons finely chopped onion
¾ teaspoon salt
¼ teaspoon freshly ground black pepper
1 egg
3 tablespoons milk
butter

1. Combine all ingredients except the butter. Shape into balls about ¾ inch in diameter.
2. Brown the balls on all sides in hot butter. Serve hot on toothpicks.

MEAT BALLS SCANDINAVIAN (6 servings)

2 tablespoons butter
3 tablespoons minced onion
1 cup fresh bread crumbs
1 cup milk (or equal parts milk and cream)
¾ pound ground round steak
¼ pound ground veal
¼ pound ground pork
1 egg
salt and freshly ground pepper
chopped fresh parsley
¼ cup flour
¾ cup cream or milk

1. Melt butter and sauté onions until golden brown. Soak bread

crumbs in milk; add meat, egg, onion, salt, pepper and parsley and mix thoroughly. Shape into balls about 1½ inches in diameter and roll in flour. Reserve 1 tablespoon of flour.

2. Melt enough additional butter in skillet to cover bottom of pan, and brown meat balls over medium heat. Shake pan occasionally to keep round shape of meat balls. Remove to serving dish and keep warm. Reserve pan juices.

3. Combine reserved flour with cream and stir gradually into pan juices, using wire whisk. Simmer for 5 minutes, stirring occasionally. Pour gravy over meat balls and serve hot.

SOUTH SEA ISLAND MEAT BALLS

(Approximately 16 meat balls or 4 to 5 servings)

1 cup soft bread crumbs
1 teaspoon salt
⅛ teaspoon black pepper
½ cup chopped onion
½ cup milk
3 teaspoons soy sauce
1 pound ground beef
¼ cup sugar
1½ tablespoons cornstarch
¼ teaspoon ground ginger
1 cup pineapple juice
2 tablespoons vinegar
1 tablespoon butter
1 8-ounce can water chestnuts, drained and cut into ¼-inch slivers
2 1-pound cans bean sprouts
1 cup coarsely chopped green pepper

1. Combine bread crumbs, salt, pepper, half the onion, milk, 2 teaspoons soy sauce and the ground beef. Form into balls, using about 2 tablespoons of the mixture for each.

2. Place meat balls in a shallow baking pan and bake in preheated 350° F. oven for about 30 minutes or until browned.

3. Combine sugar, cornstarch and ginger. Add pineapple juice, vinegar, remaining soy sauce and butter. Cook over low heat until thickened, stirring constantly. Add water chestnuts and heat.

4. Combine bean sprouts, remaining onion and green pepper. Simmer until onion is tender. Drain off liquid. Spoon bean sprout mixture on plates, top with meat balls and pour sauce over meat balls.

SWEET AND SOUR MEAT BALLS YVETTE

5 ounces prepared mustard
10 ounces currant jelly
7 ounces ketchup
2 ounces soy sauce
Tabasco sauce to taste
Meat Balls (using 1½ pounds raw beef)*

Combine all ingredients except Meat Balls in a large saucepan and heat until smooth. Add Meat Balls and simmer for ½ hour.

Approximately 1½ pints sauce for about 45 cocktail-size meat balls.

SWEET AND SOUR MEAT BALLS YVONNE

1 cup currant jelly
½ cup prepared mustard
*Meat Balls**

Combine jelly and mustard in a large saucepan. Heat and cook until smooth. Add Meat Balls and simmer for ½ hour. Sauce will be thick.

Approximately 1½ cups sauce for about 30 cocktail-size meat balls.

SWEET AND SOUR MEAT BALLS YOLANDE

1 1-pound can cranberry sauce
1 12-ounce jar chili sauce
1 onion, minced
water to fill cranberry can and chili jar
Meat Balls (using 2 pounds raw beef)*

Combine all ingredients except Meat Balls in a large saucepan, cover and simmer 45 minutes. Add Meat Balls and simmer for ½ hour.

Approximately 1 quart sauce for about 60 cocktail-size meat balls.

COOKED SHRIMP (4 servings)

For cocktails or salads

1 quart water
½ stalk celery, sliced
1 carrot, sliced
1 small white onion, sliced
juice of half a lemon
1 teaspoon salt
½ teaspoon pepper
1 pound shrimp

1. Boil all ingredients except shrimp for 15 minutes.

2. Add shrimp and simmer, covered, 2 to 5 minutes, or until they turn pink. Drain; cool, shell and devein. Refrigerate until serving time.

SHRIMP FOR HORS D'OEUVRES (8 to 10 servings)

2 pounds shrimp, cooked, shelled and deveined
*1 cup Blender Mayonnaise**
¼ cup salad oil
3 heaping tablespoons chili sauce
1 teaspoon celery seed
1 clove garlic, minced
½ medium onion, chopped fine
1 stalk of celery with leaves, chopped
2 strings of dill, chopped

Combine all ingredients. Marinate overnight. Serve on small plates.

SKEWERED SHRIMP AND BACON (18 pieces)

18 fresh or frozen shrimp, shelled and deveined
2 tablespoons olive oil
1 tablespoon lemon juice
salt and pepper to taste
paprika to taste
18 small strips bacon

1. Marinate shrimp in oil, lemon juice and seasoning for several hours.

2. Wrap each shrimp in bacon strip. Secure with wet toothpick or small skewer. Broil, turning often, until bacon is crisp and shrimp are bright pink.

DEVILED EGGS FLORENCE (8 egg halves)

4 hard-cooked eggs
1 tablespoon caviar
3 or 4 teaspoons lemon juice
*2 teaspoons Blender Mayonnaise**
2 teaspoons chopped parsley

1. Cut eggs in half lengthwise. Remove yolks and mash very fine. Combine egg yolks with caviar, lemon juice, Mayonnaise and parsley, mixing well.

2. Fill the egg whites with egg yolk mixture.

SOUPS

WE COME now to the soup, by which, it has often been said, a restaurant may be truly judged. One wonders what miracles with soup—or disasters, as the case may be—were performed in people's homes before restaurants could set such a standard. There were almost no restaurants in Paris only two hundred years ago, but it is encouraging to note that one which is known to have existed in 1765 served *only* soups. It must have set a good example. Only thirty years later, there were more than five hundred restaurants in business, serving the whole formidable variety of foods and wines for which Paris is known today everywhere in the world.

Soup was a dish close to the heart of President Kennedy, since it gave him an opportunity to be served the fish for which his New England background had given him a special appreciation. He dearly loved Boston clam chowder, and asked me to prepare it for him on many occasions.

I remember particularly a time when he asked for it three days in succession, during the course of meetings with the Prime Minister of Canada, Lester Pearson, at Hyannisport. I knew Mr. Pearson must share the President's enthusiasm for clam chowder when he asked me for the recipe, after eating it the first day. It was not surprising, then, when both the President and Mr. Pearson requested it next day, but I was truly astonished when they wanted me to make it again on the third day. I cannot remember preparing any other dish which had such consecutive popularity.

It was not so easy, however, to satisfy them a third time. In the midst of my preparations for luncheon that day, it was decided to transfer the meeting from the home of the President's father, Joseph P. Kennedy, to the house of the President. Of course that meant moving food, and pots and pans, but we were not dismayed by this task, although admittedly it was upsetting. For a chef, it was far more disturbing to be told soon afterward that the number of guests would be fifteen instead of the six we had planned for, and that the luncheon was to begin at 12:30 instead of 1 P.M.

We were whirling dervishes in the kitchen that day. I am happy to say that the first course was ready with fully eight seconds to spare. Even the soufflé came out exactly right, and that is always a precarious preparation in the best of circumstances.

Our accomplishment did not pass unnoticed. It was characteristic of Mr. Kennedy to come into the kitchen afterward and express his appreciation for what we had done. He was always ready to compliment someone for what he considered to be a good professional job. He made it easier for people to perform well by being very clear and decisive about how he wanted things done. Always he was the leader in his manner, but always he was gentlemanly and considerate.

I did everything I could to satisfy Mr. Kennedy's New England liking for good fish cookery. Quite naturally, as a Catholic, he had it every Friday, but when I traveled with him to places where an especially fresh supply was at hand, I was able to do my best. Boston and Hyannisport, as one would suppose, were ideal. I suspect the President also would have liked to have had another favorite, Boston baked beans, served to him in the White House, but as I have pointed out, the demands of a more formal cuisine would not permit it.

My recipes for soups begin herewith, and included is the one for New England Clam Chowder, South-of-Boston Style,* which so delighted the President and Mr. Pearson for three days in a row. I would like to think it played its own small part in improving international relations. At least it could not have hurt them.

NOTE: For easy reference, these soups are grouped in three categories —hot, cold and those which may be served either way.

HOT SOUPS

ALSATIAN CORN CHOWDER (10 servings)

⅛ pound salt pork, diced small
1 large onion, sliced
4 cups diced potatoes
*4 cups Chicken Broth**
4 cups light cream, scalded
3 cups fresh corn kernels, cooked
pepper to taste
dash of Tabasco

1. Render salt pork. Remove when crisp and browned and keep warm.
2. In the fat remaining in pan sauté the onion slices until they are tender. Add potatoes and Broth and cook for about 10 minutes or until potatoes are tender. Add scalded cream and corn kernels, the reserved pork, pepper and Tabasco.
3. Heat thoroughly over low heat.

BILLI-BI (6 to 8 servings)
Mussels Cream Soup

2 quarts mussels
1 cup dry white wine
5 or 6 sprigs of parsley
2 bay leaves
2 cloves garlic
1 pint milk
6 egg yolks
1 cup heavy cream
1 tablespoon butter

1. Steam mussels in skillet with wine, parsley, bay leaves and garlic. Cover skillet and place over hot fire until mussels start to open. Strain the mussels, saving the cooking stock, and let stand awhile.
2. Trim and discard horny beard from the mussels.
3. Transfer stock into a saucepan very gently, retaining only the clear portion and discarding the sediment. Add the mussels and the milk; bring to the boiling point. Pour in egg yolks, cream and butter. Heat but do not let boil.

BOUILLABAISSE MARSEILLAISE (see Fish Chapter, page 83.)

BOULA-BOULA (4 servings)

American Soup

- *2 cups green peas, freshly shelled*
- *2 cups canned green turtle soup*
- *1 tablespoon unsalted butter*
- *salt and pepper to taste*
- *1 cup sherry*
- *½ cup whipped cream, unsweetened*

1. Cook peas in salted boiling water until just tender, and drain. Put them into a blender with ½ cup turtle soup to make purée.

2. Place mixture in a saucepan, add butter, salt and pepper and blend in remaining turtle soup. Add sherry and heat just under the boiling point.

3. Pour the soup into serving cups and add a dollop of whipped cream. Place under broiler to brown the topping. Serve at once.

CABBAGE SOUP A LA RUSSE (4 servings)

- *½ pound lean beef*
- *½ pound fat pork*
- *1 large head white cabbage, shredded*
- *1 large tomato, quartered*
- *1 onion, sliced*
- *5 cups water*
- *1 bay leaf*
- *2 teaspoons salt*
- *¼ teaspoon pepper*
- *sour cream*

1. Combine meats and vegetables and add water. Add seasonings and simmer slowly for several hours or until meat is tender.

2. Remove meat from soup, cut into slices and serve with soup. Garnish soup with sour cream.

CHICKEN BROTH (1 quart)

- *1 stewing chicken, about 4 pounds*
- *1 onion stuck with 2 cloves*
- *1 stalk of celery*
- *1 sprig of parsley*
- *3 carrots*
- *1 bay leaf*
- *pinch of thyme*
- *salt and pepper to taste*

1. Wash the fowl. Place it in a large kettle and add the onion, celery, parsley, carrots, bay leaf, thyme, salt and pepper. Pour water

in kettle to cover fowl. Cover kettle and bring to a boil. Reduce heat and simmer gently for 2 hours.

2. Remove the fowl from the broth and cut the meat from the bones. (The cooked chicken meat may be used for salads.) Return the bones to the broth and simmer for another ½ hour.

CHICKEN SOUP FLANDERS (6 to 8 servings)

4-pound stewing chicken, whole
½ lemon
2 medium onions
4 cloves
½ cup diced celery
3 leeks, minced
½ cup diced carrots
1 tablespoon minced parsley
1 sprig thyme
1 bay leaf
2 teaspoons salt
¼ teaspoon pepper
2 cups dry white wine
parsley for garnish

1. Clean chicken, rub thoroughly with lemon and place in a large kettle. Add water to half cover chicken and heat to boiling.

2. Peel onions, leaving them whole, and insert 2 cloves in each onion; add to chicken with remaining ingredients except parsley. Cover kettle and simmer slowly until chicken is tender.

3. When ready to serve, remove chicken from broth and carve it, placing the carved pieces in a soup tureen. Cover with broth and garnish with parsley. Serve at once.

CHICKEN OYSTER GUMBO, SOUTHERN STYLE (8 servings)

2½- to 3-pound stewing chicken, cut up
1 pound lean beef, cubed
1 cup diced okra
2 dozen oysters
2 teaspoons salt
⅛ teaspoon pepper
1 onion, sliced
1 tablespoon fat
1½ teaspoons file (powdered sassafras)

1. Cook chicken with beef and okra in water. When broth is strong and meat is tender, remove chicken, cut meat from bones into small pieces and return to stock.

2. Add oysters with their liquor, and season to taste with salt,

pepper and onion browned in the fat. Cook until edges of the oysters curl.

3. Add file, mix thoroughly and serve immediately.

CHICKEN SHERRY CREAM (5 cups)

1 10½-ounce can cream of chicken soup
¾ cup cooked chicken, cut into cubes
1 13-ounce can red madrilène
½ cup whipping cream
½ cup sherry
chopped chives

1. Put chicken soup and cut-up chicken into blender container; cover and run on low speed until finely chopped.

2. Heat madrilène in small saucepan just until boiling. Add to chicken mixture and blend on low speed until mixed. Add whipping cream and sherry to blender and run on low speed until thoroughly combined. Pour into cups and sprinkle with chopped chives.

CONSOMME COSTA RICA (6 servings)

This was named in honor of the Alliance for Progress Conference at Costa Rica, March 17 to March 21, 1963.

1 egg yolk
1 tablespoon lemon juice
4 tablespoons Parmesan cheese
*4 cups Chicken Broth**
¾ cup cooked rice

1. Mix egg yolk, lemon juice and cheese. Fork-stir into boiling Broth. Add rice and serve.

CRAB AND TOMATO BISQUE (4 servings)

2 tablespoons butter
2 tablespoons flour
2 cups milk
½ teaspoon salt
⅛ teaspoon pepper
1 cup flaked crab meat
1 cup tomato juice

1. Melt butter in a saucepan, add flour and blend. Add milk gradually and cook slowly until thickened. Add seasonings and crab meat.

2. A few minutes before serving, heat tomato juice in another pan. When hot, add tomato juice gradually to first mixture and serve.

CRAB SOUP (8 to 10 servings)

2 tablespoons butter
½ cup diced celery
½ cup diced carrots
1 leek, diced
1 green pepper, diced
1 onion, diced
*1 quart Chicken Broth**
2 tomatoes, peeled and diced
½ teaspoon saffron
1 can king crab meat
1 tablespoon cooked rice

1. Melt butter, add vegetables and 1 cup of Broth and simmer for 10 minutes. Add tomatoes.

2. In separate pan heat remaining Broth with the saffron to boiling point. Strain saffron and Chicken Broth mixture into first mixture. Cook for 30 minutes.

3. Add crab meat and rice. Serve with crackers.

CREAM OF BROCCOLI SOUP (8 to 10 servings)

1 small onion, sliced thin
1 leek, sliced thin (white portion only)
1 small stalk of celery, sliced (without leaves)
1 tablespoon butter
½ cup water
2 teaspoons salt
pinch cayenne pepper
2 tablespoons uncooked rice
*2 cups Chicken Broth**
2 cups cooked broccoli, coarsely cut, and cooking liquid
½ cup cream or milk

1. Place onion, leek, celery, butter and water in 2-quart saucepan; simmer slowly for about 2 minutes over medium heat. Add salt, cayenne, rice and 1 cup Broth and simmer for 15 minutes. Do not boil.

2. Pour Broth-onion mixture into blender container, cover and run on high speed until liquefied. Return to saucepan.

3. Put cooked broccoli and remaining 1 cup of Broth into blender container, cover and run on high speed until broccoli is liquefied. If mixture becomes too thick to flow, add broccoli cooking liquid (½ cup) to thin. Add broccoli to onion mixture in saucepan. Add cream or milk. Heat (do not boil) and serve.

CREAM OF SPLIT PEA SOUP (6 to 8 servings)

1 cup dried split peas
2 quarts cold water
small piece fat salt pork
½ small onion
4 tablespoons butter or other fat
3 tablespoons flour
1¼ teaspoons salt
⅛ teaspoon pepper
2 cups milk

1. Pick over peas, cover with cold water and soak overnight. Drain.
2. Add cold water, pork and onion. Simmer for 4 hours, or until tender.
3. Press through a sieve or potato ricer.
4. Melt butter, add flour and stir to a smooth paste. Add pea pulp, salt, pepper and milk. If too thick, add more milk.

POTAGE CRESSONIERE (6 to 8 servings)
Cream of Watercress

¼ cup butter
1 leek, chopped
½ cup chopped onions
1 quart thinly sliced raw potatoes
1 tablespoon salt
¼ teaspoon freshly ground black pepper
¾ cup water
1 bunch watercress
1½ cups milk
1½ cups water
2 egg yolks
½ cup heavy cream

1. Heat butter in a large saucepan. Add the leek and onions and sauté until tender, about 4 minutes.
2. Add the potatoes, seasonings and ¾ cup water. Cover and bring to a boil. Reduce heat and simmer until potatoes are almost tender.
3. Cut the watercress stems into ⅛-inch lengths. Chop the leaves coarsely.
4. To the potato mixture add the watercress stems, half of the leaves, the milk and 1½ cups water. Cook for 15 minutes.
5. Place the mixture in a blender container, cover and run on high speed until puréed. Return soup to the saucepan and reheat.

6. Blend the egg yolks and cream together. Gradually stir into the soup and cook, stirring constantly, until slightly thickened. Garnish with the remaining watercress leaves and serve immediately.

FISH CHOWDER MANHATTAN (4 servings)

4 fish heads, or bones from 4 fish
2 cups water
1 small onion, chopped
1 clove garlic, minced
2 tablespoons chopped green pepper
2 tablespoons butter or olive oil
2 cups peeled, chopped ripe tomatoes
2 medium potatoes, finely diced
½ cup minced celery
1 bay leaf
1 teaspoon salt
⅛ teaspoon freshly ground black pepper

1. Wash the fish heads or bones and simmer in water for 12 minutes. Drain, reserving the broth. Pick the meat from the bones and reserve; discard the bones.

2. Sauté the onion, garlic and pepper in butter or oil until the onion is transparent.

3. Add the reserved stock, tomatoes, potatoes, celery, bay leaf, salt and pepper to taste. Cook until the potatoes are tender. Add the reserved fish meat and reheat.

MANHATTAN CLAM CHOWDER (6 servings)

1 onion, chopped
½ cup finely minced celery
1 tablespoon finely minced green pepper
1 clove of garlic, minced
2 tablespoons melted butter
1 cup diced potatoes
3 cups boiling water, salted lightly
2 cups peeled, seeded and diced fresh tomatoes
1 pint freshly opened clams, minced
salt and pepper
thyme
sage
cayenne
1 teaspoon coarsely chopped parsley
3 to 4 soda crackers, coarsely crumbled

1. Simmer the onion, celery, green pepper, and garlic in the melted butter for 20 minutes.

2. Add the potatoes and the water. Cook until the potatoes are tender.

3. Add the tomatoes, the clams and their juice, and salt, pepper, thyme, sage and cayenne to taste. Bring the chowder to a boil, add the chopped parsley and pour the soup into a tureen over the crackers.

MINESTRONE (6 to 8 servings)

½ pound dry white beans soaked in water overnight
3 quarts salted water
1 teaspoon olive oil
⅛ pound salt pork, diced small
1 clove garlic, chopped fine
1 small onion, chopped
1 leek, diced and washed
1 teaspoon chopped parsley
1 teaspoon chopped basil
1 tablespoon tomato paste
3 tomatoes, peeled, seeded and chopped
3 stalks of celery, chopped
2 carrots, sliced
2 potatoes, diced
¼ small cabbage, shredded
1 zucchini, diced
1½ quarts water
salt to taste
½ teaspoon freshly ground black pepper
1 cup elbow macaroni or ditali
6 tablespoons grated Parmesan cheese

1. Drain the beans and boil them in salted water for about 1 hour, or until tender.

2. Place the olive oil in a large kettle and add the salt pork, garlic, onion, leek, parsley and basil. Brown lightly. Add the tomato paste thinned with a little water and cook for 5 minutes. Add the tomatoes, celery, carrots, potatoes, cabbage, zucchini, water, salt and pepper and cook slowly for 45 minutes to 1 hour. Add the beans.

3. Add the macaroni and cook for 10 minutes, or until tender. Adjust the seasonings and serve immediately. Serve the cheese separately in a bowl.

NEW ENGLAND CLAM CHOWDER, SOUTH-OF-BOSTON STYLE (8 to 10 servings)

4 dozen medium hard-shelled clams
5 cups cold water
1 2-inch cube salt pork, diced
1 large onion, chopped very fine
4 medium potatoes, diced
salt and freshly ground black pepper to taste
2 cups milk, hot
1½ cups heavy cream, hot

1. Wash clams thoroughly. Place them in a deep pan with the cold water covering the clams. Bring to a boil and boil 10 minutes or until shells open.

2. Strain the broth through cheesecloth and reserve.

3. Remove the clams from their shells, clean and chop.

4. Combine salt pork and the onion in saucepan and cook gently over low heat about 3 minutes; do not brown.

5. Add broth and potatoes. Add salt and pepper to taste. Cook until potatoes are tender.

6. Add clams.

7. Remove from heat and slowly add milk and cream which have been heated. Serve immediately.

NEWPORT CHEESE SOUP (8 servings)

2 tablespoons butter
8 tablespoons flour
½ pound Cheddar cheese, diced small
*3 cups Chicken Broth**
2 cups milk, scalded
1 thin slice onion
1 cup cream, warm
salt and pepper

1. In a saucepan cook butter over low heat for 5 minutes, stirring in flour and cheese. Gradually add Broth, stirring constantly, and milk and onion. Cook a moment longer.

2. Strain the soup, return to the heat and simmer for 10 minutes, stirring constantly. Stir in cream and season to taste with salt and pepper.

SOUPE A L'OIGNON (6 to 8 servings)

Onion Soup

6 small onions, sliced very thin
2 tablespoons butter
1 teaspoon flour
*6 cups beef broth (canned) or Chicken Broth**
½ cup dry white wine, Chablis type
salt and freshly ground pepper to taste
6 slices French bread, day old
3 tablespoons grated Swiss cheese

1. Lightly brown onions in butter. Sprinkle with the flour and continue to cook. Add the beef broth, white wine, salt and freshly ground pepper to taste. Simmer the soup for 10 to 15 minutes.

2. Toast French bread on both sides and place it in a soup tureen or in individual casseroles. Pour the soup over the toast, sprinkle with grated cheese and put the tureen in a moderate oven or under the broiler to melt and brown the cheese. Serve very hot.

POTATO SOUP WITH SOUR CREAM (6 servings)

2 cups diced potatoes
1 cup boiling water
1 teaspoon salt
1 small onion, sliced
½ teaspoon pepper
2 cups sour cream
minced parsley

Combine first 5 ingredients and cook together for 15 minutes. Add cream and cook until potatoes are tender. Serve hot. Garnish with parsley.

SHRIMP BISQUE BENGAL (4 servings)

1 can frozen shrimp soup, thawed
1 can cold milk (use shrimp soup can, above, as a measure)
¼ cup parsley cluster
½ teaspoon curry powder
4 whole cooked shrimp, for garnish

1. Place first 4 ingredients in the blender. Blend for about 10 seconds.
2. Heat over very low heat. Garnish with whole shrimp.

SHRIMP CHOWDER (6 to 8 servings)

2 slices bacon, diced
1 small onion, chopped
12 raw shrimp (medium), shelled and diced
2 tablespoons kernel corn (optional)
½ cup canned cream-style corn
1 cup diced potatoes
*3 cups Court Bouillon**
¼ teaspoon paprika
salt and pepper to taste
½ cup heavy cream
½ teaspoon Worcestershire sauce

1. In a saucepan simmer the bacon, onion and shrimp for about 4 minutes. Add corn, potatoes, Court Bouillon, paprika, salt and pepper and boil for 15 minutes.

2. Just before serving add cream and Worcestershire.

VEGETABLE CHOWDER (8 servings)

3 cups diced potatoes
2 cups diced carrots
¼ pound salt pork, diced
½ cup diced onion
1 green pepper, diced
2 tablespoons flour
2 cups milk
2 cups canned tomatoes, hot
1 teaspoon salt
⅛ teaspoon pepper

1. Cover potatoes and carrots with water and cook until tender.

2. Sauté pork, onion and green pepper for about 5 minutes but do not brown; add flour and blend. Add milk and cook for 5 minutes, stirring constantly until smooth. Add potatoes, carrots and remaining ingredients; serve at once.

COLD SOUPS

ASPARAGUS SOUP (Approximately 6 servings)

1 10½-ounce can condensed cream of asparagus soup
1 cup sour cream
3 dashes Tabasco sauce
½ teaspoon celery salt
1 cup milk
1 cup crushed ice
chopped chives

1. Put all ingredients, except crushed ice and chives, in blender container; cover and run on high speed until thoroughly mixed.

2. Add ice; cover and run on high speed until ice is liquefied and soup chilled. Garnish with a sprinkle of chives.

AVOCADO SOUP CARMEL (4 servings)

2 cups peeled, cored and diced avocado
*2 cups Chicken Broth**
1 teaspoon lemon juice
1 teaspoon onion juice
1 teaspoon salt
½ teaspoon white pepper
½ cup heavy cream

1. Put all ingredients except the cream in blender. Cover and run on high speed until avocado is liquefied. Add cream and continue to blend until thoroughly mixed.

2. Chill soup for 1 hour before serving.

BRAZILIAN COLD CREAM SOUP (8 servings)

½ cup butter
6 leeks, diced
2 onions, diced
½ cup flour
3 pounds very ripe tomatoes, cut up
salt to taste
pinch of sugar
2¼ cups light cream

1. Melt butter and sauté leeks and onions until onions are wilted. Sprinkle with flour and cook for a few minutes, stirring, without

browning. Add tomatoes and simmer gently for 2 hours, stirring occasionally. Add salt and sugar.

2. Strain the soup, cool it and add cream. Serve cold.

COLD MELON SOUP (6 servings)

1 large ripe cantaloupe
½ teaspoon cinnamon
2¼ cups orange juice
2 tablespoons lime juice
fresh mint sprigs

1. Remove seeds from melon, peel and cut the pulp into cubes. Place pulp, cinnamon and ¼ cup orange juice in a blender and purée.

2. Combine remaining orange juice and lime juice and stir in the purée. Chill thoroughly and serve garnished with sprigs of mint.

CREAM SENEGALESE (Approximately 3½ cups)
Curry Soup

½ cup milk
½ cup heavy cream
1 10½-ounce can cream of chicken soup
1 heaping tablespoon shredded coconut
½ teaspoon salt
¼ apple, peeled and cored
½ teaspoon mace
1 teaspoon curry powder
1 cup crushed ice

Place all ingredients except ice in blender container; cover and run on low speed until smooth. Add ice, cover and run on high speed until ice is liquefied.

NOTE: If a thinner soup is desired, add additional milk or cream.

GAZPACHO (6 servings)

1 clove garlic, whole
½ small onion, sliced
1 small green pepper, seeded and sliced
3 ripe tomatoes, peeled, seeded and quartered
1 large cucumber, peeled and sliced
¼ teaspoon freshly ground black pepper
½ teaspoon basil
1 teaspoon salt
2 tablespoons olive oil
3 tablespoons wine vinegar
*½ cup chilled Chicken Broth**

Place all ingredients in blender and blend until mixed but not smooth. Chill until serving time.

ICED VEGETABLE SOUP (6 servings)

¾ cup minced scallions
2 leeks, thinly sliced
2 tablespoons melted butter
*3 cups Chicken Broth**
2 cups green peas
2 cups peeled and diced potatoes
½ teaspoon salt
¼ teaspoon celery seed
2 cups cream

1. Cook scallions and leeks in butter until vegetables start to take on color.
2. Add Chicken Broth, peas, potatoes, salt and celery seed and cook until they are tender.
3. Purée the vegetables and their liquid in a blender. Add 2 cups at a time until all ingredients are puréed. Cool the soup and stir in the cream. Chill before serving.

JELLIED MADRILENE CONSOMME (8 servings)

3 pints peeled, diced tomatoes
2 teaspoons chopped chives
¼ small onion, chopped
¼ cup chopped celery
1 bay leaf
2 cloves
1 teaspoon sugar
white of 1 egg
1 teaspoon salt
½ clove garlic
*1½ pints Chicken Broth**
1 teaspoon tarragon vinegar
½ teaspoon Worcestershire sauce
dash cayenne pepper
2 tablespoons unflavored gelatin softened in ⅓ cup water
lemon slices

1. Combine first 10 ingredients in a soup kettle and beat well with a wooden spoon rubbed with garlic. Heat to boiling point, reduce heat at once and simmer for ½ hour.
2. Strain through cheesecloth without pressure. Combine this with Chicken Broth and heat; add remaining ingredients except lemon.
3. A brilliant red color may be obtained by adding a little beet juice. Chill. Serve with a thin slice of lemon.

MEXICAN JELLIED VEAL CONSOMME (2 quarts)

3 pounds veal knuckle or shin bones
necks and wings of 2 chickens
3 quarts water
1 tablespoon salt
¼ teaspoon peppercorns
dash of cayenne pepper
3 stalks of celery
2 bay leaves
2 sprigs of thyme
2 cloves
1 onion
6 tablespoons minced pimiento
6 tablespoons minced green pepper

1. Wash bones and meat in running water. Place in a kettle with remaining ingredients except pimiento and green pepper. Cover and heat to boiling. Skim off any scum that rises. Simmer for 4 hours.

2. Strain through double thickness of cheesecloth. Discard solids.

3. Chill until firm. Break up with a fork and serve in chilled bouillon cups garnished on top with pimiento center surrounded by ring of minced green pepper.

SUMMER MUSHROOM SOUP (4 to 6 servings)

6 ounces mushrooms (canned), whole or chopped
2 tablespoons arrowroot or potato starch
*5 cups Chicken Broth**
½ cup heavy cream
3 egg yolks, lightly beaten
2 tablespoons chopped chives

1. Purée mushrooms and their liquid in a blender.

2. Mix arrowroot or starch with ½ cup of Broth. Heat remaining Broth to a boil and gradually stir in the ground mushrooms. Simmer for 3 minutes. Add some of the hot liquid to the arrowroot; return to the pan and bring to a boil, stirring.

3. Combine cream and egg yolks and add to the soup while beating with a wire whisk. Heat, beating, until the soup just thickens. Do not boil. Cool and chill. Serve with sprinkle of chives.

VICHYSSOISE (8 servings)

6 leeks (white part only), sliced thin
2 small onions, sliced thin
1 stalk of celery, diced
½ cup water
*4 cups Chicken Broth**
5 potatoes, diced
2 cups scalded milk
1 teaspoon salt
white pepper to taste
1 cup cream
chopped chives
Worcestershire sauce (optional)

1. Cook leeks, onions and celery slowly in ½ cup water for 5 minutes.

2. Add the Chicken Broth and the potatoes and cook for 15 minutes longer.

3. Add the scalded milk and bring soup to the boiling point. Season with salt and pepper and purée soup in an electric blender, using 2 cups at a time.

4. Chill thoroughly, add the cream and serve in chilled cups. Garnish with a sprinkling of chopped chives on each portion. (Worcestershire sauce may be added to taste.)

HOT or COLD SOUPS

HOT or COLD CREAM BOURBONNAISE (6 to 8 servings)

Named in honor of the French royal family whose members became rulers in France, Spain and Italy.

3 leeks (white part only), cut up
2 tablespoons melted butter
3 tablespoons water
2 potatoes, sliced
*1 quart Chicken Broth**
salt and pepper to taste
1 cup light cream
2 tablespoons chives

1. Slowly simmer the leeks in melted butter and water for about 5 minutes.

2. Combine potatoes and leek mixture in a saucepan with Chicken Broth and cook for 15 to 20 minutes.

3. Transfer to the container of an electric blender. Cover and run on high speed, ½ at a time, until liquefied. Add salt and pepper to taste.

For hot soup, add cream.

For cold soup, chill and add cream and chives.

CREAM OF CHICKEN SOUP BURMESE (4 servings)

1 10½-ounce can cream of chicken soup
1 can cold milk (use soup can, above, as measure)
2 teaspoons curry powder
3 tablespoons lemon juice
½ banana, puréed or thoroughly mashed

1. Combine all ingredients in a saucepan. Heat thoroughly.

2. Serve hot or cold.

EGGS

AMERICANS like to begin their day with eggs, in contrast to Frenchmen, who prefer café au lait or hot chocolate and some bread or rolls with jam—the familiar "Continental" breakfast—when they arise.

Eggs are traditional and usual on the American breakfast table, but people everywhere tend to be individual about what they eat in the morning, and there are many variations from the eggs-and-toast, eggs-and-bacon or eggs-and-sausage routine.

At the White House, for example, the Kennedys were not especially fond of the more elaborate egg dishes. Mrs. Kennedy's customary breakfast was orange juice, scrambled eggs, two strips of bacon, a little honey and a glass of skimmed milk. Occasionally she had tea or coffee instead. Little John often had breakfast with her, and usually ate all her honey and bacon, but she did not seem to mind—not only because he was her adored son, but because she was not in any case a large eater.

The President's breakfast seldom varied. Nearly every day he had a large glass of orange juice, toast with jam, two four-and-a-half-minute eggs, some strips of broiled bacon and coffee with cream and sugar. Much as he appeared to enjoy his breakfasts, I am sure Mr. Kennedy enjoyed even more the appearances of Caroline and John, who would rush in, shouting, "Good morning, Daddy," and hug and kiss him, both talking and laughing at once.

Mr. Kennedy shared his wife's liking for soufflés, especially at luncheon, but there was a day when he learned that a soufflé waits for no man, not even a President. His secretary, Mrs. Lincoln, called me and said the President would like to have a soufflé for lunch at 12:30 P.M. Knowing how busy Mr. Kennedy's days were, I understood that he would hardly be able to curtail an important conference because a soufflé was falling, and so I drew up a plan of action as a good general would do. I prepared the ingredients for four soufflés, the first one to be ready as he had requested, at 12:30.

I placed it in the oven on schedule. It rose majestically and was ready to be served on time. But the President was not ready and my first soufflé fell with that disheartening sinking so familiar to housewives. I put number two and number three in the oven fifteen minutes apart, but still the President was not ready for lunch and they too collapsed dismally, uneaten.

There was nothing to do. I could only hope that my last soufflé would reach the President's table. While suspense gripped the kitchen, it rose to its splendid zenith and at that moment word came from the President that he was ready. I almost collapsed with relief. Busy as he was, Mr. Kennedy must have understood about soufflés and what the delay must have done to the kitchen, because he sent me a message of appreciation—reward enough for any chef!

In the fourth recipe of this section, I have tried to spare you the tragedy which so nearly overtook me. It is one for a soufflé which may be *reheated* and *repuffed,* so that if your dinner is delayed for some reason you will not have to undergo the agony of the soufflé-maker.

SOUFFLE MARTHE (4 servings)

⅓ cup butter
3 tablespoons flour
1 cup milk
4 eggs, separated
salt and pepper to taste
1½ cups asparagus tips

1. Melt butter, blend in flour and stir constantly. When mixture is smooth, gradually add milk, stirring until the mixture thickens. Remove from heat and cool slightly before adding the beaten egg yolks. Add salt and pepper and stir well.

2. Fold in stiffly beaten egg whites.

3. Arrange asparagus tips in a well-buttered soufflé dish and pour the mixture over the tips. Bake in a preheated 350° F. oven for about 35 minutes, or until golden brown.

SOUFFLE VICTOIRE (4 servings)

4 tablespoons butter
4 tablespoons flour
1 cup milk
1 teaspoon Dijon-type mustard
1 cup freshly grated Parmesan cheese
1 cup freshly grated Swiss cheese
¼ teaspoon freshly ground black pepper
dash of cayenne pepper
4 eggs, separated

1. Melt the butter and blend in the flour. Bring the milk to a boil and add, all at once. Cook, stirring vigorously, until the sauce is thickened and smooth. Stir in the mustard.

2. Remove from heat and stir in the cheeses until they are melted. Season with peppers. Cool slightly. Stir in egg yolks which have been beaten lightly.

3. Beat the egg whites until stiff and fold gently into the cheese mixture. Turn into a well-buttered 6-cup soufflé dish.

4. Bake in preheated 375° F. oven until the soufflé has risen and is golden brown, approximately 25 to 30 minutes.

SPINACH CASSEROLE SUZANNE (8 servings)

This dish is a bit complicated, but well worth the effort.

4 eggs, separated
1 teaspoon melted butter
⅛ inch anchovy paste
3 cups cooked spinach, finely chopped
⅓ cup bread, softened in ¼ cup cold milk
salt and pepper to taste
dash freshly ground nutmeg
dash ground cloves
1 tablespoon grated Swiss cheese
2 tablespoons chopped parsley
2 tablespoons grated onion

FILLING

4 large mushrooms, chopped fine
½ pound chopped beef
3 tablespoons butter
1 tablespoon grated onion
1 tablespoon chopped chives
salt and pepper to taste
nutmeg to taste

NOTE: The filling must be prepared before the spinach-egg mixture comes out of the oven.

1. Beat egg yolks until light. Stir in butter mixed with anchovy paste. Add cooked, well-drained spinach and bread which has been softened in cold milk. Season with salt, pepper, nutmeg and cloves and mix thoroughly. Stir in grated cheese, parsley and onion.

2. Beat egg white until stiff and fold into spinach mixture.

3. Spread mixture in a 10×14-inch pan lined with paper and buttered. Bake in preheated 375° F. oven until firm (about 15 minutes). Remove at once from the oven and cut off the hard edges. Spread at once with filling and roll as for jelly roll.

FILLING

1. Cook mushrooms and beef in butter until meat loses its red color. Add onion and chives and season with salt, pepper and nutmeg. To serve, cut into 1½-inch slices.

I've described the perils of the falling soufflé. Here is a recipe I recently developed for one that really may be *reheated* and *repuffed,* so that latecomers need not worry you.

VEGETABLE, CHEESE OR SEA FOOD SOUFFLE (4 servings)

3 tablespoons margarine or butter
2 tablespoons cornstarch
½ teaspoon salt
¼ teaspoon pepper
1 cup milk
1 cup grated cheese; or 1 cup chopped shrimp; or sea food, flaked; or chopped vegetables
4 well-beaten egg yolks
4 stiffly beaten egg whites

1. Melt 3 tablespoons butter in saucepan, and blend in 2 tablespoons cornstarch, salt and pepper.

2. Remove from heat. Slowly stir in 1 cup milk. Cook and stir over medium heat until thickened.

3. Stir in cheese, sea food or vegetables. Stir in beaten egg yolks, then fold in beaten egg whites.

4. Bake in greased, heatproof 2-quart casserole set in pan of hot water in 350° F. oven for 1¼ hours.

TO REPUFF: Leave soufflé in casserole and set in pan of hot water. Reheat in 350° F. oven until repuffed, about 20 to 30 minutes.

SHIRRED EGGS ALBERT (1 serving)

4 tablespoons fine bread crumbs, buttered
2 eggs
2 tablespoons chopped cooked mushrooms

1. Line a buttered shirred-egg dish with 2 tablespoons bread crumbs. Very carefully break eggs into the dish.

2. Cover the white of the egg with chopped mushrooms and remaining crumbs. Bake in preheated 275° F. oven for approximately 10 to 12 minutes, until the white is milky but still creamy.

SHIRRED EGGS ROBERT (1 serving)

pâté de foie gras, *sufficient to barely cover bottom of shirred-egg dish*
1 teaspoon finely chopped green olives
1 teaspoon finely chopped chives
2 eggs
salt and white pepper to taste

1. Spread *pâté de foie gras* on bottom of shirred-egg dish which has been buttered. Sprinkle over this the olives and chives.

2. Carefully break the eggs into dish, one at a time. Season with salt and pepper and cook over a very low heat until the eggs are set.

SCRAMBLED EGGS CARMAUX (8 servings)

¾ cup diced cooked lobster meat
3 tablespoons melted butter
dash of paprika
1½ teaspoons curry powder
¼ teaspoon salt
7 eggs
⅓ cup heavy sweet cream

1. Sauté lobster in melted butter until heated. Stir almost constantly but do not let come to a boil. Season with paprika and curry powder mixed with salt.

2. Beat the eggs as for an omelet, adding cream. Pour over the lobster mixture, stirring thoroughly and gently over low heat until eggs begin to set.

SCRAMBLED EGGS NIEVRE (8 servings)

3 tablespoons melted butter
4 ounces grated Parmesan cheese
1 tablespoon finely minced shallot
1 tablespoon finely minced chives
1 cup dry white wine
8 eggs, well beaten
salt and pepper to taste
dash of nutmeg, freshly grated

1. To the melted butter in a saucepan stir in the grated cheese alternately with the shallots and chives. Cook over low heat until heated. Gradually stir in the wine and cook until smooth.

2. Pour in the eggs seasoned with salt, pepper and nutmeg. Cook, stirring thoroughly and gently, until the eggs are set.

OMELETTE (2 servings)

4 eggs
1 teaspoon salt
⅛ teaspoon pepper
2 tablespoons milk or cream
1 tablespoon butter

1. Beat together lightly the eggs, salt, pepper and milk or cream.

2. In a 9-inch skillet melt the butter until it sizzles. Be careful not to burn. Pour in egg mixture. As mixture cooks on bottom and sides, prick it with a fork so that the egg on top will penetrate the cooked surface and run under the sides. When set but still moist, fold over. Let stand a few minutes to brown, and turn onto a hot dish.

MUSHROOM OMELET (2 servings)

1 cup thinly sliced mushrooms
2 tablespoons melted butter
salt and pepper to taste
*recipe for Omelette**

1. Sauté mushrooms in melted butter for 5 minutes. Add salt and pepper to taste.

2. Add to omelet mixture and cook as directed in Omelette recipe.

OMELETTE GRUYERE (2 servings)

4 eggs
1 teaspoon salt
⅛ teaspoon pepper
1 tablespoon heavy cream
¼ cup grated Gruyère cheese
1 tablespoon butter

1. Beat the eggs, salt, pepper and cream. Stir in the cheese.

2. Melt the butter in a 9-inch skillet until it sizzles. Pour in the egg mixture and cook as directed in recipe for Omelette.* May be served with ham or crisp bacon if desired.

OMELETTE LOUIS (6 servings)

6 eggs, separated
¾ teaspoon salt
¼ teaspoon nutmeg
⅛ teaspoon white pepper
¾ cup cottage cheese
⅓ cup cold milk
3 tablespoons finely chopped green pepper
1 tablespoon finely chopped parsley
1 tablespoon finely chopped onion
1 tablespoon finely chopped chives
3 tablespoons butter
3 tablespoons grated Gruyère cheese
paprika to taste

1. Place egg yolks, salt, nutmeg, pepper, cottage cheese and milk in blender container. Cover and run at high speed for 1 minute. Pour into a bowl. Add green pepper, parsley, onion and chives.

2. Fold in stiffly beaten egg whites.

3. In a light frying pan, heat 2 tablespoons of the butter. Pour in the egg mixture and cook as an Omelette. When mixture just begins to set and the bottom is lightly browned, fold omelet over.

4. Turn out on a hot platter, brush with 1 tablespoon of melted butter, sprinkle grated cheese over top of omelet and place under the broiler to melt the cheese. Sprinkle with a little paprika.

OMELETTE MONTEREY (6 to 7 servings)

1 medium onion, sliced
1 tablespoon oil
1 tablespoon butter
4 ounces mushrooms, sliced
10 eggs, beaten
1 tablespoon chopped chives
1 clove garlic, chopped
salt and pepper to taste
1 avocado, diced

1. Cook onion in the oil and butter until onion is wilted. Stir in the mushrooms and cook for a few minutes.

2. To the beaten eggs add the chives and garlic and mix with the onion and mushrooms. Add salt and pepper.

3. Using the above mixture, make an Omelette* in the usual manner, and just before folding it place the avocado in the center and roll it.

OMELETTE NONTRON (8 servings)

12 artichoke bottoms, canned or freshly cooked
3 tablespoons melted butter
*½ cup Béchamel Sauce**
8 eggs

1. Mince the artichokes and sauté in melted butter for 5 minutes, stirring occasionally.

2. Stir in Béchamel Sauce.

3. Prepare an Omelette* in the usual manner, and when the eggs are just beginning to set, place the artichoke mixture in the center. Fold the omelet and slide it onto a hot serving platter.

OMELETTE A L'OIGNON (2 to 3 servings)

Onion Omelet

4 eggs
salt and pepper to taste
4 tablespoons butter
1 medium sweet onion, sliced very thin

1. Lightly beat eggs with salt and pepper.

2. Melt 2 tablespoons butter in a skillet and sauté onions about 5 minutes. Remove onions to a deep bowl. Add eggs and beat well.

3. Melt balance of butter in skillet and pour in egg mixture. Cook as directed in recipe for Omelette.*

SPANISH OMELET (6 servings)

6 fresh tomatoes
3 tablespoons cooking oil
1 onion, chopped
1 green pepper, chopped
1 clove garlic, minced
3 sprigs of parsley, chopped
½ teaspoon thyme
½ bay leaf
salt and freshly ground black pepper

1. Peel tomatoes and cut in half. Gently press out the seeds and liquid. Chop tomatoes.

2. In a pan heat the oil and add the onion, green pepper, garlic and parsley. Sauté for 5 minutes. Add tomatoes and season with thyme and bay leaf. Add salt and pepper to taste. Gently simmer the mixture until vegetables are tender, approximately 10 minutes. Discard bay leaf. This can be used to fill and garnish 6 3-egg omelets. (See recipe for Omelette.*)

EGGS BENEDICT (6 servings)

3 English muffins
6 slices broiled ham
*6 Poached Eggs**
*Blender Hollandaise Sauce**

1. Split English muffins and toast them.

2. Cut ham the same size as the muffin; place on muffin. Carefully slip egg on ham and cover with Hollandaise Sauce.

POACHED EGGS

water to cover eggs
½ teaspoon salt
pepper to taste
½ tablespoon lemon juice or vinegar
1 or 2 eggs per person

1. Heat water to simmering in a shallow pan; add salt, pepper and vinegar.

2. Carefully break egg into a cup and gently slip it into water. Cook eggs below boiling point for about 5 minutes or until white is firm and a film has formed over the yolk. Remove egg with a skimmer.

POACHED EGGS LILLE (6 servings)

3 raw potatoes
4 tablespoons melted butter
salt and pepper to taste
dash of freshly ground nutmeg
⅓ cup grated Gruyère cheese
6 eggs
heavy sweet cream

1. Cut potatoes into thin slices and sauté in melted butter until tender and browned on both sides. Stir frequently over medium heat. Season with salt, pepper and nutmeg.

2. Spread cooked potatoes on the bottom of a buttered baking dish and sprinkle with grated cheese. Break the eggs on top of the cheese, leaving space between the eggs. Add salt and pepper to taste and cover the eggs with the cream. Bake in a preheated 375° F. oven for about 10 minutes or until the eggs are set.

POACHED EGGS NIMES (4 servings)

1 tablespoon melted butter
½ cup dry white wine
4 eggs
salt and pepper
dash of cayenne pepper
2 tablespoons grated Roquefort cheese

1. To melted butter in a skillet add wine.

2. Slip in eggs one at a time. Season with salt, pepper and cayenne. Poach until whites are almost firm. Sprinkle with cheese and cook until the cheese is melted. May be served on hot buttered toast.

EGGS A LA MENTON (6 servings)

3 ounces grated Swiss cheese, plus additional ⅓ cup
6 eggs
salt and white pepper to taste
1 tablespoon finely chopped parsley
1 tablespoon finely chopped chives
1 tablespoon finely chopped chervil
1 tablespoon finely chopped onion
1½ tablespoons unsalted butter

1. Sprinkle a buttered earthenware baking dish with the 3 ounces of

grated cheese. Carefully break the eggs over the cheese and season with salt and pepper.

2. Cover all with the additional ⅓ cup grated cheese mixed with parsley, chives, chervil and onion.

3. Dot with the butter and bake in preheated oven at 350° F. until bubbly and browned.

EGGS PACIFIC (6 servings)

12 hard-cooked eggs, shelled and sliced
1 pound shrimp, cooked and shelled
3 tablespoons butter
3 tablespoons flour
1⅔ cups light cream
2 teaspoons prepared mustard
1 teaspoon salt
dash of pepper
1 tablespoon dry white wine
1 tablespoon capers, drained
2 tablespoons chopped parsley
¼ teaspoon thyme
½ cup shredded Swiss cheese

1. Butter a 2-quart baking dish and arrange half the eggs on the bottom. Sprinkle the shrimp over the eggs, and top with the remaining eggs.

2. Melt butter and stir in flour; cook for about 1 minute. Gradually add cream, stirring. Blend well. Stir in mustard, salt, pepper, wine, capers, parsley and thyme. Pour the sauce over the eggs. Sprinkle with cheese and bake in preheated oven at 425° F. for about 15 minutes until bubbly.

STUFFED EGGS (12 stuffed halves)

6 hard-cooked eggs
12 cubes ham, olive or pimiento (optional)
3 tablespoons butter, room temperature
dash of Worcestershire sauce
salt and pepper to taste
*2 tablespoons Blender Mayonnaise**

1. Slice eggs in half, lengthwise or crosswise. Trim off a bit from round bottom of eggs. Remove yolks. Arrange eggs on a rack. To each cavity add a cube of ham, olive or pimiento as desired.

2. Beat yolks with electric mixer. Add remaining ingredients and beat well until very smooth. Anchovy paste, lemon juice or dry mustard may be added to yolk mixture. Fill cavities, covering cubes.

STUFFED EGGS CALIFORNIA (6 servings)

1 small can smoked sardines, drained
6 hard-cooked eggs
6 ripe olives, chopped
1 tablespoon lemon juice
salt and pepper to taste
paprika to taste
*Blender Mayonnaise**
watercress

1. Thoroughly mash sardines.

2. Cut eggs in half lengthwise, remove the yolks and mash. Add the sardines, olives, lemon juice, seasoning and enough Mayonnaise to moisten.

3. Fill the egg whites with sardine mixture and serve on bed of watercress.

STUFFED EGGS NANETTE (6 servings)

6 hard-cooked eggs
3 tablespoons pâté de foie gras
1 teaspoon very finely chopped black truffle
1 teaspoon butter, room temperature
½ teaspoon finely chopped chervil
*2 cups Béchamel Sauce**
6 teaspoons grated Parmesan cheese

1. Cut eggs in halves, remove yolks and blend them with the *pâté de foie gras,* truffle, butter and chervil.

2. Fill egg whites with this mixture. Put the 2 halves of each egg together and place each whole egg in an individual casserole which has been buttered.

3. Divide the Béchamel Sauce into 6 equal portions and pour, covering each egg with the sauce. Sprinkle grated cheese over each egg. Brown quickly under the broiler.

FISH AND SEA FOOD

IF MY recipes for fish and sea food which follow should seem overnumerous to you, I hope you will forgive my enthusiasm. In the French cuisine, fish and its preparation is one of the major accomplishments. It is, indeed, a high art to present fish on the table, with appropriate wines and sauces, so that one can truly say, "I have dined well," even if he should eat no more that meal.

We should eat food for no better reason than because we enjoy it, but it is nice to know that in the case of fish it is also good for us. Fish are second only to agricultural products as man's most important source of food. We have more than thirty thousand kinds to choose from in the world. Annually, the fisheries of the globe bring in nearly a hundred billion pounds.

The use and preparation of sea food has a history thousands of years old. No doubt, prehistoric man was the first to learn that fish was excellent food, although he ate it raw. By the time of the Roman Empire, cuisine had reached such a point that those gourmets and gastronomes of Rome who loved and could afford a superior table were able to set before guests delightful fish dishes brought from the Mediterranean and artfully prepared, as the descriptions they have left behind tell us. One of these records that Emperor Elagabalus, about 220 A.D., maintained a special fleet of fishing boats solely to catch conger eels. The finest of the catch were kept in tubs and carefully fattened for their roe, which were used as caviar. Another Emperor, Domitian, thought so much of his household's cuisine that he interrupted a debate in the Senate to ask the Senators their advice about which sauce he should serve over the snails at a royal banquet. It is not recorded what the Senators told him, nor whether their advice was confined to snail sauces.

Fish, including eels, is still one of the glories of Roman cuisine, but in France we believe that sea food is elevated to its highest and proper pinnacle by the sauces which accompany it, or by such special preparations as the cooking of *lupe de mer,* the Mediterranean equivalent of the Atlantic sea bass, with sticks of fennel to give it a remarkable and unusual flavor.

The importance of fish to French gastronomy can only be measured by the often-told story of King Louis XIV's maitre d', Vatel, who committed suicide at an untimely thirty-six years of age because the fishmonger failed to deliver his order on time. Ironically, it arrived only a few minutes after his death.

Later monarchs have been less demanding of their kitchens. When I was at the Normandy Hotel in Deauville, the former King of Egypt, Farouk, came often with his retinue. I was told by the waiters that he seemed to enjoy particularly the New Delhi Lobster* I prepared for him, and often ordered double portions. One evening he came to the kitchen with another gentleman to compliment me and to ask me for the recipe, which of course I gladly gave him. You will find it among the fish recipes in this section.

If they are well prepared, sea food dishes can be delightful—and done superbly, they will please the most difficult gourmet. An absolute necessity in the preparation of any such dish is that the fish be fresh. Make sure the gills are bright red, the flesh firm, the smell clean and without any unpleasant odor, the eyes not dull or deeply embedded.

When you have thus prepared yourself, try one of the following recipes. They are a challenge to your creative abilities in the kitchen, and I believe you will find them most satisfying.

BOUILLABAISSE MARSEILLAISE (10 to 12 servings)

1½ pounds red snapper
1½ pounds sea bass
1½ pounds striped bass
1 pound halibut
2 live lobsters (about 1½ pounds each)
1 pound mussels in shells
1 pound uncooked, peeled shrimp
4 tablespoons olive oil or vegetable oil
1 medium onion, chopped
6 ripe tomatoes, peeled and chopped
1 tablespoon tomato paste
4 cloves garlic, chopped
1 head of fresh fennel, sliced thin
1 white leek, sliced thin
1 stalk of celery, sliced thin
1 teaspoon saffron
*1 quart Court Bouillon**
1 bay leaf
dash of thyme
1 cup Chablis wine
salt and pepper to taste
1 tablespoon Pernod
French bread, sliced thickly and gently rubbed with garlic
1 tablespoon chopped parsley

1. Skin, clean and filet all the fish into 3- or 4-inch pieces. Cut the lobsters into pieces, including the heads.

2. In large saucepan heat the oil. Stir in onion, tomatoes, tomato paste, garlic, fennel, leek, celery and saffron. Cook for 2 minutes. Add Court Bouillon, bay leaf, thyme, wine, salt and pepper.

3. Add the filets, lobsters, mussels and shrimp to the mixture. Bring the liquid to a boil and simmer for 15 minutes. Add Pernod to liquid and mix gently.

4. Toast bread and place in the bottom of a deep, round platter. Pour the fish broth over these slices.

5. On another platter, arrange all the sea food in an attractive manner and sprinkle with parsley.

CRAB AND RICE, ITALIAN STYLE (4 servings)

1 cup uncooked rice
2 medium onions, chopped
3 tablespoons olive oil
2 8-ounce cans tomato sauce
⅓ cup chopped parsley
1 clove garlic, minced
1 pound crab meat
grated Parmesan cheese

1. Cook rice and onions in olive oil until the rice is translucent. Add tomato sauce, cover and steam until rice is done.

2. Add parsley, garlic, crab meat and cheese. Cook over low heat until all ingredients are hot and the cheese has melted into them.

CRAB CARIB (6 servings)

3 firm avocados
6 tablespoons garlic vinegar
2 tablespoons butter
2 tablespoons flour
1 cup cream, scalded
salt to taste
1½ cups crab meat
1 tablespoon capers, drained
dash of Tabasco sauce
6 tablespoons grated Cheddar cheese

1. Do not peel avocados. Cut in half lengthwise and remove pits. Sprinkle with 1 tablespoon vinegar for each half and let stand for 30 minutes.

2. Melt butter and blend in flour. Add scalded cream. Cook, stirring, until smooth and thickened. Add salt, crab meat, capers and Tabasco sauce.

3. Stuff avocados with crab mixture and sprinkle each with a tablespoon of cheese. Bake in preheated oven at 375° F. until thoroughly heated, approximately 20 minutes.

CRAB MEAT VALENTINE (4 to 6 servings)

1 pound crab meat
2 tablespoons butter
½ cup sherry wine
2 tablespoons flour
2 cups light cream
salt and pepper
2 packages frozen asparagus
1 cup whipped cream
4 tablespoons grated Parmesan cheese

1. Sauté crab meat lightly in butter. Add sherry and simmer until reduced by one-half.

2. Add flour and cream, season and cook until thickened. Fork-stir, keeping crab in lumps.

3. Cook and drain asparagus.

4. Place asparagus in bottom of a buttered casserole. Pour crab mixture over asparagus, spread with whipped cream, sprinkle with cheese and brown under a low flame.

CRAB-STUFFED FISH WITH CUCUMBER SAUCE
(4 to 6 servings)

1 3-pound red snapper or striped bass
¼ cup butter
¼ cup chopped onion
3 tablespoons chopped celery
½ pound crab meat, cooked
2 tablespoons chopped parsley
salt and pepper to taste
1 cup fresh white bread crumbs
¼ cup milk or cream

1. Have fish cleaned and ready for stuffing. Rinse and dry.
2. Melt butter and cook onion and celery until tender.
3. Add crab meat, parsley, salt and pepper, bread crumbs and milk or cream. Mix well.
4. Fill cavity of fish loosely and sew up.
5. Place in a buttered baking dish and dot with butter.
6. Bake in 400° F. oven about 35 minutes or until fish flakes easily.
7. Remove thread. Serve with Cucumber Sauce.

CUCUMBER SAUCE

3 tablespoons flour
3 tablespoons melted butter
¼ cup clam juice
1 cup milk
¼ cup cream
½ cup chopped cucumber

1. Stir flour into melted butter.
2. Add clam juice and milk. Stir until sauce thickens.
3. Simmer 15 minutes, stirring occasionally.
4. Just before serving, stir in cream and cucumber.

CRABES MOUS AMANDINES (6 servings)
Soft-shelled Crabs with Almonds

18 soft-shelled crabs
¾ cup butter
salt and pepper to taste
1 cup blanched, shredded almonds

1. Wash crabs and pat dry. Melt butter in a large skillet. Sauté crabs, shell side down, for 5 minutes. Turn crabs over and cook 3 minutes longer. Add salt and pepper to taste.

2. Place crabs on a heated platter.

3. Add almonds to the pan juices and sauté them until they are golden. Pour the almonds and the pan juices over the crabs.

FLOUNDER AIGLON (3 servings)

2 tablespoons melted butter
½ cup julienne of celery (thin strips)
¼ cup julienne of mushrooms
1 small truffle, cut julienne
½ cup white wine
*½ cup Court Bouillon**
¼ cup heavy cream
3 flounder fillets
chopped parsley

1. Melt butter and simmer celery and mushrooms for about 5 minutes.

2. Add truffle, wine, Court Bouillon and cream.

3. Lay the fillets side by side on a buttered baking dish and pour the sauce on top.

4. Bake the fish in a preheated moderately hot oven (400° F.) for about 10 minutes. Sprinkle with chopped parsley and serve.

FILLETS OF HADDOCK IN PINK SAUCE (6 servings)

½ cup butter
3 tablespoons flour
½ cup dry white wine
1 cup cream
salt and freshly ground black pepper
paprika
4 tablespoons sherry
6 haddock fillets
chopped parsley

1. Preheat oven to moderate (325° F.)

2. Heat the butter, stir in the flour and cook until slightly colored.

3. Add the wine and stir until smooth.

4. Gradually add the cream and continue stirring until smooth and moderately thick. Cook for 5 minutes and season to taste with salt, pepper and paprika.

5. Add the sherry.

6. Place the fillets in a greased baking dish and pour the sauce over them. Bake, uncovered, for 25 to 30 minutes. Remove to heated serving platter and sprinkle liberally with chopped parsley.

TURBOTIN A LA DUGLERE (6 to 8 servings) PLATE II

Halibut Duglère

The American equivalent of the *turbotin* is the chicken halibut.

1 turbotin, or chicken halibut, 4 to 6 pounds	*1 cup dry white wine*
1 teaspoon chopped onion	*salt and pepper to taste*
2 cups peeled, seeded, chopped tomatoes	*1 cup unsalted butter*
	1 tablespoon chopped parsley
	Puff Paste for garnish*

1. Have the fish cleaned, trimmed and filleted.
2. Place the fish fillets in a buttered baking dish and cover with the onion, tomatoes and wine.
3. Add salt and pepper to taste.
4. Cover the fish with baking-pan parchment liner paper and place the dish in a preheated moderate oven (350° F.) to poach for about 20 minutes, until the flesh flakes at the touch of a fork.
5. Transfer the fish carefully to a serving platter.
6. Over high heat, reduce the cooking liquid in the baking dish to a thick purée.
7. Gradually stir in the butter.
8. Add parsley.
9. Pour the sauce over the fish. Garnish the platter with crescents of Puff Paste.

HALIBUT ST. TROPEZ (6 servings)

6 halibut steaks, 1 inch thick	*1 tablespoon olive oil*
salt and pepper to taste	*grated Swiss cheese*
paprika to taste	*dry bread crumbs*
2 eggs, lightly beaten	*4 tablespoons butter*
2 tablespoons milk	*1 clove garlic*

1. Season halibut steaks with salt, pepper and paprika.
2. Combine eggs, milk and olive oil. Roll steaks in this mixture, then roll in grated cheese. Roll again in egg mixture, then roll in bread crumbs.
3. Melt butter, add garlic, cook 2 minutes and remove garlic. Fry

the steaks in the butter over low heat, turning often, until well browned on both sides.

HALIBUT IN WINE SAUCE (6 servings)

2 pounds halibut
2 tablespoons butter
2 tablespoons minced shallots
salt and pepper
½ pound mushrooms, sliced
⅔ cup dry white wine

1. Place halibut in a shallow pan and dot with butter. Sprinkle with shallots and add salt and pepper. Top with mushrooms and pour wine over all.

2. Cover tightly with foil and bake in preheated oven at 325° F. for 30 minutes.

LOBSTER AMERICAINE (4 servings)

4 live lobsters, 1½ pounds each
¼ cup vegetable oil
1 tablespoon butter
1 tablespoon chopped shallots
1 tablespoon finely diced carrots
½ tablespoon finely diced celery
1 small clove garlic, chopped
½ cup cognac or brandy
2 cups dry white wine, Chablis type
*2 cups Court Bouillon**
*½ cup Pisa Tomato Sauce**
*1 cup Brown Sauce**
4 tomatoes, peeled, seeded and chopped
salt and pepper to taste
1 tablespoon butter, room temperature
1 tablespoon flour
1 teaspoon chopped tarragon
1 tablespoon chopped parsley

1. Cut the live lobsters into pieces, reserving the liquid and intestines; discard the stomach sac.

2. In skillet heat the oil and butter, add the lobsters and cook until the meat has stiffened and the shells are red.

3. Add shallots, carrots, celery and garlic and stir. Add half of the brandy and set aflame.

4. When flame goes out, add white wine, Court Bouillon, Tomato Sauce, Brown Sauce, chopped tomatoes, salt and pepper and cook for 20 minutes.

5. Remove the lobster to serving dishes and keep hot.

6. Mix butter, flour, lobster liquid and intestines until it becomes a paste.

7. Stir the mixture into the sauce and let cook for 2 minutes. Add half of the chopped tarragon and half of parsley. Pour sauce over the lobster, add remaining brandy and sprinkle with the remaining tarragon and parsley. Serve very hot.

HOMARD A LA NEWBURGH (6 servings)

Lobster Newburgh

4 live lobsters, 1¼ pounds each
1 tablespoon vinegar per quart water
1 tablespoon unsalted butter, melted
1 tablespoon paprika
salt and pepper to taste
pinch of cayenne pepper
½ cup sherry wine
1 cup cream
3 egg yolks

1. Plunge the live lobsters into boiling salted water, add vinegar and cook them for 20 minutes. Chill in running cold water.

2. Crack the shells and carefully remove the meat from the tail and claws. Remove the black intestinal vein in the tail and cut the tail into ½-inch-thick slices.

3. Toss the lobster meat over a hot fire in the melted butter for a few minutes and sprinkle with paprika. Toss until the meat acquires a fine red color. Add salt, pepper and a little cayenne pepper. Simmer with sherry wine for a few minutes longer and add half the cream.

4. Stir in the egg yolks, blended with the remaining cream, and remove the pan from the heat so that the sauce will thicken without danger of curdling. From step 3 on, lobster and sauce may be prepared and served in a chafing dish.

LOBSTER SUPREME (4 servings)

4 tablespoons butter
2 tablespoons flour
½ teaspoon salt
½ teaspoon paprika
1½ cups hot milk
2 egg yolks
2 tablespoons lemon juice or sherry wine
2 cups cooked diced lobster meat

1. Melt butter in a saucepan, add the flour and stir until smooth.

Add seasoning and hot milk and stir until thoroughly mixed and thickened. Remove from heat.

2. Beat in egg yolks one at a time. Stir in lemon juice or sherry and diced lobster. Heat through.

HOMARD THERMIDOR (4 servings)

Lobster Thermidor

2 live lobsters, 1½ pounds each
1 tablespoon vinegar per quart water
½ pound mushrooms, diced
2 tablespoons butter
1½ tablespoons flour
1 teaspoon dry mustard, diluted with a little white wine
1 cup milk, hot
salt and pepper
cayenne pepper
½ cup cream, hot
grated Swiss cheese

1. Boil the live lobsters for 15 to 18 minutes in salted water and vinegar. Place under cold water faucet and chill the lobsters thoroughly. Cut the lobsters in half lengthwise. Remove the claws and tail meat and cut it in large dice. Wash and rinse the body shells carefully.

2. Combine the mushrooms with 1 teaspoon butter. Cook, covered, for 6 minutes, and drain, reserving the liquid. Combine the mushrooms with the lobster meat.

3. Melt the rest of the butter, stir in the flour and cook the *roux* for a minute or two, stirring constantly. Do not allow the *roux* to brown.

4. Add the mustard and gradually stir in the hot milk and the mushroom liquid. Cook for 2 minutes, stirring constantly, and season with salt, pepper and cayenne pepper to taste.

5. Add the hot cream and simmer for a minute or so longer.

6. Strain the sauce through a fine sieve over the lobster and mushrooms.

7. Fill the shells with the mixture, sprinkle with finely grated Swiss cheese and set in a very hot oven to brown the topping.

NEW DELHI LOBSTER (4 servings)

2 medium onions, chopped
3 tablespoons butter or oil
1 large clove garlic, chopped
1 tablespoon curry powder
juice of 1 lemon
1 tablespoon grated lemon peel
1 cup light cream
salt and pepper
1 pound cooked lobster meat, diced

1. Sauté onion until yellow in melted butter or oil. Add garlic.
2. Add curry powder and blend well. Add lemon juice and peel. Cook and stir until smooth. Add cream and seasonings, stirring until smooth again.
3. Add lobster meat and heat thoroughly.

BAKED STUFFED MACKEREL (4 servings)

1 large onion, minced
½ green pepper, chopped
½ cup finely chopped celery
4 tablespoons butter
3 cups mashed potatoes (about 1½ pounds when raw)
1 teaspoon salt, or to taste
¼ teaspoon freshly ground black pepper
¼ teaspoon sage
¼ teaspoon thyme
1 2½-pound mackerel

1. Preheat oven to 375° F.
2. Cook the onion, green pepper and celery in 2 tablespoons of the butter until the onion is transparent. Mix with the potatoes and seasonings and stuff into the mackerel. Sew or skewer closed.
3. Place the fish in a buttered baking dish. Score lightly in several places. Melt the remaining butter and sprinkle over the fish. Bake until fish flakes easily when tested with a fork—about 45 minutes.

FILETS DE MAQUEREAUX PECHEUR (2 servings)
Fillets of Mackerel, Fisherman's Style

6 clams
2 scallions, chopped
salt and pepper to taste
2 tablespoons fresh bread crumbs, or enough to make a paste
2 fillets of mackerel
¼ cup white wine
1 tablespoon butter

1. Open the clams and remove meat. Chop and strain clam meat, saving the clam juice. Mix clams, scallions, salt, pepper and bread crumbs to a paste.

2. Lay the fillets side by side in a shallow pan. Spread the paste on top of the fish. Add the wine and clam juice. Dot with butter. Bake in preheated 350° F. oven for 15 minutes.

MOULES MARINIERE (2 to 3 servings)
Stewed Mussels

1 quart mussels
¼ cup dry white wine
½ teaspoon chopped shallots or green onions
½ teaspoon chopped onion
½ teaspoon chopped parsley
freshly ground black pepper
1 teaspoon heavy cream
1 tablespoon butter blended with 1 teaspoon flour

1. Scrub the mussels thoroughly.

2. Place them in a kettle with the wine and chopped vegetables. Add freshly ground pepper to taste. Cover the kettle tightly and cook over high heat until all the shells are open (about 5 minutes).

3. Drain in a colander, saving the liquid, and put mussels in a serving dish to keep warm.

4. Return liquid to kettle and let settle for 1 or 2 minutes. Pour liquid very slowly into another saucepan. Reduce over high heat to one third its original volume. Add cream.

5. Thicken the sauce by stirring in the butter blended with flour. Cook for a minute or two longer and pour the sauce over the mussels.

HUITRES CASINO (2 servings)

Oysters Casino

12 oysters
1 tablespoon chopped green pepper
1 tablespoon melted butter
2 tablespoons diced pimientos
juice of ½ lemon
salt and pepper
2 slices bacon, cut into 1½-inch strips
dry bread crumbs

1. Open large oysters and leave the meat on the deep half shell.
2. Cook the green pepper in the butter, blend in the pimientos and lemon juice and season with salt and pepper.
3. Cover each oyster with a piece of bacon and some of the seasoned butter.
4. Sprinkle with dry bread crumbs.
5. Bake in a preheated hot oven (450° F.) for about 7 minutes. A bed of rock salt makes it easy to balance the oyster shells on the baking pan.

FLAMING PERCH (4 servings)

1 3- to 4-pound perch
2 teaspoons salt
3 tablespoons melted butter
2 small bunches fennel greens
⅓ cup brandy, heated

1. Wash perch and dry thoroughly. Rub with salt inside and out. Dip the fish in the melted butter and grill over an open fire for about 10 minutes, basting often with melted butter. The fish is done when it flakes easily.
2. Place the fish in a shallow baking dish and cover it with the fennel greens which have been washed and thoroughly dried.
3. Pour brandy over the greens and set aflame.

FILETS DE POMPANO HELOISE (Serves 6)

2 shallots or green onions, chopped
½ cup very finely diced mushrooms
6 pompano fillets
salt and pepper
2 cups dry white wine
juice of ½ lemon
2 tablespoons butter

1. Sprinkle the shallots and mushrooms on a buttered baking dish.

2. Season the pompano fillets with salt and pepper and lay them on the mushrooms side by side.

3. Add the wine and lemon juice and cover the fish with a piece of buttered brown paper.

4. Bake in a preheated moderate oven (350° F.) for about 15 minutes, until the fish flakes readily when touched with a fork.

5. Pour the cooking liquid into a saucepan and reduce it over high heat to one fourth its original volume.

6. Remove the pan and swirl in the butter.

7. Adjust seasoning and pour the sauce over the fish in the baking dish.

8. Place the dish under the broiler for a minute or two to glaze the sauce.

BAKED RED SNAPPER FLORIDA (6 to 8 servings)

1 4- to 5-pound red snapper
salt
6 tablespoons butter
½ small onion, minced
1 cup day-old bread crumbs or cubes
½ cup fine cracker crumbs
½ teaspoon basil or dill
2 teaspoons chopped parsley
¼ teaspoon salt
freshly ground black pepper to taste
1 grapefruit, sectioned, with its juice
1 orange, sectioned

1. Preheat oven to 400° F.

2. Sprinkle the fish inside and out with salt.

3. In skillet melt 4 tablespoons of the butter, add the onion and cook until it is transparent.

4. Add the bread and cracker crumbs, the basil, parsley, ¼ teaspoon salt and pepper and mix well.

5. Stuff the fish with the mixture and close with skewers and string.

6. Place the fish in a greased, foil-lined pan, and bake for about 40 minutes or until it flakes easily. Brush frequently with the grapefruit juice and the remaining butter.

7. Three minutes before removing the fish from the oven, arrange the grapefruit and orange sections on top of fish and brush with the remaining butter mixture or additional butter.

POACHED SALMON STEAK (6 servings)

2 tablespoons butter
⅓ cup chopped onion
⅓ cup chopped celery
1 quart water
½ cup vinegar
1 bay leaf
1 pinch thyme
salt
peppercorns
1 3-pound salmon steak
Blender Hollandaise or Mayonnaise**

1. In a large skillet heat the butter, add vegetables and cook 5 minutes. Add water, vinegar, bay leaf, thyme and seasonings and simmer for 5 minutes.
2. Wrap the salmon in cheesecloth and place in the liquid. Lower the heat, cover and simmer gently for about 25 minutes, or 8 minutes per pound.
3. Remove the salmon carefully, unwrap and serve hot with Hollandaise Sauce or cold with Mayonnaise.

CURRIED SCALLOPS (6 servings)

2 pounds scallops
seasoned flour
8 tablespoons butter
6 shallots or green onions, finely chopped
1½ tablespoons curry powder
⅓ cup dry white wine

1. Wash and dry scallops.
2. Dust lightly with seasoned flour.
3. Melt butter in skillet and in it sauté shallots for 3 minutes.
4. Add scallops and cook quickly, turning often to brown on all sides.
5. Sprinkle with curry powder, add wine and mix well. Serve on boiled rice garnished with sautéed almonds.

SCALLOPS ANTOINE (6 servings)

2 pounds scallops
2 cups dry white wine
¼ cup butter
¼ cup finely chopped shallots
½ pound mushrooms, sliced
2 tablespoons flour
2 tablespoons heavy cream
2 tablespoons chopped parsley
½ cup buttered bread crumbs

1. Place fish and wine in a skillet with a tight cover and simmer for about 5 minutes or until tender. Drain and reserve liquid.

2. Melt butter and sauté shallots and mushrooms for 3 to 5 minutes. Stir in flour and gradually stir in reserved liquid and cream. Bring to a boil, stirring.

3. Add fish and parsley to sauce and pour into a shallow casserole. Top with bread crumbs and place under broiler to brown lightly.

SCALLOPS BRUNI (4 to 6 servings)

2 ounces butter
½ cup chopped onion
½ cup chopped leeks (white part only)
1 pound raw scallops, cut into cubes
2 tablespoons flour
*1 unbaked 9-inch Pastry Shell**
4 eggs, slightly beaten
2 cups heavy cream, scalded
½ teaspoon salt
¼ teaspoon black pepper
⅛ teaspoon nutmeg

1. Melt butter in a skillet and add the onion and leeks. Sauté for 5 minutes.

2. Sprinkle the scallops with flour and add to the onion and leeks in the pan. Fry over high heat for about 5 minutes. Place mixture in Pastry Shell.

3. Blend the eggs and the cream. Add salt, pepper and nutmeg. Pour over the scallops. Bake in preheated oven at 375° F. until light brown and set.

SCALLOPS EN BROCHETTE (4 servings)

Skewered Scallops

2 pounds scallops
salt and pepper to taste
1½ cups dry vermouth
½ cup chopped fennel leaves
cherry tomatoes
salad oil

1. Wash and dry scallops and season with salt and pepper.

2. Combine vermouth and fennel leaves and marinate scallops for about 2 hours in this mixture.

3. Alternate scallops and tomatoes on skewers and roll them in oil.

4. Grill slowly until scallops are a light golden color.

SCALLOPS SARIAT (4 to 6 servings)

8 tablespoons butter
1 small carrot, finely chopped
1 onion, finely chopped
2 shallots, finely chopped
2 sprigs of parsley, finely chopped
pinch of powdered thyme
1 bay leaf
2 pounds scallops
1 cup dry white wine
3 tomatoes, peeled, seeded and chopped
¼ cup brandy

1. In 4 tablespoons of butter gently sauté all the vegetables except tomatoes until they are lightly browned. Add thyme and bay leaf and cook over low heat for about 15 minutes.

2. Wash and dry scallops and add to vegetable mixture. Cook until scallops are lightly browned. Add wine and tomatoes and simmer for 10 minutes. Add the brandy to the pan and set it aflame.

3. Remove the scallops and keep warm. Reduce pan juices to 1½ cups. Add remaining 4 tablespoons butter and cook 2 minutes longer. Return scallops to the sauce to heat thoroughly.

SCALLOPS ST. YVES (1 serving)

1 mushroom, diced
½ teaspoon chopped chives
1 tablespoon dry bread crumbs
salt and pepper to taste
1 tablespoon dry white wine
½ tablespoon melted butter
6 to 8 scallops
1 scallop shell or shirred-egg dish

1. Mix mushroom, chives, bread crumbs, salt, pepper, wine and butter together.

2. Combine this with the scallops and fill the shell. A sprinkling of bread crumbs may be put on top of filling.

3. Bake in preheated 350° F. oven for 20 minutes.

BOSTON SCROD, NEW ORLEANS STYLE (2 servings)

1 tablespoon butter
1 medium onion, sliced
1 green pepper, sliced thin
4 mushrooms, sliced
1 stalk of celery, sliced thin
3 tomatoes, peeled, seeded and diced
*½ cup Pisa Tomato Sauce**
½ clove garlic, chopped
½ cup dry white wine, Chablis type
salt and pepper to taste
2 portions Boston scrod
1 tablespoon chopped parsley

1. In saucepan melt butter and add onion, green pepper, mushrooms and celery. Stir and cook for 1 minute. Add tomatoes, Tomato Sauce, garlic, wine, salt and pepper. Cook for 10 minutes.

2. Lay the fish in a pyrex baking dish, pour sauce over and bake in preheated oven at 350° F. for about 15 minutes.

3. Sprinkle parsley on top before serving.

SHAD ROE ANGEVINE (4 servings)

3 tablespoons unsalted butter
2 tablespoons finely chopped shallots
¼ cup canned sorrel
1½ cups dry white wine
4 pairs shad roe
salt and white pepper to taste
1¼ cups heavy cream

1. In a skillet heat the butter, place the shallots, sorrel and wine in it and arrange the roe on top. Sprinkle with salt and pepper.

2. Cover the pan and bring mixture to a boil. Reduce the heat and simmer about 20 minutes.

3. Remove the roe to a warm plate and keep warm.

4. Add the cream to remaining sauce, bring to a boil, reduce the heat and cook down to the consistency of a thin white sauce, leaving the skillet uncovered. Adjust the seasonings and spoon the sauce over the roe.

SHAD ROE POLONAISE (2 to 4 servings)

¼ cup butter
2 medium shad roe
salt and pepper
2 teaspoons lemon juice
1 hard-cooked egg, chopped
1 tablespoon chopped parsley
2 teaspoons chopped chives
1 tablespoon bread crumbs

1. In a skillet heat the butter and add the shad roe. Season with salt and pepper. Cook the roe on both sides, with a lid to prevent spattering, for about 12 minutes. Turn once carefully.

2. When the roe is cooked through, transfer to a hot platter.

3. Add the remaining ingredients to the skillet. Heat, stirring, and pour over the shad roe.

CHILLED SHRIMP SHANGHAI (4 servings)

½ cup soy sauce
¼ to ½ cup lemon juice
1 teaspoon ground ginger
24 shrimp, cooked, shelled, deveined and chilled
1 bunch watercress

1. Combine soy sauce, lemon juice and ginger and mix well.

2. Arrange shrimp and watercress in chilled platter. Dip into sauce.

ORIENTAL SHRIMP (6 servings)

1½ pounds shrimp, shelled and deveined
4 tablespoons vegetable fat
2 onions, sliced
1 green pepper, thinly sliced
½ cup pineapple chunks
½ cup sugar
½ cup vinegar
1 tablespoon soy sauce
1 teaspoon dry mustard
1 tablespoon cornstarch
¼ cup water
rice

1. Sauté the shrimp in melted fat until cooked (about 5 minutes). Remove from the pan. Add the onions, green pepper and pineapple. Cook for 1 minute.

2. Combine the sugar and vinegar, add to the pan and bring to a boil.

3. Add soy sauce and mustard. Combine the cornstarch and water. Stir into sauce. Cook and stir until the mixture thickens, and boil for 1 minute. Add the shrimp. Serve with rice.

SHRIMP AMANDINE BOMBAY (4 to 6 servings)

¼ cup butter
1 small carrot, scraped and cut into small cubes
1 tablespoon finely chopped onion
1 tablespoon finely chopped shallot
¼ teaspoon dried thyme
½ bay leaf
1½ pounds raw shrimp, shelled and deveined
1 cup dry white wine
½ teaspoon curry powder
2 tomatoes, peeled, seeded and chopped
½ teaspoon salt
½ cup chopped blanched almonds
½ cup heavy cream

1. Melt butter in a heavy skillet and add carrot, onion, shallot, thyme and bay leaf. Cook until onion is transparent, or about 5 minutes.

2. Add shrimp and cook, stirring until the shrimp are pink, or about 5 minutes. Add wine, curry powder and tomatoes and simmer 10 minutes longer. Add salt.

3. Remove shrimp to a warm dish. Strain sauce and add almonds and cream. Heat thoroughly, but do not boil. Return shrimp to sauce. Reheat and serve immediately.

SHRIMP AND LOBSTER MEDITERRANEAN (4 servings)

1 large live lobster
3 tablespoons olive oil
2 pounds raw shrimp, shelled and deveined
2 cloves garlic, chopped
2 teaspoons chopped parsley
2 cups dry white wine
salt to taste

1. Cut lobster into pieces with a heavy knife. Sauté in olive oil until lobster pieces are red on all sides. Add shrimp, garlic and parsley. Cook, stirring frequently, for about 3 minutes, until vegetables begin to soften.

2. Add wine and salt to taste. Bring to a boil and simmer over low heat for about 15 to 20 minutes.

SHRIMP D'ORAL (6 servings)

¼ cup butter
1 cup chopped onion
2 to 3 teaspoons curry powder
½ teaspoon salt
⅛ teaspoon ginger
⅛ teaspoon chili powder
3 tablespoons flour
1 bottle (8 ounces) clam juice
2 pounds raw shrimp, shelled and deveined
1 tablespoon lemon juice

1. In hot butter in a large skillet sauté onion and curry until onion is tender, about 5 minutes. Remove from heat.

2. Add salt, ginger, chili powder and flour and mix well. Stir in clam juice and bring to a boil, stirring. Reduce heat and simmer for 5 minutes.

3. Stir in shrimp and lemon juice and simmer until tender.

SHRIMP FRANCESCA (4 servings)

6 tablespoons flour
2 tablespoons grated Parmesan cheese
1 teaspoon salt
1 pound raw shrimp
6 medium green peppers
½ cup oil
1 clove garlic, minced
¼ cup dry white wine
¾ teaspoon salt
pepper to taste

1. Mix flour, cheese and salt in a paper bag. Add shrimp and shake to coat.

2. Remove seeds from green peppers and cut into narrow strips.

3. Heat oil and toss in shrimp and minced garlic. Cook for 5 minutes until golden. Remove shrimp. Put peppers in the pan. Cover and cook for 10 to 15 minutes until tender.

4. Return the shrimp and add wine, salt and pepper and heat.

SHRIMP MARGARET (4 servings)

6 slices day-old bread
1 pound shrimp, cooked, shelled and deveined
½ pound Cheddar cheese, diced
4 tablespoons melted butter
3 whole eggs, beaten
¼ teaspoon dry mustard
salt and pepper to taste
cayenne pepper to taste
2 cups milk

1. Trim the bread and cut it into cubes.
2. Arrange layers of bread, shrimp and cheese in a greased casserole and pour the melted butter over all.
3. Beat the eggs and add mustard, salt, pepper and cayenne pepper to taste. Stir in the milk and pour this mixture over the shrimp, bread and cheese layers.
4. Bake in preheated 350° F. oven for 1 hour.

SHRIMP NAPOLI (4 to 6 servings)

6 tablespoons butter
3 tablespoons olive oil
½ cup chopped onion
1 clove garlic, minced
1½ cups raw rice
¾ cup white wine
*2½ cups boiling Chicken Broth**
1 pound raw shrimp, shelled and deveined
1½ teaspoons salt
pepper to taste
¼ teaspoon cayenne pepper
¼ cup grated Parmesan cheese

1. Heat 4 tablespoons of butter and the oil in a heavy casserole. Add the onion and cook until shiny. Add the garlic and the rice and cook till the rice just starts to take on color. Add wine and cook over medium heat until wine is absorbed.
2. Add one-half of the Broth and cover. Cook gently for 15 minutes without stirring. Add the shrimp, salt, pepper, cayenne pepper and remaining Broth. Stir lightly with a fork. Cover. Simmer until rice is tender. Stir in cheese and remaining butter. Serve immediately.

SHRIMP NEWBURGH (4 servings)

4 tablespoons butter
4 tablespoons flour
1½ cups milk
3 tablespoons sherry
1½ cups cooked or canned shrimp, deveined
1 tablespoon butter
paprika
rice

1. Melt 4 tablespoons butter in small saucepan on medium heat. Add flour slowly, stirring constantly until flour is cooked. Remove from heat and let cool slightly.

2. Bring milk to boiling point in small saucepan over high heat. Add milk slowly to butter and flour, stirring mixture with portable mixer until thick and smooth. Place mixture over medium heat.

3. Put sherry in medium bowl and add hot sauce slowly while beating with portable mixer. Pour mixture back into saucepan and heat slowly.

4. Simmer shrimp in 1 tablespoon butter and sprinkle lightly with paprika. Put shrimp into hot sauce and serve with rice.

SHRIMP RATATOUILLE (6 servings)

¼ cup olive oil
4 cloves garlic, minced
1 pound sweet onions, sliced in thin rings
1 tablespoon salt
½ teaspoon freshly ground pepper
1 pound green peppers, cut in strips
1 medium eggplant, sliced ¼ inch thick and sprinkled with 1½ tablespoons lemon juice
1 pound (small) zucchini, sliced thin
2 pounds tomatoes, peeled and sliced thin
2 pounds shrimp, shelled and deveined
¼ cup olive oil

1. In a large casserole heat ¼ cup olive oil. Add half the garlic

and simmer 1 minute. Add half the onions and cook 1 minute more. Sprinkle a little salt and pepper over the mixture.

2. To make layers: Use half of each of remaining ingredients for each layer and sprinkle with salt, pepper and olive oil. There should be 2 layers.

3. Bring to a boil. Reduce heat and simmer, covered, for 20 minutes. Remove cover and cook to reduce sauce—about 10 minutes.

4. Sauce may be thickened by adding 2 teaspoons butter and 2 teaspoons flour.

SHRIMP RIMINI (4 servings)

DRESSING

1 egg yolk
½ cup olive oil
¼ cup salad oil
¼ cup wine vinegar
2 tablespoons prepared mustard
2 tablespoons minced parsley
2 tablespoons chopped chives
1 tablespoon minced shallots
1 package frozen artichoke hearts, cooked, drained and chilled
24 shrimp, cooked, shelled and deveined

Blend all dressing ingredients well. Add artichoke hearts and shrimp. Marinate in the refrigerator about 4 hours, turning often.

SHRIMP SOUTH-OF-THE-BORDER STYLE (4 to 6 servings)

1½ pounds raw shrimp, shelled and deveined
3 tablespoons peanut oil
2 medium onions, sliced
1 clove garlic, finely minced
4 stalks of celery, chopped
1½ tablespoons flour
2½ cups canned tomatoes
1 bay leaf
½ teaspoon thyme
1 tablespoon chili powder
½ pound fresh mushrooms, sliced and cooked in butter until wilted
2 pimientos, chopped
salt and pepper to taste

1. Wash the shrimp well and dry them thoroughly.

2. Heat the oil in a large skillet and add the onions, garlic and about two-thirds of the celery. Cook until the vegetables are tender.

3. Sprinkle in the flour and continue cooking, stirring constantly, until mixture is lightly browned. Add tomatoes, bay leaf, thyme, chili

powder, mushrooms and pimientos. Season to taste with salt and pepper and cook for 10 minutes.

4. Add the shrimp and remaining celery and simmer 10 minutes longer.

SHRIMP WITH HERBS (4 servings)

2 pounds shrimp, shelled and deveined
3 cloves garlic, finely chopped
¼ cup chopped parsley
1 teaspoon basil
1 teaspoon dry mustard
1 teaspoon salt
½ cup olive oil
juice of 1 lemon

1. Place shrimp in a bowl, add remaining ingredients which have been thoroughly mixed, and marinate for several hours at room temperature.

2. Broil 4 or 5 minutes, turning once.

ENGLISH SOLE ARLESIENNE (3 to 4 servings)

6 fillets of English sole or 1½ pounds fillets of flounder
½ cup tomatoes, peeled, seeded and diced
2 bottom parts of artichokes, fresh or canned, diced
½ cup mushrooms, diced
½ cup white wine
2 tablespoons butter
salt and pepper
chopped parsley

1. Flatten the sole lightly with the flat of a knife and lay the fillets on a buttered pan.

2. Place the tomatoes, artichokes and mushrooms on top, add the wine and dot with butter. Salt and pepper to taste.

3. Bake in preheated 400° F. oven for about 10 minutes. Sprinkle chopped parsley on top before serving.

FILLETS OF SOLE NORMANDE (4 servings)

8 fillets of English sole
salt and pepper to taste
1 tablespoon finely chopped shallots
4 small uncooked shrimp, shelled and deveined
8 mussels, washed and scrubbed
4 medium mushroom caps
½ cup dry white wine, Chablis type
1 teaspoon lemon juice
½ cup heavy cream
2 egg yolks
2 slices bread, toasted and cut in triangles

1. Lay the sole fillets side by side on a buttered baking dish and sprinkle them with salt and pepper. Add shallots, shrimp, mussels, mushrooms, wine and lemon juice.
2. Cover and bake in preheated oven at 350° F. for 15 minutes.
3. Remove the sole, shrimp, mushrooms and mussels. Take mussels out of the shells. Keep all warm.
4. Pour the cooking juices in a saucepan and add cream. Bring to a boil. Add egg yolks. Heat all together without boiling, stirring constantly, and strain over the fish.
5. Serve with toast triangles.

FILETS DE SOLE VERONIQUE (6 servings)

6 sole fillets
salt and pepper
*1 cup Court Bouillon**
½ cup white wine
1 cup white grapes, skinned and seeded
½ cup cream
2 tablespoons butter

1. Flatten the sole fillets lightly with the flat of a knife and fold them in half.
2. Season with salt and pepper and lay the fillets side by side on a buttered pan. Pour the Court Bouillon and white wine over the fish.
3. Cook gently for 10 minutes, until the fish is done.
4. Remove the sole to a platter and garnish with the grapes.
5. Reduce the cooking liquor in pan over high heat to one-fourth its original volume.
6. Add cream and slowly swirl in the butter, off the heat. Adjust the seasoning.

7. Pour the sauce over the fillets and grapes and set the platter under the broiler to glaze the sauce.

SOLE D'ANTIN (4 servings)

2 tablespoons butter
2 tablespoons finely chopped onion
4 fillets of sole or flounder
¼ cup bottled clam juice
½ cup dry white wine or water
3 tomatoes, peeled, seeded and diced
5 mushrooms, sliced
2 tablespoons minced parsley
½ clove garlic, chopped
salt to taste
⅛ teaspoon freshly ground black pepper
2 tablespoons heavy cream

1. In a skillet heat the butter, add the onion and cook until it is transparent.
2. Arrange the fillets in a baking dish and pour the clam juice and wine over them.
3. Add the tomatoes, mushrooms, parsley, garlic, salt and pepper.
4. Bake in preheated oven at 350° F. for 10 minutes.
5. Remove the fillets to a serving dish and keep warm.
6. Pour sauce from baking dish into pan and stir over high heat for 2 or 3 minutes until slightly reduced.
7. Add cream and stir.
8. Pour the sauce over the fillets.

SOLE DORIA (4 servings)

1½ cups dry vermouth
3 tablespoons chopped shallots or green onions
1 cucumber, seeded, cut 1 inch long and ¼ inch thick
8 small fillets of sole
salt and freshly ground pepper
1¼ cups butter, cut into small pieces
6 egg yolks
2 tablespoons heavy cream

1. In a skillet simmer the vermouth, shallots and cucumber for 5 minutes.
2. Add the sole and poach gently until the fish flakes easily.

There should be enough of the wine to cover the fish. Add more wine if necessary.

3. Place the fish in a flat baking dish, season with salt and pepper and keep warm.

4. Boil the liquid until it is reduced to ½ cup.

5. In the top of a double boiler, mix the cooking liquid, butter and egg yolks.

6. Whisk the sauce over simmering water until it thickens.

7. Add the heavy cream and pour the sauce over the fish.

8. Set under a hot broiler for a few seconds to glaze top, and serve at once.

SOLE DIEPPOISE (6 servings)

1 pint mussels, scrubbed well and debearded
2 tablespoons white wine, Chablis type
6 small mushrooms
1 tablespoon water
½ teaspoon lemon juice
6 small fillets of sole
1 small jar shrimp
½ cup butter
1 tablespoon flour
2 egg yolks
½ cup heavy cream
salt and pepper

1. Place the mussels in a saucepan with the wine, cover and steam until the shells open. Drain, reserving the liquid.

2. Cook the mushrooms in the water and lemon juice about 2 minutes. Drain, reserving the liquid.

3. Place the fillets in a saucepan with 1½ cups of the mixed liquids from the mussels and mushrooms. If there is not enough liquid to make 1½ cups, add enough water or white wine to fill. Simmer gently for 10 minutes. Remove the fish to a serving dish, arrange the mussels, mushrooms and shrimp around it and keep warm.

4. In a saucepan heat 2 tablespoons of the butter, add the flour and cook, stirring, until golden. Add the cooking liquid from the fish, stirring vigorously, and boil for about 4 minutes.

5. Mix the egg yolks with the cream, add to the sauce and bring to the boiling point, stirring constantly. Do not let it boil. Add the remaining butter, salt and pepper and strain through a fine sieve over the fish.

SOLE MEUNIERE (3 servings)

6 fillets of English sole
½ cup beer or milk
seasoned flour (flour seasoned with ½ teaspoon salt and ⅛ teaspoon pepper)
peanut oil
3 tablespoons butter
lemon juice
finely chopped parsley
1 medium lemon, sliced
chopped parsley
paprika

1. Place fillets in shallow dish, add beer or milk and let stand for about 15 minutes.

2. Pat the fillets dry and dredge in seasoned flour.

3. Add peanut oil to a skillet to a depth of ¼ inch. When hot, cook the fillets on both sides until golden brown.

4. Transfer the fillets to a hot dish and discard the oil in the skillet.

5. Add the butter to the skillet and when it starts to brown, pour it over the fillets.

6. Sprinkle with lemon juice and chopped parsley and garnish with lemon slices dipped in half parsley and half paprika.

TRUITES DE RIVIERE AU BLEU (3 servings)
Boiled Brook Trout

3 live brook trout, about 1 pound each
*1 quart Court Bouillon**

1. Remove the trout from the water and tap them on the head to render them unconscious. Cut the fins off and clean the fish.

2. Place the fish on a rack and slowly lower them into kettle of boiling Court Bouillon. Reduce the heat to prevent the boiling from causing the trout to break.

3. Boil for 8 to 10 minutes, depending upon the size of the fish. Serve with melted butter and boiled potatoes.

TRUITES AMANDINES (2 servings)

Brook Trout with Almonds

2 brook trout, about 1 pound each
salt and pepper to taste
cold milk
flour
5 tablespoons unsalted butter
2 tablespoons blanched, shredded almonds
2 teaspoons lemon juice

1. Season trout with salt and pepper. Dip in milk and roll in flour. Sauté over low heat in 3 tablespoons of butter until brown on both sides. Remove trout and keep hot.

2. To butter remaining in pan add 2 more tablespoons of the butter and heat to foaming point. Stir in the almonds and cook for 1 minute. Rock the pan constantly while cooking almonds.

3. Sprinkle each fish with lemon juice and pour the butter-almond mixture over the fish.

POULTRY AND GAME BIRDS

WHAT is an absolute necessity for fish is also true for poultry. It must be absolutely fresh. Not even the most skillful preparation will disguise its failings in this respect.

When you buy fowl, take particular care in the selection of what you buy. It should, first, have tender flesh and be elastic without being flabby. The breastbone should give when it is moved from side to side between thumb and forefinger. The skin should be loose and white.

Most especially, make sure your bird is free from offensive odor. Even if it is wrapped in clear plastic, as so many markets sell it today, do not be hesitant about opening the package and smelling, or asking the manager to let you smell it before it is wrapped up if he is selling it without a container. I have taken the trouble to emphasize this point only because I know how frequently chickens can spoil in this era of large-scale cold storage of edibles. The dangers to health and gastronomy are obvious.

If a recipe calls for the addition of cooking liquor, be careful not to use too much, or the delicate flavor will be dissipated. And, if you have never done so, try one of the dishes which blend some other delicacy with the bird, as is the case with the recipe for Baby Pheasant Souvaroff,* which you will find in this chapter, where *pâté de foie gras* becomes a delightful part of the dish. Ordinarily, one thinks of pâté as something to precede the meal, or to go with the drinks, but this gourmet specialty, which was invented more than two hundred years ago in Normandy by the chef of the Marechal de Contades, can be used effectively in many dishes. The Alsatians have made pâté a regional specialty since the original recipe of 1762 came into being.

A favorite chicken dish of the Kennedys in their family dining, and often served at important White House functions, was Poulet a l'Estragon*—that is, chicken with tarragon. The recipe I used for it opens this section.

POULET A L'ESTRAGON (4 servings)

Chicken with Tarragon

1 chicken, 3 pounds
2 tablespoons flour
salt and pepper to taste
6 ounces (¾ cup) melted butter
2 or 3 shallots
½ cup dry white wine
*½ cup Chicken Broth**
1 bay leaf
pinch thyme
2 sprigs of parsley
1 small bunch fresh tarragon

1. Cut chicken into 8 or 10 pieces (or leave whole).

2. Combine flour, salt and pepper. Coat chicken with flour mixture. (Reserve any leftover flour.) Brown lightly on all sides in melted butter for 4 or 5 minutes.

3. Cut shallots very fine and spread over chicken. Simmer for a few minutes. Add wine, Chicken Broth and the herbs, using only the stems of the tarragon and saving leaves for the sauce. Cover and simmer for 25 minutes or until chicken is tender. If chicken is cooked whole, simmer about 45 minutes, turning frequently. When tender, remove and keep hot.

SAUCE

1 cup heavy cream
tarragon leaves

1. To the pan juices, add cream and any flour not used in coating chicken. Simmer gently until sauce thickens.

2. Strain sauce over chicken. Garnish with tarragon leaves, whole or chopped.

BAKED CHICKEN WITH FRUIT SAUCE (6 servings)

- *1 roasting chicken, about 4 pounds, cut in serving pieces*
- *½ cup dry white wine*
- *¼ cup lime juice*
- *¼ cup soy sauce*
- *1 cup finely chopped onions*
- *4 cloves garlic, crushed*
- *½ teaspoon oregano*
- *½ teaspoon thyme*
- *1 teaspoon curry powder*
- *1 teaspoon ground ginger*
- *2 tablespoons butter*
- *1 tablespoon salad oil*
- *2 tablespoons flour*
- *1 cup canned kumquats, halved*
- *2 egg yolks, lightly beaten*
- *salt to taste*

1. Place chicken pieces in a large, shallow baking dish. Combine the next 9 ingredients and pour over chicken. Cover and allow to marinate about 8 hours, turning 2 times. Drain chicken and reserve marinade.

2. Heat butter and oil in large frying pan, brown chicken pieces and return to the baking dish. Stir flour into the fat remaining in the pan and cook, stirring, until bubbly. Gradually stir in marinade and cook until thickened. Pour sauce over chicken, cover dish with foil and place in a preheated 350° F. oven for 1 hour, or until tender.

3. Remove chicken from sauce and place in a shallow serving dish. Arrange kumquats around and on chicken and keep warm.

4. Pour sauce from baking dish into a small saucepan and bring to a boil. Blend some of the hot liquid with the egg yolks, then return mixture to pan. Cook, stirring constantly, until sauce is thickened. Do not boil. Add salt to taste and pour sauce over chicken.

BREAST OF CHICKEN A LA REINE ELISABETH (6 servings)

PEANUT BUTTER

2 cups salted peanuts

Put shelled, salted peanuts in blender container; cover and run on low speed until finely chopped, then move to high speed until smooth. Stop blender when necessary and push peanuts from sides of container toward blades. Makes about 1½ cups.

BUTTER FILLING

½ cup unsalted butter, room temperature
½ cup fresh Peanut Butter

1. Measure ½ cup butter and ½ cup smooth fresh Peanut Butter into a clean blender container; cover and run on low speed just until mixed. Stop blender, if necessary, and push the ingredients toward the blades with a rubber spatula.

2. Empty mixture into a small bowl and chill in the refrigerator for 45 minutes or in freezer for 15 minutes.

3. Form mixture into 6 rolls, 3×½ inches. Wrap rolls in aluminum foil and freeze.

CHICKEN BREASTS

3 fresh chicken breasts, boned and halved
salt and white pepper to taste
½ pound butter, clarified
1 egg, slightly beaten
1 tablespoon salad oil
1 cup flour
soft bread crumbs

1. To prepare each breast half, carefully remove all skin. Using a smooth-surfaced meat hammer or a rolling pin, flatten each breast and "fillet," cut side up, to about ¼ inch thick; be careful not to tear meat. Lightly salt and pepper chicken.

2. Place butter roll lengthwise on each breast half. Roll and fold each breast so that the butter is completely enclosed. Wrap in wax paper or aluminum foil; chill in the refrigerator.

3. Clarify butter by melting in top of double boiler. Pour off butter, leaving impurities in the bottom of the pan.

4. Mix egg and oil. Spread flour in shallow pan. Remove chicken breasts from refrigerator. To coat evenly, roll each breast in the flour. Dip each breast into the egg-oil mixture. Roll chicken generously in bread crumbs rendered fine in blender. Chicken breast must be well sealed to retain butter.

5. Using about ¼ cup clarified butter in heavy frypan, cook 1 or 2 chicken rolls, turning until evenly golden brown. Place browned chicken in oven pan. Repeat with remaining chicken. Oven should be preheated to 350° F. Bake for 10 to 15 minutes or until chicken is tender. Make Sauce Supreme while chicken bakes.

SAUCE SUPREME

1 tablespoon butter
2 tablespoons flour
*1 cup Chicken Broth**
3 tablespoons heavy cream

1. Melt butter in small, heavy saucepan and stir in flour. Cook, stirring constantly with a whisk, for 1 minute. Add Chicken Broth gradually and cook for 15 minutes on low heat.

2. Add cream and strain through cheesecloth. Keep sauce hot until serving time.

TO SERVE

6 slices bread
6 slices Virginia ham

1. Toast 6 slices of bread; cut in heart shape.

2. Warm the 6 slices of Virginia ham on both sides in frypan.

3. Place toast on serving plate; lay ham on toast and top with baked chicken breast. Serve with Sauce Supreme on the side or spooned over each serving.

BREAST OF CHICKEN, INDIAN STYLE (4 servings)

2 tablespoons chopped onion
2 tablespoons chopped celery
3 tablespoons butter
¼ teaspoon salt
2 teaspoons curry powder
3 tablespoons flour
1 cup milk
½ cup cream
1 tablespoon sherry
¼ cup diced pickled peaches
4 chicken breasts
*1 cup Chicken Broth**
croutons
grated Parmesan cheese

1. Sauté onions and celery in butter until onions are yellow. Add salt and curry powder and mix thoroughly. Add flour and cook until bubbly. Add milk and cream, stir briskly until smooth and thick and cook until all starchy flavor is gone. Add sherry and fruit.

2. Poach chicken in Broth. Add to the curry sauce and simmer for 10 minutes. Spoon over croutons sprinkled with Parmesan cheese.

I recall the occasion when I first prepared Suprême de Volaille Gismonda at the White House. It was a luncheon for Prince Rainier and Princess Grace of Monaco, in May of 1961. The menu follows:

PULIGNY MONTRACHET 1958	SOFT-SHELL CRAB AMANDINE*
CHATEAU CORTON	SUPREME DE VOLAILLE GISMONDA*
	SALADE MIMOSA*
DOM PERIGNON 1952	STRAWBERRIES ROMANOFF
	PETITS FOURS SEC
	DEMITASSE

Now, here is the recipe for Suprême de Volaille Gismonda:

SUPREME DE VOLAILLE GISMONDA (4 servings)
Breast of Chicken with Mushrooms and Spinach

4 chicken breasts, boned
salt to taste
white pepper to taste
flour for dredging
1 tablespoon water
1 egg, beaten
¼ cup grated Parmesan cheese
¾ cup white bread crumbs
3 tablespoons butter
1 pound cooked spinach, coarsely chopped
¼ pound mushrooms, sliced
*2 tablespoons Brown Sauce**
chopped fresh parsley

1. Remove skin from chicken breasts and pound meat to flatten. Season with salt and pepper and dredge with flour.

2. Add water to beaten egg and dip the meat in this mixture. Combine cheese and crumbs; coat the meat.

3. Heat 2 tablespoons of butter in skillet and brown meat on both sides, about 10 minutes on each side.

4. Make a bed of coarsely chopped spinach on serving platter, arrange chicken breast on top and keep hot.

5. To the skillet add remaining butter and sauté mushrooms until tender. Spoon over chicken, pour Brown Sauce around the chicken and sprinkle with chopped parsley.

CHICKEN AND BEEF, COUNTRY STYLE (6 servings)

1 pound beef stew meat
6 chicken drumsticks
3½ cups boiling water
3 teaspoons salt
1 teaspoon lemon juice
12 small white onions
6 carrots, sliced
1 cup sliced celery
1 cup fresh snap beans, cut into 2-inch pieces
3 ears fresh corn, cut into 2-inch lengths
¼ teaspoon freshly ground pepper
3 tablespoons flour
⅓ cup cold water

1. Trim excess fat from the beef and cut the meat into 1-inch cubes. Brown the beef and chicken in a Dutch oven or heavy saucepan, using the fat trimmed from the beef. Remove the chicken and reserve.

2. Add the boiling water, salt and lemon juice to the pan, cover and cook slowly until the meat is tender, about 1 hour.

3. Add the chicken and onions and cook for 15 minutes. Add the carrots, celery and beans and cook for another 10 minutes.

4. Add the corn and pepper and cook 10 minutes longer. Thicken with the flour and water mixed to a smooth paste.

CHICKEN AND NOODLES IN CREAMY SAUCE (4 servings)

1 chicken, about 3 pounds, cut up
¼ cup flour
1 teaspoon paprika
1 teaspoon salt
¼ teaspoon pepper
3 tablespoons salad oil
1 medium onion, chopped
1 clove garlic, minced
½ cup water
3 tablespoons lemon juice
1 bouillon cube
1 cup sour cream
1 package (8 ounces) noodles, cooked and drained

1. Shake chicken in seasoned flour and reserve the flour.

2. Brown chicken in oil and drain on paper towel.

3. Sauté onion and garlic. Return chicken to pan and add water, juice and bouillon cube. Cover and simmer for 30 minutes.

4. Remove from heat. Remove chicken, stir in 1 tablespoon seasoned flour and gradually blend in sour cream. Add noodles and toss to coat.

CHICKEN AND PINEAPPLE IN CHINESE SAUCE (4 servings)

1 chicken, about 3½ pounds, cut up
¼ cup flour
¼ teaspoon freshly ground pepper
¼ teaspoon monosodium glutamate
6 tablespoons salad oil
⅓ cup soy sauce
2 green peppers, cut into strips
2 medium onions, chopped
⅓ cup crushed pineapple

1. Dredge the chicken pieces in the flour mixed with pepper and monosodium glutamate.

2. Heat 3 tablespoons of oil, add chicken pieces and brown on both sides. Add the soy sauce, cover and cook for 10 minutes. Remove the chicken.

3. Heat the remaining oil, add the green peppers and onions and cook until the pepper is wilted. Return chicken to pan, add pineapple, cover and cook until chicken is tender.

CHICKEN BALTIMORE (4 servings)

2 2-pound frying chickens, cut in pieces
flour to dredge
2 tablespoons butter
1 small onion, chopped fine
*1 cup Chicken Broth**
salt and pepper to taste
1 cup heavy cream
1 cup corn, cooked
8 slices of bacon (broiled or sautéed)

1. Dredge the chicken lightly with flour.

2. In a large skillet, melt the butter, add the pieces of chicken and brown lightly on all sides. Add onion and Broth. Season with salt and pepper and cook slowly until tender (approximately 20 minutes).

3. Remove chicken to platter and keep warm.

4. Add the cream to the skillet, reduce heat and cook down to a creamy consistency. Stir in the corn and pour over the chicken. Top with bacon.

CHICKEN BASQUAISE (4 servings)

1 chicken, 2½ pounds, cut in serving pieces
salt and pepper to taste
3 tablespoons vegetable oil
1 medium onion, sliced
4 tomatoes, peeled, seeded and chopped
2 green peppers, seeded and sliced
1 clove garlic, minced
6 mushrooms, sliced
½ cup diced Virginia ham
½ cup dry white wine
*½ cup Brown Sauce**
1 tablespoon diced pimientos
1 tablespoon chopped parsley

1. Season chicken with salt and pepper.
2. In skillet heat the oil, add the chicken and brown on both sides.
3. Add onion, tomatoes, green peppers, garlic, mushrooms and ham and simmer for 4 minutes.
4. Add wine and Brown Sauce and cook for 30 minutes or until tender.
5. Before serving, sprinkle pimientos and parsley on top.

CHICKEN BEAUVAIS (2 servings)

1 frying chicken, about 3 pounds, cut in half
2 tablespoons butter
4 thin slices lemon
2 tablespoons dry sherry
½ cup heavy cream
4 thin slices Gruyère cheese
salt and pepper to taste

1. Place chicken, skin side up, in shallow roasting pan. Dot with butter and bake in preheated 350° F. oven, placing pan near top of the oven, for about 30 minutes. Place 2 slices of lemon on each half of chicken.
2. Mix sherry and cream and pour over the chicken. Cook about 1 hour longer, or until chicken is tender and crisp. Remove lemon slices and place 2 slices of cheese over each half of chicken. Bake until cheese melts. A little Chicken Broth* may be added to pan if juices begin to evaporate.
3. Remove chicken to heated serving platter. Add salt and pepper to juices in pan and pour over chicken.

CHICKEN BOMBAY (4 servings)

1 fryer, about 3 pounds, cut up
¼ cup flour mixed with 1 teaspoon salt and ¼ teaspoon pepper
4 tablespoons butter
⅓ cup diced onion
⅓ cup diced green pepper
1 clove garlic, minced
1½ teaspoons curry powder
½ teaspoon thyme
2 cups stewed tomatoes
blanched toasted almonds

1. Dredge chicken pieces in seasoned flour.
2. Heat butter and brown chicken on all sides.
3. Remove the chicken. Add the onion, pepper, garlic, curry powder and thyme. Cook briefly, stirring. Add tomatoes with liquid from the can. Return the chicken, skin side up. Cover and cook until tender. Serve with almonds.

CHICKEN BREAST FLORIO (8 servings)

8 chicken breasts
salt and pepper to taste
sprinkling of marjoram
5 tablespoons butter
1 pound mushrooms, cut into small pieces
12 ounces noodles, uncooked
*2 cups Béchamel Sauce**
1 cup cold milk
*1 cup Chicken Broth**
*1 cup Blender Hollandaise**
½ cup dry white wine
grated Parmesan cheese

1. Season breasts with salt, pepper and a sprinkling of marjoram. Sauté in 2 tablespoons butter until fully cooked.
2. Season mushrooms to taste and sauté in 2 tablespoons butter.
3. Cook noodles and drain. Add a tablespoon of butter and toss well.
4. To Bechamel Sauce add cold milk and Chicken Broth. Cook until thickened. Blend Hollandaise and Béchamel sauces together and add wine.
5. Butter a casserole. Place noodles on bottom, then mushrooms and then the breasts. Pour sauce over all. Sprinkle generously with grated cheese and place under broiler to brown.

POULET SAUTE A LA CREOLE (2 to 3 servings)

Chicken, Creole Style

1 chicken, 2½ pounds
salt and pepper
flour
2 tablespoons clarified butter (made by melting in top of double boiler)
1 onion
3 tomatoes, peeled and sliced
1 green pepper, seeded and sliced thin
2 garlic cloves, crushed
bouquet of 1 sprig of parsley, 1 sprig of thyme, bit of bay leaf tied together with white kitchen thread
*½ cup Chicken Broth**
½ cup sherry
salt and pepper

1. Have the chicken quartered and season the pieces with salt and pepper. Sprinkle them lightly with flour and brown them on all sides in the butter. Remove the chicken and keep it warm.

2. Slice the onion and brown it in the butter. Add the tomatoes, green pepper, garlic and the bouquet.

3. Simmer all together for 15 to 20 minutes. Add the Broth and wine, bring the liquid to a boil and season well with salt and pepper.

4. Return the chicken to the pan, cover and cook for 20 minutes until the chicken is very tender. Serve with rice.

CHICKEN DIABLO (3 to 4 servings)

1 2½-pound fryer, cut up
salt and pepper
½ cup salad oil
2 tablespoons flour
*1 cup hot water or Chicken Broth**
1½ teaspoons dry mustard
2 teaspoons Worcestershire sauce
2 teaspoons ketchup
paprika

1. Season chicken with salt and pepper and brown in oil; remove from pan.

2. Stir flour into fat; add hot water or Chicken Broth; cook until mixture thickens, stirring constantly. Add remaining 4 ingredients to cooked sauce.

3. Place chicken in sauce, cover pan and simmer until chicken is tender, about 1 hour.

CHICKEN FRANCAISE (4 to 6 servings)

½ pound ham, cut in small cubes
¼ cup butter
3- to 4-pound chicken, cut up
½ cup flour
5 white onions, quartered
1 clove garlic, crushed
1 tablespoon chopped parsley
¼ teaspoon dried thyme
1 cup chopped mushrooms
salt and pepper
2 tablespoons brandy
1 cup dry red wine

1. Sauté ham cubes in butter for a few minutes.
2. Dredge chicken pieces in flour, then brown in the butter, turning to cook on all sides. Add onions, garlic, parsley, thyme and mushrooms. Add about 1 teaspoon salt and ¼ teaspoon pepper. Cover and keep over low heat until all vegetables are thoroughly heated.
3. Remove cover and add brandy and wine. Bring just to boiling point, then adjust heat to keep at a simmer, cover and cook for 1 hour.

POULARDE FRANCILLON (4 servings)
Chicken Frances

1 4-pound chicken, seasoned with salt and pepper
4 ounces (½ cup) unsalted butter, melted
1 medium-sized onion, cut in cubes
1 carrot, cut in cubes
1 celery stalk, cut in cubes
1 clove garlic
pinch thyme
1 bay leaf
1 chicken neck, cut in small pieces
1 pint dry champagne
1½ pints (3 cups) heavy cream

1. Roll seasoned chicken in melted butter. Roast in preheated oven at 350° F. about 1 hour.
2. At the same time, place the cubed vegetables, garlic, thyme, bay leaf and chicken neck around the chicken. Be sure to baste the chicken very often while cooking with remaining melted butter.
3. When three-quarters done, add the dry champagne and cover. When cooked, remove the chicken and add the cream to the remain-

ing ingredients. Cook until sauce is fairly thick and smooth, then press through a strainer. Correct seasoning. Serve very hot.

CHICKEN HELENE (4 servings)

1 2½- to 3-pound chicken, cut up
flour seasoned with salt and pepper
6 tablespoons butter
2 tablespoons flour
*¾ cup Chicken Broth**
½ cup dry white wine
¼ cup thinly sliced green onions, including tops
½ cup sliced fresh mushrooms, sautéed in butter
1 9-ounce package frozen artichoke hearts, cooked and drained

1. Dust chicken with seasoned flour. Melt 4 tablespoons of the butter in a shallow baking pan. Place chicken in pan, skin side down; bake, uncovered, in preheated 350° F. oven for 45 minutes, or until almost tender.

2. Meanwhile, melt remaining butter in saucepan. Stir in flour. Add Broth and wine; cook, stirring constantly, until thickened and smooth.

3. Remove chicken from oven. Turn pieces over; sprinkle with onions, mushrooms and artichokes. Pour sauce over the top. Return to oven, reduce heat to 325° F. and bake 25 to 30 minutes longer.

POULET SAUTE CHASSEUR (6 to 8 servings)

Chicken, Hunter's Style

6 ounces (¾ cup) butter
3 chickens, 2½ pounds each, cut in pieces
5 shallots, chopped
1 onion, chopped
1 cup dry white wine
1 12-ounce can stewed tomatoes
½ pound mushrooms, sliced
12 ounces Chicken Broth (or canned)*
salt and pepper to taste
1 tablespoon flour
1 teaspoon chopped tarragon leaves
1 bay leaf
pinch thyme

1. Put 4 ounces of butter in a deep pan. When butter is hot, cook the chicken till golden brown, then add the shallots and onion, and cook slowly for 3 or 4 minutes. Add wine, stewed tomatoes,

mushrooms, Broth, salt and pepper to taste. Cook slowly for 25 minutes.

2. Remove the chicken pieces and keep warm. If desired trim off wing tips and exposed bones.

3. Boil the sauce slowly and thicken with 2 ounces of the butter blended with 1 tablespoon of flour. Boil sauce slowly for 5 minutes, add chopped tarragon leaves, bay leaf and thyme. Pour over the chicken pieces.

Serve with boiled potatoes or rice.

CHICKEN IN WHISKEY (4 to 6 servings)

1 4-pound roasting chicken, cut up
1 tablespoon flour
2 tablespoons olive oil
4 tablespoons butter
2 shallots, chopped
1 medium onion, chopped
2 ounces whiskey
1 cup heavy cream
*½ cup Brown Sauce**

1. Dredge chicken with flour.

2. In a heavy skillet, heat oil and butter and brown chicken. Add shallots and chopped onion. Cover and simmer for 50 minutes or until chicken is tender.

3. Remove chicken and keep warm.

4. To pan add whiskey, cream and Brown Sauce. Bring to boiling point, reduce heat and return chicken to skillet. Keep warm until serving time.

CHICKEN JAMBALAYA (8 servings)

2 tablespoons salad oil
1 cup chopped onion
1 cup chopped green pepper
2 cloves garlic, minced
1 cup diced cooked chicken
1 cup diced cooked ham
12 tiny pork sausages
1 No. 2 can tomatoes
1 cup raw white rice
*1½ cups Chicken Broth**
½ teaspoon thyme
1 tablespoon chopped parsley
1 teaspoon salt

1. Heat oil, add vegetables and cook slowly, stirring often until tender.

2. Add meats. Cook for 5 minutes.

3. Add balance of ingredients, turn into a casserole, cover and cook for 1 hour in preheated oven at 350° F.

CHICKEN MADRAS (4 servings)

1 fryer, about 3 pounds, cut up
salt and pepper
¼ cup (½ stick) butter
2 small onions, finely chopped
2 green apples, peeled and diced
2 tablespoons curry powder
2 tablespoons flour
*1½ cups Chicken Broth**

1. Season chicken with salt and pepper. Brown in melted butter. Remove from pan.

2. Add onions and apples and sauté until onions are tender. Sprinkle with curry powder and flour. Cook, stirring, for 2 minutes.

3. Stir in Broth and bring to a boil. Add chicken, cover and cook over low heat for 30 to 40 minutes until tender. If sauce is too thick, add more stock.

CHICKEN MADRID (3 to 4 servings)

1 2- to 2½-pound chicken
seasoned flour
2 tablespoons melted butter
1 cup chopped onion
2 cloves garlic, minced
½ cup diced green pepper
⅓ cup pimiento, cut in strips
1 cup uncooked rice
*1½ cups Chicken Broth**
1½ teaspoons turmeric
dash of chili powder
1 teaspoon salt
pepper

1. Cut chicken in serving pieces, roll in seasoned flour and brown in butter. Remove from skillet.

2. Cook onion, garlic and green pepper in remaining butter until onion is golden. Add pimiento and rice; stir over low heat for about 2 minutes. Add remaining ingredients. Heat to boiling.

3. Pour mixture into 2-quart casserole; arrange chicken on top. Bake in moderate preheated oven, 350° F., for about 1½ hours.

CHICKEN MANDARIN STYLE (4 to 6 servings)

½ cup soy sauce
½ cup honey
½ cup Scotch whiskey
3 tablespoons lemon juice
*½ cup Chicken Broth**
¼ teaspoon ginger
1 roasting chicken, about 4 pounds, washed and dried

1. Blend all ingredients (except chicken) for sauce, and brush generously inside chicken. Let stand at room temperature for 1 hour.

2. Arrange chicken on spit. Brush sauce on outside of chicken. Roast 4 to 5 inches from heat for about 1½ hours, or until done, basting often with sauce.

CHICKEN NAPOLI (4 servings)

1 3-pound chicken, cut in pieces
1 teaspoon monosodium glutamate
¼ cup flour
1 teaspoon salt
⅛ teaspoon pepper
2 tablespoons grated Parmesan cheese
½ teaspoon paprika
¼ cup butter
1 6-ounce can sliced mushrooms, drained, with liquid reserved
1 pound zucchini squash, cut in ½-inch slices

1. Sprinkle chicken with half the monosodium glutamate and let stand for 15 minutes.

2. Combine the flour, half the salt, all the pepper, cheese and paprika and coat the chicken with the mixture.

3. Melt butter in a skillet and brown chicken pieces on all sides.

4. Add water to reserved mushroom liquid to make ⅔ cup. Add to skillet. Cover and simmer for about 20 minutes, until chicken is just about tender.

5. Add mushrooms and zucchini to skillet. Sprinkle remaining monosodium glutamate and salt. Cover and cook for about 10 minutes longer or until chicken is tender.

CHICKEN PIE EMPIRE (4 servings)

1 small onion, chopped
4 tablespoons butter
½ pound spinach, shredded
⅓ cup uncooked rice
*⅔ cup Chicken Broth**
salt and pepper to taste
1 3½-pound chicken for roasting, whole
6 mushrooms, sliced
2 tomatoes, sliced
*½ cup Brown Sauce**
*¼ cup Chicken Broth**
1 teaspoon Worcestershire sauce
4 slices bacon, cooked
1 Pâté Brisée (dough)*
1 egg, beaten

1. Simmer the onions in half of the butter for 2 minutes. Stir in the spinach.

2. To the Chicken Broth add rice and salt and pepper to taste. Cover and bake in preheated 350° F. oven for 18 to 20 minutes. Cool.

3. Mix the rice and spinach and stuff the chicken, closing opening with skewers. Roast chicken for 1½ hours or until tender at 350° F.

4. Sauté mushrooms and tomatoes in remaining butter.

5. Remove the chicken from the roasting pan. Add Brown Sauce, Broth and Worcestershire sauce to the pan and mix.

6. Place the chicken in a pie dish and cover with the mushrooms, tomatoes and bacon. Pour the sauce over.

7. Wet the edges of the pie dish with water. Cover with Pâté Brisée dough. Roll out scraps of dough and cut with an oval cutter. Decorate top of pie. Brush top with beaten egg. Bake at 400° F. for about 10 minutes or until brown.

CHICKEN ROQUEFORT

1 chicken, about 3 pounds, cut up
½ stick (¼ cup), butter melted
1 cup sour cream
¼ cup crumbled Roquefort cheese
1 teaspoon Worcestershire sauce
paprika

1. Brown chicken in butter.

2. Mix sour cream, Roquefort cheese and Worcestershire sauce

and pour over chicken in a casserole. Sprinkle with paprika. Bake in preheated oven at 325° F. for about 30 minutes.

CHICKEN SAN FRANCISCO (4 servings)

1 2- to 2½-pound chicken, cut up
grated rind and juice of 2 medium oranges
1 tablespoon grated onion
½ teaspoon salt
½ teaspoon dry mustard
⅛ teaspoon pepper
dash of Tabasco sauce
¾ cup flour
1 teaspoon paprika
½ cup salad oil

1. Arrange chicken in a single layer in a shallow dish. Combine the orange rind, orange juice, onion, salt, dry mustard, pepper and Tabasco. Pour mixture over chicken. Marinate for 1 to 3 hours.

2. Drain, reserving marinade for gravy.

3. Combine flour and paprika and coat chicken thoroughly with this mixture. Save any leftover flour mixture for gravy.

4. Brown chicken in heavy skillet containing ½ inch of hot oil. Turn occasionally to brown evenly.

5. When chicken is lightly browned (15 to 20 minutes), add 1 tablespoon of water and cover skillet tightly. Cook slowly until thickest pieces are fork-tender. Turn chicken as necessary to brown and cook evenly.

6. Uncover and continue cooking slowly to re-crisp coating (about 5 minutes). Remove chicken to warm platter and prepare gravy, using the marinade mixture as part of the liquid.

GRAVY

1 tablespoon butter
2 tablespoons flour (leftover)
1 cup liquid (use marinade and add water or Chicken Broth as needed)*

1. Melt butter in the skillet and stir in the flour. Cook, stirring constantly for about 2 minutes.

2. Gradually add the liquid, cook, stirring until the sauce thickens and becomes smooth. Scrape bottom of the skillet to remove chicken particles. These add flavor to the gravy.

CHICKEN SAVANNAH (4 to 6 servings)

4 tablespoons butter
4 tablespoons flour
*2 cups Chicken Broth**
½ cup light cream
¼ cup dry sherry
8 ounces fine noodles, cooked and drained
2 cups cooked chicken
1 can sliced mushrooms
¼ cup slivered almonds
¼ cup grated Parmesan or Gruyère cheese
1 teaspoon butter

1. Melt butter in a saucepan, add flour and stir until smooth. Add Chicken Broth and light cream and cook until thickened and smooth. Add sherry.

2. Place noodles in a buttered casserole and add chicken, mushrooms and cream sauce.

3. Sprinkle with almonds, cheese and butter. Bake in preheated oven at 350° F. until bubbly and nuts are brown.

CHICKEN SORRENTO (4 servings)

1 chicken, about 3½ pounds, cut up
3 tablespoons salad oil
2 tablespoons chopped parsley
½ stalk of celery, sliced
½ clove garlic, minced
1 teaspoon salt
½ teaspoon pepper
2 bay leaves
½ cup white wine
2 tablespoons water

1. Brown chicken pieces in hot oil. Transfer to a casserole.

2. Sauté the vegetables in same pan and add salt, pepper and bay leaves. Stir in the wine and water. Bring to a boil and pour over the chicken. Bake in preheated oven at 350° F. for 45 minutes or until chicken is tender.

POULET VALLE D'AUGE (4 servings)

Chicken Valley d'Auge

2 tablespoons butter
1 chicken, 2½ pounds, cut in pieces
salt and pepper to taste
1 small onion, chopped
2 tablespoons Calvados or applejack (apple brandy)
½ cup cider
1 cup heavy cream
2 egg yolks
8 small onions, cooked
12 baby carrots, cooked
12 small mushrooms

1. In a large skillet heat the butter and add the chicken which has been salted and peppered. Cook for 2 minutes. Do not brown.
2. Add chopped onion and simmer for 2 minutes. Add the Calvados and cider, cover tightly and cook over low heat for 45 minutes or until tender.
3. Remove the chicken to a warm platter and keep hot. Slowly stir the cream into the pan and bring to a boil. Add the egg yolks, stirring constantly. Let mixture simmer for 1 minute. Do not let it boil.
4. Combine and heat the onions, carrots and mushrooms. Drain off any liquid. Arrange vegetables on top of chicken.
5. Pour the sauce over the chicken.

CHICKEN VERONA (4 servings)

1 cup fine dry bread crumbs
⅓ cup grated Parmesan cheese
¼ cup minced parsley
2 teaspoons salt
¼ teaspoon pepper
pinch of mustard
¾ cup (1½ sticks or 6 ounces) butter, melted
1 clove garlic, minced
1 chicken, about 3 pounds, cut up

1. Mix bread crumbs with cheese, parsley, salt, pepper and mustard.
2. Mix the melted butter and garlic.
3. Dip the chicken pieces into the melted butter, dredge in the crumb mixture and arrange in a single layer in a shallow baking pan. Sprinkle the remaining butter over the top. Bake in preheated oven at 350° F. for about 45 minutes.

CHICKEN WITH CHEESE (4 servings)

1 2½-pound chicken, cut up
flour mixed with salt and pepper for dredging
4 tablespoons butter
1 pint heavy cream
2 eggs
2 egg yolks
3 tablespoons grated Parmesan cheese
3 tablespoons grated sharp Cheddar cheese
bread crumbs

1. Dredge the chicken pieces lightly in seasoned flour. Cook in the butter until golden brown on all sides. Pour the cream over the top and cook, covered, slowly until tender, about 40 minutes.

2. Transfer the chicken pieces to a shallow heatproof casserole. Lightly beat the eggs and yolks and add the pan liquid, beating. Pour over the chicken. Sprinkle with a mixture of the cheese and bread crumbs and place under a preheated broiler until the surface is browned.

CHICKEN WITH HERBS (6 to 8 servings)

¼ pound butter
1 tablespoon minced parsley
¼ teaspoon tarragon
½ teaspoon marjoram
3 broilers, about 3 pounds each, halved
1 cup dry white wine
½ cup salad oil
¼ cup soy sauce
1 clove garlic, crushed
¼ teaspoon salt

1. Combine the butter, parsley, tarragon and marjoram and rub in under the skin of the chickens.

2. Combine the remaining ingredients and place chickens in the marinade. Refrigerate overnight.

3. Broil chickens, basting often with marinade, until tender.

4. Cut into quarters for serving.

CHICKEN WITH LEMON (3 to 4 servings)

2- to 3-pound chicken, quartered
4 tablespoons melted butter
1 tablespoon flour
*1 cup Chicken Broth**
3 sprigs of parsley
pinch thyme
1 bay leaf
1 teaspoon Kitchen Bouquet
salt and pepper to taste
1 lemon, diced
1 lemon, sliced (optional)

1. Brown chicken in butter. Remove chicken from pan.

2. Add the flour and mix it with the butter. Then add Chicken Broth, parsley, thyme, bay leaf, Kitchen Bouquet, salt and pepper. Add diced lemon, return the chicken to the pan and cook for 30 minutes or until tender.

3. One sliced lemon may be used for decoration around the platter.

COQ AU VIN (4 servings)

Chicken with Wine

1 chicken, 3 pounds, cut into serving pieces
salt and pepper to taste
3 tablespoons butter
2 tablespoons finely chopped shallots
2 tablespoons cognac or brandy
1 bottle (1 pint, 8 ounces) red Burgundy wine
4 sprigs of parsley
1 bay leaf
pinch thyme
12 small onions
12 small mushroom caps
3 slices salt pork cut in ½-inch pieces
4 teaspoons melted butter
pinch sugar
1 tablespoon butter
1 tablespoon flour
4 slices of toasted white bread cut in heart shapes

1. Season the chicken with salt and pepper. In a large skillet melt the butter and brown the chicken on all sides. Sprinkle with shallots.

2. Pour off the butter, add the cognac and flame it. Add wine, parsley, bay leaf and thyme. Cover and simmer for about 35 minutes, until the chicken is tender.

3. While the chicken is cooking, brown the onions, mushrooms and salt pork in melted butter and sugar.

4. Remove the chicken to a hot serving platter and garnish with the onions, mushrooms and pork.

5. Combine the 1 tablespoon butter and the flour to make a paste (this is called: Beurre Manie) and add to the gravy in the pan. Stir with a whisk to obtain thickness. Strain the gravy over the chicken.

6. Place the bread around the platter for decoration.

CHICKEN WITH WINE AND ALMONDS (4 servings)

1 chicken, about 3 pounds, cut up
⅔ cup slivered almonds
3 tablespoons melted butter
1 cup white wine
salt and pepper
⅓ cup chopped parsley

1. Sauté chicken and almonds in butter until the chicken is a golden color on all sides.

2. Add wine and seasoning. Cover and simmer for about 40 minutes. Add parsley.

DELAWARE CHICKEN STEW (6 servings)

2 onions, sliced
2 tablespoons bacon fat
1 2½-pound fryer, cut up
salt and pepper
3 cups water
3 tomatoes, peeled and quartered
½ cup sherry
2 teaspoons Worcestershire sauce
1 pound fresh Lima beans
½ cup okra
3 ears green corn
2 tablespoons butter
½ cup bread crumbs

1. Sauté onions in bacon fat. Season chicken and brown on all sides in bacon fat.

2. Pour off fat and place chicken and onions in heavy kettle. Add water, tomatoes, sherry and Worcestershire sauce.

3. Cook slowly over low heat for ½ hour. Add Lima beans, okra and corn cut from the cob. Simmer for 1 hour, add butter and bread crumbs and cook ½ hour longer.

EAST INDIAN CHICKEN (6 servings)

½ cup butter
2 small fryers, about 2½ pounds each, cut up
salt and pepper to taste
⅛ teaspoon saffron
2 tablespoons tomato purée
1½ cups light cream

1. Melt butter in a heavy skillet and in it sauté chicken until golden brown on all sides.

2. Season with salt, pepper and saffron and add tomato purée and cream. Blend well, cover and simmer gently for 15 minutes.

3. Remove cover and cook until sauce is reduced by half.

FAR EASTERN CHICKEN (6 servings)

2½ cups bread cubes, toasted
2 cups bean sprouts
⅔ cup sliced water chestnuts
½ cup sliced mushrooms
1 teaspoon salt
2½ to 3 cups diced cooked chicken
¼ cup sugar
2 tablespoons cornstarch
¾ cup pineapple juice
¼ cup imported soy sauce
2 tablespoons vinegar
¼ cup toasted almonds

1. Combine bread cubes, sprouts, water chestnuts, mushrooms, salt and chicken. Set aside.

2. Combine sugar and cornstarch in a small pan. Stir in the juice and soy sauce. Bring to a boil, stirring, and cook for 2 to 3 minutes once it is thickened. Remove from heat and add the vinegar.

3. Place the chicken mixture in a greased 1½-quart casserole. Pour sauce over and top with almonds. Bake in 350° F. oven for 30 minutes.

FRIED CHICKEN BALTIMORE (4 to 5 servings)

2 frying chickens, about 2½ pounds each, cut up
¾ cup flour
1 teaspoon salt
¼ teaspoon pepper
3 tablespoons shortening
1 cup water

1. Wash and dry chickens carefully. Shake in bag with flour, salt and pepper. Brown chicken quickly in shortening. Reduce heat, add water and simmer slowly, covered, until tender, about 30 minutes.

2. Remove lid and let chicken fry slowly. Garnish with corn fritters and broiled bacon.

FRIED CHICKEN FREDERICK (4 servings)

1 2½-pound frying chicken, cup up
salt and pepper
flour
paprika
5 or 6 tablespoons salad oil
1 clove garlic, minced
¼ cup meat broth (may be made with a bouillon cube)
½ pint sour cream

1. Roll chicken in salt, pepper, flour and a little paprika.

2. Heat oil until very hot in heavy skillet and add chicken. Brown quickly on all sides. Add garlic.

3. Remove skillet from fire and add broth. Pour sour cream over top. Don't stir; the cream will seep down through the chicken as it is baking.

4. Place skillet, tightly covered, in a moderate preheated oven (350° F.) and cook for 30 minutes.

FRIED CHICKEN VIENNESE (4 servings)

1 medium onion, chopped
1 small clove garlic, crushed
6 tablespoons olive oil
1 tablespoon salt
¼ teaspoon black pepper
1 tablespoon lemon juice or vinegar
1 teaspoon sugar
½ teaspoon paprika
1 chicken, about 3 pounds, cut up
1 cup dry bread crumbs mixed with 2 teaspoons salt
1 egg, beaten, mixed with 2 tablespoons water
4 tablespoons shortening

1. Combine first 8 ingredients and mix thoroughly. Marinate chicken pieces in mixture for about 3 hours.

2. Drain chicken. Dip chicken pieces in bread crumbs and then in egg, then dip again in bread crumbs.

3. Fry chicken in deep fat. As soon as chicken is light brown, remove. Place in a baking dish and bake in preheated oven at 375° F. for 50 to 60 minutes.

HONEYED CHICKEN (2 servings)

¼ cup honey
¼ cup prepared mustard
1 tablespoon fresh, frozen or canned lemon juice
1 teaspoon salt
1 1½- to 2-pound chicken, halved
½ teaspoon salt
3 tablespoons butter

1. Combine first 4 ingredients and set aside. Sprinkle chicken with ½ teaspoon salt.

2. In a foil-lined pan in a preheated 350° F. oven, melt butter, then remove pan. In it, arrange chicken, skin side down, and brush on some of honey mixture. Bake 30 minutes, brushing occasionally with honey mixture. Turn chicken; bake about 30 minutes longer or until tender, continuing to brush chicken occasionally until almost all of honey mixture is used up.

3. Just before serving, drizzle chicken with remaining honey mixture.

OLD-FASHIONED BOILED CHICKEN DINNER (6 to 8 servings)

PLATE III

4-pound chicken for stewing
white wine (optional)
1 bay leaf
pinch thyme
1 teaspoon black pepper
2 whole cloves
1 teaspoon salt
3 medium potatoes, peeled, or 6 small new potatoes, scraped
6 small onions
4 white turnips
3 leeks
12 small carrots
3 stalks of celery, cut into 2½-inch pieces, tied together
parsley for garnish

1. Cover chicken with water (or white wine). Tie bay leaf, thyme, pepper and cloves together and wrap in cheesecloth. Add to chicken and bring water to a boil. Skim off any froth that rises to the top. Reduce heat and simmer for 45 minutes.

2. Add salt and all the vegetables except parsley. Simmer until chicken and vegetables are tender. Discard the cheesecloth with the spices. Serve chicken with the vegetables and garnish with parsley.

POULET ROTI BEAU SEJOUR (4 to 6 servings)

Roast Chicken

3 tablespoons unsalted butter
1 clove garlic
½ teaspoon powdered thyme (fresh thyme may be used for better flavor)
1 plump roaster, about 5 pounds
salt and pepper

1. Melt 1 tablespoon butter and add the garlic and thyme. Pour this inside the chicken. Truss the legs and wings close to the body with kitchen string.

2. Sprinkle the bird inside and out with salt and pepper, brush with remaining butter and roast it in a moderately hot preheated oven (375° F.) for about 1½ hours, basting frequently and turning it from time to time to insure even browning.

3. Test the bird for doneness; any tinge of red in the juice indicates that further cooking is necessary.

SAUTEED CHICKEN KATY (4 servings)

3-pound roasting chicken
salt and pepper to taste
2 tablespoons butter
1 small onion, chopped
½ pound mushrooms, sliced
½ cup dry sherry or dry white wine
1 pint heavy cream
2 egg yolks
pinch of chopped parsley

1. Cut chicken in 8 pieces. Season with salt and pepper.

2. Melt butter in a deep skillet and cook chicken over fairly high heat, turning pieces to brown on all sides. Turn heat to medium and cover. Simmer for 7 to 9 minutes. Add chopped onion and sliced mushrooms. Cover and cook gently for about 10 minutes. Add wine and continue cooking gently, with pan covered, for 15 more minutes. Chicken should be well cooked. Place chicken on serving platter and keep hot.

3. Add the cream mixed with lightly stirred egg yolks to liquid in skillet. Simmer—but do not boil—for about 4 to 5 minutes. Correct seasoning. Pour gravy over chicken and sprinkle with chopped parsley. Serve on fresh hot toast triangles.

SHERRIED CHICKEN (4 servings)

½ cup flour
2 teaspoons salt
1 3-pound chicken, cut in serving pieces
¾ cup butter
½ cup dry sherry
2 tablespoons soy sauce
2 tablespoons lemon juice
¼ cup finely chopped preserved ginger

1. Combine flour and salt and coat chicken pieces with the mixture.

2. Melt ½ cup of butter, brown chicken on all sides and place chicken pieces in a covered baking dish.

3. In a saucepan combine remaining butter, sherry, soy sauce, lemon juice and ginger. Bring to a boil, stirring, and pour over the chicken. Bake in a preheated 350° F. oven for about 1 hour or until tender. Turn chicken once during baking.

SPICY CHICKEN WITH ASPARAGUS (6 servings)

4½ cups (about 4 cans) canned condensed cream of mushroom soup
1½ cups heavy cream
1½ teaspoons curry powder
few drops Tabasco sauce
6 tablespoons chopped pimiento
16 slices cooked chicken
1½ pounds cooked asparagus
6 tablespoons grated Parmesan cheese

1. Combine first 5 ingredients, heat thoroughly and stir until smooth.

2. Place chicken and asparagus in greased shallow baking dish and pour sauce over them. Sprinkle with Parmesan cheese. Bake in preheated oven at 400° F. for about 20 minutes.

CANARD A L'ORANGE (4 servings)
Duckling with Orange

1 duck, 4 to 5 pounds
½ cup sugar
1 tablespoon wine vinegar
juice of 2 oranges
½ cup Grand Marnier
*1 cup Brown Sauce**
¼ cup shredded orange peel
pinch of salt

1. Roast duck for 1½ hours at 350° F.

2. Combine sugar and vinegar in pan. Heat until sugar melts. Add the orange juice and reduce over high heat to one-fourth the original quantity. Add Grand Marnier and Brown Sauce and bring to a boil.

3. Cook shredded orange peel in water to cover, and salt, until orange peel is tender. Strain and add to the gravy.

4. Remove duck to a hot platter and pour the sauce over it.

DUCK MEXICAN STYLE (4 servings)

6 ripe tomatoes, peeled and quartered
4 tablespoons butter
salt and pepper
1 pound mushrooms, quartered
2 cups shredded cooked duck meat
2 teaspoons grated orange rind
cooked buttered rice

1. Cook tomatoes in 2 tablespoons butter until they are soft and season with salt and pepper. Keep tomatoes warm.

2. In another saucepan, brown mushrooms in remaining 2 tablespoons of butter. Add duck meat, orange rind and salt and pepper to taste. Heat the mixture through.

3. Serve the duck in the center of a ring of cooked buttered rice and surround the rice with the sautéed tomatoes.

CANARD AUX PECHES (4 servings)
Duck with Peaches

1 duck, 4 to 5 pounds
1 teaspoon butter
1 teaspoon chopped shallots
1 quart can peach halves, drained, with liquid reserved
¼ cup peach liqueur or Triple Sec
*1 cup Brown Sauce**
¼ cup currant jelly
confectioners' sugar

1. Roast duck for 1½ hours in preheated oven at 350° F.

2. Melt butter in saucepan, brown shallots and add the juice from the peaches and the liqueur. Reduce liquid over high heat to one-half the original quantity. Add Brown Sauce and currant jelly, bring to a boil and remove from heat.

3. Place peaches in a baking dish, sprinkle with confectioners' sugar and bake in oven until nicely browned.

4. Remove duck to a hot platter, arrange the peaches on top or around and pour the sauce on top.

ROAST DUCKLING (4 servings)

1 5-pound duckling
salt and pepper
lemon juice
celery leaves
1 onion, sliced
1½ cups dry white wine
1 tablespoon honey (optional)

1. Wash the duckling thoroughly inside and out with cold water, dry it and sprinkle with salt and pepper. Rub the cavity with lemon juice and insert a few celery leaves and the onion. Prick the skin. Place the duckling breast side up on a rack in a roasting pan and cook in a moderately slow preheated oven (325° F.) for ½ hour.

2. Drain the fat from the pan, add 1½ cups of wine and continue to roast, basting often, until it is tender. Allow about 30 minutes cooking time per pound.

3. If a very crisp skin is desired, brush the duck with honey 15 minutes before taking it from the oven, and do not baste again.

ROAST DUCKLING WITH BRANDIED KUMQUATS (4 servings)

*recipe for Roast Duckling**
12½-ounce jar of preserved kumquats
2 tablespoons brandy

1. Follow the recipe for Roast Duckling. Half an hour before the duck is done, heat kumquats in their syrup, allowing the syrup to reduce slightly.

2. Drain the syrup from the kumquats and add brandy.

3. Pour off the fat from the pan juices. Add the kumquat syrup and baste the duck frequently until it is done.

4. Arrange the duck on a platter, pour the sauce over it and garnish it with kumquats.

PENNSYLVANIA DUTCH DUCK (6 servings)

1 6-pound duck
2 quarts sauerkraut
1 cup water
3 tablespoons sugar

1. Prepare duck for roasting as described in recipe for Roast Duckling.*

2. Place in pan and add sauerkraut, water and sugar. Cover and bake in moderate preheated oven (325° F.) until tender and brown, allowing 20 to 25 minutes per pound.

ROAST STUFFED GOOSE WITH BAKED STUFFED APPLES
(8 servings)

8-pound goose, with giblets
2 quarts bread crumbs
2 onions, chopped
2 tablespoons butter, room temperature
1 teaspoon sage
2 teaspoons salt
dash of pepper
additional salt
6 to 8 apples
¼ cup brown sugar
3 cooked, mashed and seasoned sweet potatoes

1. Cook the giblets in water until tender, chop and mix with bread crumbs, onions, butter, sage, salt and pepper. Reserve for stuffing.

2. Clean and wash goose thoroughly, but do not stuff. Prick through skin into fat layer around legs and wings. Heat in moderate preheated oven (375° F.) for 15 minutes. Cool to room temperature and repeat 2 more times. Drain off fat. Rub inside of goose with salt, stuff with giblet mixture and truss.

3. Place in roaster and roast uncovered in slow oven (325° F.) until tender, about 25 minutes per pound.

4. Wash and core apples; sprinkle with brown sugar, stuff with seasoned sweet potatoes and place in pan with goose 1 hour before goose is done. Serve hot with goose.

BABY PHEASANT SOUVAROFF (6 servings)

6 baby pheasants, 1 pound each
3 tablespoons melted butter
3 tablespoons cognac or brandy
¼ cup dry sherry
*1½ cups Brown Sauce**
½ cup heavy cream
4 tablespoons imported foie gras (*goose livers*)
1 tablespoon diced small black truffles

1. Roast pheasants for about 30 minutes at 350° F. Baste every 10 minutes with melted butter.

2. Remove pheasants and keep hot. Pour drippings from roasting pan into a skillet. Add the cognac and flame it. Add the sherry, Brown Sauce and heavy cream. Bring to boiling point.

3. Place the pheasants in an oven-proof tureen, spread with *foie gras,* sprinkle with truffles and pour the gravy on top.

4. Cover and bake in preheated 300° F. oven for 10 minutes.

GULF COAST ROAST PIGEON (4 servings)

6 slices bacon
¾ cup chopped celery
1 onion, chopped
2 cups uncooked rice
*4 cups Chicken Broth**
4 eggs
salt and pepper
4 pigeons
mustard pickle juice

1. Dice bacon and fry until crisp. Remove bacon and brown celery and onion in drippings.

2. Boil rice in Chicken Broth until tender and add bacon, celery and onion. Beat eggs and add rice. Season with salt and pepper.

3. Dress pigeons, fill with part of rice mixture and place on mounds of remaining rice. Bake in slow preheated oven (325° F.) from 45 to 60 minutes, basting frequently with mustard pickle juice.

QUAIL IN WINE SAUCE (6 servings)

½ cup shortening
2 small onions, minced
2 whole cloves
1 teaspoon peppercorns
2 cloves garlic, cut fine
½ bay leaf
6 quail, cleaned and trussed
2 cups white wine
½ teaspoon salt
⅛ teaspoon pepper
few grains cayenne pepper
1 teaspoon minced chives
2 cups cream

1. Melt shortening and add onions, cloves, peppercorns, garlic and bay leaf; cook for several minutes.

2. Add quail and brown on all sides. Add wine, salt, pepper, cayenne and chives and simmer until tender, about 30 minutes.

3. Remove quail to hot serving dish. Strain sauce, add cream and heat to boiling point. Pour over quail.

ROCK CORNISH HEN BAVARIAN (4 servings)

4 Cornish hens
salt and pepper to taste
2 tablespoons melted butter
1 small onion, chopped
1 teaspoon paprika
½ cup dry white wine
¼ teaspoon cornstarch
½ cup heavy cream
¼ cup raisins
½ cup sour cream

1. Sprinkle hens with salt and pepper and roast for about 30 minutes in preheated oven at 350° F. Baste with melted butter every 10 minutes.

2. Remove hens from roasting pan to heated platter and pour drippings into a skillet. Add onion and simmer for a few minutes until tender. Stir paprika into the onion. Pour in the wine and cook over high heat until reduced by about half the original quantity.

3. Combine cornstarch with heavy cream and add to the skillet. Add raisins and bring to the boiling point. Reduce heat, add sour cream and heat but do not boil again. Serve hens with hot sauce.

BRAISED SQUAB WITH YOUNG PEAS (2 servings)

2 squabs
2 tablespoons butter
1 small Boston lettuce, shredded
1 package frozen peas with tiny onions (10 or 12 ounces)
1 carrot, sliced
2 ¼-inch-thick slices bacon, cut into pieces ¼ inch long

1. Brown the squabs in butter. When brown, add shredded lettuce, peas and onions, carrots and 2 tablespoons of water. Cook slowly for ¾ hour.

2. Brown bacon in frying pan, strain off fat and add bacon to the squabs. Cook 15 minutes longer.

SQUABS IN CASSEROLE (4 servings)

4 young squabs
salt and pepper
4 ounces butter, melted
8 small potatoes, peeled
1 12-ounce can tiny onions, drained
1 teaspoon white sugar
1 ounce brandy
2 ounces dry white cooking wine
*2 ounces water or Chicken Broth**
6 mushrooms, quartered
1 tablespoon melted butter

1. Sprinkle squabs with salt and pepper, place in a deep roasting pan and brush with half the butter. Cook in a preheated 350° F. oven for 15 minutes, add potatoes and cook 20 minutes longer. Turn squabs over during cooking. When squabs are a golden brown, place in a covered serving dish.

2. While squabs are roasting, put onions in skillet with remaining butter, sprinkle with 1 teaspoon white sugar and cook over high heat until brown.

3. In same roasting pan, add brandy, white wine and water or Broth, cook for 5 minutes and pour mixture over squabs.

4. Sauté mushrooms in butter. Surround squabs with all vegetables.

ROAST TURKEY (Allow ¾ to 1 pound per serving)

1. Place stuffed turkey on a rack in an open roasting pan, breast side up. Rub butter over the entire turkey. Season inside and out with salt and pepper to taste.

2. Roast in preheated oven at 325° F. Baste once or twice with the drippings in the pan.

ROASTING TIME

4- to 8-pound turkey	3 to 4 hours
8- to 12-pound turkey	4 to 4½ hours
12- to 16-pound turkey	4½ to 5½ hours

To test for doneness, move the leg joint up and down. It should give readily.

CHESTNUT STUFFING

4 pounds chestnuts
4 teaspoons salad oil
6 cups beef broth
1 onion, chopped
2 tablespoons butter
½ pound sausage meat
1 teaspoon chopped parsley
½ teaspoon powdered thyme
salt and pepper to taste
¾ cup soft bread crumbs
½ cup cognac

1. Cut a gash in the flat side of each chestnut. Heat the oil, add the chestnuts and cook over high heat for 3 minutes, shaking the pan constantly. Drain and cool. Remove the shells and inner skins.

2. Cook the chestnuts in the broth until tender, about 20 minutes. Drain and reserve the broth for soup. Chop half the nuts coarsely and mash the rest.

3. Cook the onion in butter until golden. Add sausage and seasonings and cook, stirring, 4 to 5 minutes. Add the chestnuts.

4. Soften the bread crumbs in water. Squeeze out excess water and add to the chestnut mixture. Add cognac and mix thoroughly.

Sufficient stuffing for 12-pound turkey.

TURKEY AND AVOCADO IN CREAMY WINE SAUCE
(4 servings)

4 tablespoons butter
4 tablespoons flour
1 teaspoon salt
dash of nutmeg
dash of cayenne pepper
1 egg yolk, slightly beaten
*1½ cups turkey or Chicken Broth**
1 tablespoon lemon juice
3 tablespoons dry sherry
2 cups diced cooked turkey
1 medium avocado, peeled and diced

1. Melt butter in a medium-sized saucepan and blend in flour and seasonings.

2. Combine egg yolk and Broth and add gradually to flour mixture. Cook over medium heat, stirring, until mixture thickens and comes to a boil. Stir in lemon juice, sherry and turkey.

3. Just before serving, add avocado to sauce and heat through.

TURKEY SOUFFLE (8 servings)

2 tablespoons shortening
2 tablespoons flour
⅛ teaspoon pepper
1 teaspoon salt
¼ teaspoon paprika
*1½ cups milk or Chicken Broth**
½ cup soft bread crumbs
3 eggs, separated and beaten
2 cups chopped cooked turkey
1 teaspoon lemon juice
chopped parsley, green or red pepper or pimiento

1. Melt shortening and blend in flour, pepper, salt and paprika. Add milk and cook until thickened, stirring constantly. Add crumbs, pour the mixture over beaten egg yolks and add turkey and lemon juice. Cool.

2. Fold in stiffly beaten egg white and parsley, pepper or pimiento. Pour into greased mold or individual cups. Set in pan of hot water and cook in moderate preheated oven (350° F.) for 20 to 35 minutes or until firm.

MEATS

I HAVE remarked more than once in these pages how gracious President Kennedy was to me, and how thoughtful in complimenting me when I had done something particularly pleasing to him. I must add, however, that he did not hesitate to tell me if he was *not* pleased, but even then he was so pleasant about it that one could not be really abashed.

Setting down my meat recipes is an appropriate place to tell you of one of the very few cases of Presidential displeasure I had to endure. Like any other man, Mr. Kennedy liked to have his steak done exactly the way he ordered it. I had not been long in the White House when he came into the kitchen one day with a steak I had prepared for him, and confronted me sternly. "Chef," he said, "I like my steak *broiled,* medium rare."

"But it *is* broiled, Mr. President," I answered respectfully.

"Well, it looks fried to me," he insisted. "It's a little shiny on top."

"That's because I just brushed the top with a little butter to give the steak a better aspect," I explained. "Look, Mr. President, you can see the marks of the grill on the steak."

Mr. Kennedy smiled. "I guess you're right," he said. "Thank you, Chef."

As time went on he was less formal and came to call me René, as Mrs. Kennedy did. But always he was courteous, smiling and pleasant, as he was even when I had displeased him. He was especially relaxed whenever we traveled anywhere, and if he found a moment when he was not busy, he would chat with me.

My trouble with the President's steak, however, recalls still another "steak story," again with a happy ending. It is a story that I think will particularly please Frenchmen.

At a luncheon following a diplomatic conference between Prime Minister Lester Pearson, of Canada, and President Johnson, on January 22, 1964, I had served a menu which attracted the special attention of one of the guests, Senator Wayne Morse, of Oregon. In a subsequent newsletter to his constituents, the Senator told them of the conference and the luncheon, and he reproduced the menu, on which there was a dish called "Filet Mignon Choron." A voter who read this letter wrote to declare that "Choron" was misspelled, that it should be "Cheron." He described the dish and said he had made it himself when he cooked at the Blackstone and Sherman hotels and the South Shore Country Club in Chicago.

No detail is too small for Senator Morse. He wrote to Mike Manatos, Administrative Assistant to the President, remarking that his duplication of the White House menu in his newsletter had "aroused a great deal of interest among the readers," and inquired whether "the White House chef could cast some light on this matter." Naturally, Mr. Manatos asked me what I had to say.

I told him that the spelling was indeed correct, and that it referred to garnished artichokes with asparagus tips and peas and a Madeira sauce. It had been named, I noted, for Alexander Etienne Choron, a composer and author who lived from 1772 to 1834.

This information was duly relayed to Senator Morse, who sent it along to his constituent, and you will find the recipe for this dish in the section on sauces.

I could not help but admire President Kennedy's common-sense approach to problems involving the convenience and comfort of others. For instance, it was customary, before his administration, for arriving dignitaries to be greeted at Union Station, where the red carpet was literally rolled out, or at Washington National Airport, where the President waited at the foot of an airplane ramp. At both places, the customary dress was high hat and cutaway.

President Kennedy instituted a more sensible procedure, which avoided the necessity of the welcoming delegation having to stand and wait, often in very unpleasant weather. Under his regime, very often the arriving kings, presidents or prime ministers would be taken first to historic Williamsburg, Virginia, where they could rest and relax from their journey in the quiet elegance of this restored eighteenth-century town. Next morning they would be flown by helicopter to the White House, where they were met first by Angier Biddle Duke, who was in charge of protocol for the State Department. A few minutes before the helicopters landed, President Kennedy would be notified and would leave in time to greet the visitors on the traditional red carpet, as they disembarked from the automobile convoy used to convey them from the helicopter landing site to the south White House portico.

Soon after that, my part in entertaining the visitors would begin. In preparing appropriate meals for these important visitors, I was always conscious of the pressure to make sure that every dish prepared was perfect not only in taste but in its appeal to the eye. A professional chef learns to take this kind of pressure in stride. If he does not, soon he will no longer be a chef.

It was necessary, too, for the table settings to be as appealing as the food. The White House dinner plates we used were dignified and attractive in design—an eagle on a white base. On more formal occasions we used the Eisenhower service, which had gold stars surrounding the seal of the United States on a white base, with a gold-figured rim.

At these and other Washington dinners it might not have been inappropriate to borrow an old Roman custom, in which a single rose was placed on the table to indicate to guests that anything which was said during the dinner would not be repeated later, thus giving rise to our phrase, *sub rosa,* meaning literally "under the rose," or confidential.

To give you some idea of the care and thought which went into a menu for visiting dignitaries, permit me to recall a luncheon I prepared for the late Prime Minister Nehru, of India, and Madame Gandhi, given on November 6, 1961, at Newport. The logistics of this occasion were not made easier by the fact that the gentlemen dined together downstairs in the Newport house, while Mrs. Kennedy and Madame Gandhi had their meal upstairs, creating a small problem in serving, if not in the preparation.

To begin, I served them the New England chowder celebrated earlier in this book. It was accompanied by that most pleasant Italian wine, a Soave Bertani. Next came Cailles Veronique (quail in a special sauce, with its delicate touch of grape), and with it a California wine, Almadén Pinot Noir. Glazed carrots and a Mimosa Salad* accompanied this entree. Dessert was Bavarian cream mold with oranges, its sweetness tempered by the splendid champagne served with it, a Cuvée Dom Perignon 1952. Petits fours with almonds were also at hand, and demitasse followed.

But let us come now to the entrees for your own table, the recipes for meat dishes, which follow.

BEEF STEW WITH WINE (3 servings)

- *1½ teaspoons salt*
- *¼ teaspoon pepper*
- *¼ cup flour*
- *1 pound round of beef, cut in 2-inch cubes*
- *2 tablespoons butter or salad oil*
- *1 cup water*
- *½ cup dry red wine*
- *6 small white onions*
- *3 medium potatoes, cut in half*
- *2 carrots, cut ¾ inch long*

1. Mix salt, pepper and flour together. Roll beef in the flour mixture.

2. Melt the butter in a heavy saucepan and sauté the beef on all sides. Add water and wine and simmer for 1 hour.

3. Add onions, potatoes and carrots and simmer ½ hour longer or until meat is tender.

BOEUF AU VIN ROUGE (6 to 8 servings)

Beef with Red Wine

- *3 pounds rump of beef*
- *2 tablespoons melted butter*
- *4 cups canned tomatoes*
- *4 medium onions, sliced*
- *3 carrots, sliced*
- *1 stalk of celery*
- *2 cups red wine*
- *2 cloves garlic, halved*
- *½ teaspoon whole black peppercorns*
- *⅛ teaspoon thyme*
- *1 bay leaf*
- *salt to taste*
- *beef broth*

1. Brown meat on all sides in melted butter in a skillet.

2. Transfer meat to a rack in a covered roaster or Dutch oven. Add tomatoes, onions, carrots, celery, wine and seasonings. Add broth to cover the meat.

3. Roast at 350° for about 2½ hours or until meat is tender. Remove meat to a hot platter and strain the broth. Serve the broth hot with the meat.

BOEUF MIROTON (4 servings)

Boiled Beef with Onions and Sauce

3 tablespoons butter
4 cups thinly sliced onions
2 tablespoons flour
2 cups rich beef broth (canned)
salt and freshly ground black pepper to taste
1 teaspoon wine vinegar
1½ pounds leftover boiled beef, sliced

1. Melt butter in a heatproof casserole. Add the onions and cook, stirring, until the onions are golden. Sprinkle with flour and add the beef broth gradually while stirring. When sauce has thickened, add salt, pepper and vinegar. Partly cover the casserole with a lid and simmer for 15 minutes.

2. Add sliced beef to sauce, cover and simmer for 30 minutes.

BOILED SHIN OF BEEF (4 to 6 servings)

1 4- to 5-pound shin of beef
water or beef broth (canned) to cover
2 carrots, scraped and quartered
1 medium onion, whole
2 stalks of celery, sliced
½ teaspoon dried thyme or 2 sprigs fresh thyme
3 sprigs of parsley
1 bay leaf
1 leek
salt to taste
12 peppercorns

1. Combine all ingredients in a kettle or large saucepan.

2. Bring to a boil and simmer for about 3 hours or until meat is tender.

BRAISED BEEF ROAST (8 to 10 servings)

boned rump or sirloin roast, 4 to 5 pounds
flour
salt and pepper
2 onions, sliced
2 carrots, sliced
1 stalk of celery
¼ cup brandy
1 can (8 ounces) tomato purée
2 cups beef broth (canned)
1 cup white wine
pinch of thyme
¼ bay leaf, crumbled
salt and pepper

1. Rub meat with flour, salt and pepper. Brown all sides in a Dutch oven over high heat. Drain off fat.

2. Add onions, carrots and celery, lower heat and cook until golden. Add brandy, tomato purée, broth, wine, herbs and seasoning. Braise, covered, in preheated 350° F. oven for about 3½ hours. Add more broth if needed. Remove meat. Press gravy through sieve and heat.

3. Slice and serve with gravy.

BRAISED SHORT RIBS ALADDIN (8 servings)

6 pounds short ribs of beef
flour for dredging
salt and pepper to taste
2 eggs, beaten
sesame seeds
3 ounces butter
1 cup tomato purée
2 tablespoons chili powder
4 cloves garlic, minced
2 tablespoons chopped parsley
1 teaspoon cumin seed
½ teaspoon ground coriander
2 hot chili peppers
½ cup beef broth (canned)
½ cup pitted ripe olives, sliced
½ cup blanched almonds

1. Dredge the ribs in the flour seasoned with salt and pepper. Dip them in the beaten eggs and roll in the sesame seeds.

2. Melt the butter in a skillet and brown the ribs on all sides.

3. Transfer the ribs to a roasting pan and add the purée, chili powder, garlic, parsley, cumin seed, coriander, chili peppers and broth. Cover and bake in preheated oven at 300° F. for 2 hours, basting frequently. Add the olives and almonds. Continue cooking until meat is tender.

FILET MIGNON ESSEX (4 servings)

4 filet mignons (5 ounces each)
1 tablespoon butter
¼ cup champagne
*½ cup Brown Sauce**
1 small can Morilles (a type of mushroom), or other mushrooms
¼ cup heavy cream
4 slices toasted bread, cut the same size as the filets

1. Sauté the filets in butter for 4 to 5 minutes or according to the way you like your meat. Remove meat and keep warm.

2. Heat the champagne, Brown Sauce, mushrooms and cream to boiling point.

3. Place the toast on your serving dishes. Lay a filet on top of the toast and spread the sauce on. Serve.

FILET OF BEEF WELLINGTON (12 to 15 servings)

I PASTRY TO COVER BEEF

4 cups sifted flour
½ teaspoon salt
½ pound butter
3 egg yolks
¾ cup cold water

1. Sift the flour and salt onto a marble slab or pastry board. Make a little hole in center, add half of the butter, the egg yolks and the water; mix to make the dough. Chill the dough for 1 hour.

2. Roll into a square and put the other half of the butter in the center. Fold all 4 sides of the dough over the butter to enclose it completely. Roll the dough out into a rectangle 3 times as long as it is wide. Fold the left-hand third over the middle and the right-hand third over the left, thus making 3 layers. This process of rolling and folding is called a "turn." Make another turn and chill the dough for 20 minutes. Make 2 more turns and chill for 30 minutes before using. The dough will keep in the refrigerator, wrapped in a dry cloth and a wet towel, for several days.

II THREE POUNDS BEEF TENDERLOIN, TRIMMED

1. Have the butcher trim a beef tenderloin and tie it to keep it in shape.

2. Roast the meat in a buttered pan in very hot preheated oven (475° F.) for 7 minutes and remove it at once from the oven to cool.

III D'UXELLES' OF MUSHROOMS

½ pound mushrooms
1 teaspoon lemon juice
2 tablespoons melted butter
salt and pepper to taste
4 ounces goose livers, diced

1. Grind mushrooms with fine plate of meat grinder. Sprinkle immediately with lemon juice to maintain mushrooms' light color.

2. Cook in small amount of melted butter (2 tablespoons) and add salt and pepper to taste. Cool completely and add diced goose livers; mix well.

IV FINAL STEPS

1. Roll the pastry into a rectangle ⅜ inch thick and large enough to envelop the filet of beef.

2. Cover the center of the rectangle with a portion of the D'Uxelles' of mushrooms.

3. Place the filet, which should be cold, on the center of the pastry. Coat the filet with the remaining mushroom mixture. Wrap the beef carefully with the pastry to make a loaf. Trim pastry and save trimmings.

4. Place loaf in a greased pan, seam side down. Roll out pastry trimmings and cut out shapes (i.e., leaf). Garnish the top of the loaf with cutouts. Brush with beaten egg to ensure a high gloss. Let meat stand for 1 hour, refrigerated. Bake in preheated 400° F. oven for 40 to 50 minutes or until pastry is nicely browned. Serve hot. To be served with Madeira Sauce* mixed with chopped truffles.

HOME-STYLE BEEF STROGANOFF (4 servings)

1 tablespoon butter
1 tablespoon chopped shallots or white onions
10 fresh mushrooms, sliced
1 tablespoon dry white wine
2 tablespoons sherry wine
½ teaspoon paprika
salt and white pepper to taste
1 cup light cream
1 can cream of mushroom soup
1½ tablespoons vegetable oil
1 pound steak (tenderloin, sirloin or rump, cut into narrow strips about 2 inches long and ½ inch thick)
salt and pepper to taste
¼ cup sour cream

1. In a saucepan melt butter and sauté shallots and mushrooms for a few minutes. Add white wine, sherry, paprika, salt, pepper, cream and mushroom soup. Simmer for 5 minutes.

2. In a separate pan, heat oil and add the meat, salt and pepper. Brown meat quickly on both sides.

3. Remove the meat from the pan. Add the meat to the sauce. Do not let the meat and the sauce boil. Simmer until meat is tender. Add the sour cream and mix thoroughly.

BROILED KEBABS (4 servings)

2 pounds lean, tender beef or lamb
¼ cup olive oil
2 tablespoons lemon juice
1 teaspoon salt
¼ teaspoon pepper
bay leaf
pinch thyme
pinch rosemary
1 can (1 pound) white onions
2 green peppers, cut in quarters

1. Cut meat into 1½-inch cubes.

2. Combine oil, lemon juice and seasoning in bowl. Add meat and marinate several hours or overnight.

3. Skewer meat, onions and peppers. Broil 15 minutes, turning occasionally.

DAUBE PROVENCAL (6 servings)

Marinated Beef Stew

3 pounds round of beef, cut into 2-inch cubes
1 teaspoon salt
¼ teaspoon freshly ground pepper
1 whole allspice
¼ cup wine vinegar
1 clove garlic, chopped
4 cups dry red wine
2 tablespoons lard or butter
12 small white onions
½ pound diced salt pork
2 carrots, cut ¾ inch long
2 stalks of celery, cut ½ inch long
1 bay leaf
pinch thyme

1. Combine the beef, salt and pepper, allspice, vinegar, garlic and 2 cups of wine. Let stand for 2 hours, turning occasionally.

2. Remove meat, strain the marinade and reserve. Dry the meat.

3. Heat lard in a casserole, add onions, salt pork, carrots and celery. Cook until the onions are golden. Add the meat and brown on all sides. Add bay leaf, thyme, reserved marinade and remaining wine. When stew reaches the boiling point, cover the casserole and bake until tender, approximately 2 hours, in preheated 375° F. oven.

ORIENTAL MARINADE FOR MEATS (3 cups marinade)

Marinating any kind of beef in this superb sauce will enhance its flavor enormously. The meat should be left immersed in the marinade for at least 2 hours and turned frequently.

1 cup red wine
½ cup soy sauce
1 cup orange or pineapple juice
1 teaspoon thyme
1 teaspoon rosemary
¼ cup Worcestershire sauce
1 cup finely chopped onions
1 teaspoon pepper
2 cloves garlic, crushed

Combine all ingredients and blend well.

MEAT BALLS

1 pound lean beef, finely ground
1½ teaspoons salt
freshly ground black pepper to taste
⅓ cup bread crumbs

Mix beef with seasonings and crumbs and form into balls of desired size.

About 30 tiny cocktail-size meat balls or, about 20 walnut-size meat balls

NOTE: For larger yields, increase all ingredients proportionately.

OVEN POT ROAST (6 servings)

3 pounds brisket of beef or chuck roast
1 teaspoon salt
pepper to taste
1 onion, sliced
2 stalks of celery, whole
½ cup chili sauce
¼ cup water
1 can beer, 12 ounces
¼ cup chopped parsley

1. Place beef in a casserole, season with salt and pepper and place onion, celery, chili sauce and water on top of meat. Roast, uncovered, in preheated oven at 325° F. for 1 hour.

2. Pour beer over the meat and bake, covered, for about 3 hours or until tender.

3. Remove meat and keep hot. Strain fat off gravy, add parsley to gravy and serve with meat.

STEAK AU POIVRE (4 servings)
Peppered Steak

salt
3 tablespoons freshly ground pepper
4 sirloin steaks (individual portions)
3 tablespoons butter
¼ cup cognac
*½ cup Brown Sauce**

1. Salt and pepper both sides of steaks.

2. In a skillet, melt butter and sauté steaks to extent desired (rare, medium or well done).

3. Remove steaks, retain in hot serving dish and discard butter from skillet. Add cognac in skillet used for steaks and ignite it. When the flame goes out, add Brown Sauce and bring to a boil. Pour over the steaks and serve.

SPANISH SHORT RIBS OF BEEF (6 servings)

1 tablespoon dry mustard
2 tablespoons water
1 onion, finely chopped
1 clove garlic, minced
1 tablespoon lemon juice
2 tablespoons wine vinegar
¼ cup olive oil
1 tablespoon salt
pepper to taste
1½ teaspoons chili powder
¼ teaspoon cayenne pepper
3 pounds lean ribs of beef
2 tablespoons flour
3 tablespoons water

1. Combine mustard and water and let stand for 10 minutes. Add onion, garlic, lemon juice, vinegar, oil, salt and pepper, chili powder and cayenne to the mustard. Pour over the meat, cover and refrigerate for 12 hours. Turn the meat occasionally.

2. Drain the meat and place in a casserole. Bake for 20 minutes in preheated oven at 450° F. Add marinade to casserole, lower heat to 350° F. and cook, uncovered, for 1 hour or until tender. Baste frequently.

3. Remove meat and keep hot. Add flour mixed with the water, stir and cook for 1 or 2 minutes until thickened. Serve gravy hot with meat.

TOP SIRLOIN LEMON POT ROAST (10 servings)

½ cup lemon juice
3 slices lemon, quartered
2 tablespoons minced onion
1 clove garlic, sliced
½ teaspoon salt
½ teaspoon celery salt
½ teaspoon pepper
¼ teaspoon thyme
1 5-pound top sirloin roast
flour
3 tablespoons melted butter

1. Combine lemon juice, lemon, onion, garlic, salt, celery salt, pepper and thyme. Refrigerate for 24 hours.

2. Sprinkle meat with flour and brown on all sides in melted butter in a heavy saucepan.

3. Add lemon mixture, cover and simmer for 3 hours or until the meat is tender.

ASPARAGUS AND HAM AU GRATIN (4 servings)

1 pound asparagus, washed and trimmed
½ tablespoon butter
1 tablespoon flour
¼ teaspoon salt
⅛ teaspoon white pepper
pinch grated nutmeg
¼ cup grated Parmesan cheese
12 to 14 ounces cooked ham, in one piece
4 eggs, hard-cooked and halved
1 tablespoon chopped parsley

1. Cook asparagus in small amount of salted boiling water, drain and reserve liquid.

2. In a heavy saucepan melt butter. Blend in flour. Gradually stir in ⅔ cup of asparagus liquid. Add salt, pepper and nutmeg. Cook for 3 minutes. Remove pan from heat. Stir in grated cheese.

3. Cut ham into 1-inch cubes and put in a lightly buttered casserole. Top with asparagus. Arrange halved eggs in a crown over asparagus. Sprinkle eggs with parsley. Cover with sauce and bake in preheated oven at 375° F. for 10 minutes.

FLAGEOLETS AVEC JAMBON (4 servings)

French Stew

2 tablespoons butter
¼-pound piece of bacon, cut into 1-inch cubes
½ pound smoked cooked ham, cut into cubes
1 small hot Italian sausage, cut into thin slices
4 tablespoons tomato sauce
1 small onion, chopped
1 14½-ounce can French flageolets (green beans)

1. Melt 1 tablespoon butter and sauté the bacon, ham and sausage for 15 minutes. Drain meat and set aside.

2. In a heavy saucepan, heat tomato sauce and remaining butter. Add chopped onion, flageolets and meat. Simmer for 10 minutes, stirring occasionally.

MOUSSE OF HAM (Approximately 10 servings) PLATE VI

2 tablespoons butter
2 tablespoons flour
1½ teaspoons gelatin, softened in
1 cup Chicken Broth, heated*
1 pound cooked ham, cubed (½-inch cubes)
2 tablespoons sherry
¼ teaspoon white pepper
1½ cups cream for whipping
1 13-ounce can red madrilene
1½ teaspoons gelatin

1. Melt butter in small saucepan until bubbling. Add flour and mix well with wire whisk. When flour begins to bubble, add gelatin and Chicken Broth. Mix and cook on high heat until thick.

2. Put sauce, ham, sherry and white pepper in blender; cover and run on high speed until smooth. If necessary, stop blender and push ingredients toward blades with a rubber spatula. Chill thoroughly.

3. Whip cream with food mixer until soft-peak consistency. Fold small portions of ham mixture into whipped cream gradually. Chill in refrigerator for 15 minutes.

4. Heat madrilene and gelatin in saucepan until gelatin is dissolved. Chill by placing in pan of ice cubes.

5. Chill a 1-quart mold. Pour madrilene mixture into mold and rotate to cover. Pour off excess and re-chill mold. Repeat process until

mold is covered with about ¼ inch of madrilene mixture. Pour remaining mixture into a small square pan and chill. Carefully pour ham mixture into mold, reserving about 1 cup for decoration. Refrigerate mold for about 6 hours.

6. To decorate mold, cut four slices of boiled ham in half and then in half diagonally. Carefully roll into cone shapes. Place the 1 cup of reserved ham mixture in pastry tube and fill the ham cones. Place around mold. Cut hardened gelatin into triangles and place between ham cones.

PILAF AU JAMBON AMANDINE (4 servings)

Rice Pilaf with Ham and Almonds

*2½ cups Chicken Broth**
½ cup dry white wine
6 tablespoons butter
¾ pound ham steak, diced
¼ pound mushrooms, thinly sliced
1½ cups raw rice
salt and pepper to taste
½ cup finely diced celery
2 teaspoons salad oil
2 tablespoons grated Parmesan cheese
¾ cup almonds, blanched and toasted

1. Combine Broth and wine in a saucepan and bring to a boil.

2. Melt 2 tablespoons of butter in a 2-quart casserole. Over low heat, brown the ham in the butter for 2 minutes, stirring constantly to brown evenly. Add mushrooms and brown for 2 minutes.

3. Add remaining butter to casserole and melt. Add rice and brown for 5 minutes, stirring. Add the boiling Broth with wine, salt and pepper.

4. Cover casserole tightly and simmer 20 to 30 minutes or until rice is fluffy and liquid is absorbed.

5. While rice is cooking, sauté celery in oil for 1 minute and add to cooked rice. Sprinkle rice with cheese and almonds and heat 2 minutes longer.

Pâté de Faisan Truffe en Crout
(Pâté of Pheasant in Crust with Truffles)

Turbotin à la Duglère (Halibut Duglère)

Old-fashioned Boiled Chicken Dinner

Purée Favorite. Rack of Lamb Jacqueline with Mint Sauce
Pommes Dauphine (Dauphine Potatoes)

Asparagus with a Variety of Sauces: Maltaise, Hollandaise, Vinaigrette, and Melted Butter

Mousse of Ham and Maître Jean's Caesar Salad

Floating Island and Madeleines

Gâteau d'Abricot à l'Orange (Orange-flavored Cheesecake with Apricots)
and Parfait aux Framboises Noyau (Champagne Parfait with Raspberries)

VIRGINIA HAM A LA VERDON (20 servings)

1 14- to 16-pound Virginia ham
2 slices onion
2 carrots, sliced
1 stalk of celery, diced
1 bay leaf
1 teaspoon thyme
quartered apricots or peaches (about 12 whole apricots or peaches)
whole cloves
1 cup brown sugar or molasses
1 cup vinegar
*2 quarts Brown Sauce**
¼ cup sherry wine

1. Soak Virginia ham according to packer's instructions. After soaking, place ham (skin side down) in a large steam kettle or deep pot and cover with cold water. Simmer for about 15 minutes per pound. Add additional hot water to keep the ham covered at all times.

2. When ham is completely cooked, remove from water and allow to cool. Remove the skin by lifting the skin around the edge of the butt (large) end with a sharp knife. With a clean cloth in each hand, grasp the hock bone in one hand and, starting at the butt end, pull the skin toward the hock, being careful not to tear the fat. Leave 4 inches of skin on the hock bone. Trim excess layers of fat with a sharp knife.

3. Place prepared ham in a large roasting pan. Spread a layer of onion, carrot and celery around ham and season with bay leaf and sprinkle of thyme. With a sharp knife, cut a diamond pattern in ham fat. Decorate crown of ham with quartered apricots or peaches secured with whole cloves. Cover ham with brown sugar or molasses. Roast in preheated oven at 375° F. until ham is glazed and heated through. Baste ham as necessary.

4. Remove ham from roasting pan and place in a covered pan to keep hot. Add vinegar, Brown Sauce and sherry to the pan. Cook slowly over medium heat for 10 minutes.

5. Strain the sauce and skim off grease. Serve hot in a sauce bowl.

FLAMED PORK CHOPS HENRI (4 servings)

1 small onion, finely chopped
2 cloves garlic, finely chopped
1 cup bread crumbs
6 tablespoons melted butter
1 teaspoon tarragon
¼ cup finely chopped cooked tongue
½ cup pine nuts
¼ cup cognac
½ teaspoon salt
½ teaspoon pepper
4 pork chops, 3 inches thick
1 tablespoon melted butter
¼ cup dry white wine
salt and pepper to taste
¼ cup cognac, warm
1 cup heavy cream

1. Combine onion and garlic. Heat bread crumbs in melted butter and add to onion mixture. Add tarragon, tongue, nuts, ¼ cup cognac, salt and pepper.

2. Have butcher cut a pocket in each pork chop. Fill the pockets with the bread crumb stuffing and fasten the chops with small skewers.

3. Brown the pork chops in the melted butter, add wine and season with salt and pepper. Cover the pan and simmer for 45 minutes or until the meat is tender.

4. Pour the ¼ cup warmed cognac over the chops and set aflame. Remove the chops to a heated platter.

5. Add cream to the pan juices and blend thoroughly. Serve the sauce hot over the pork chops.

PAELLA VALENCIA (8 to 10 servings)

¼ cup olive oil
1 chicken, 2½ pounds, cut in 8 pieces
1 medium onion, chopped
1¼ cups rice
½ cup smoked ham
18 slices chorizo *(Spanish sausage) or smoked sausage*
2 cloves garlic, chopped
1 teaspoon saffron
3 lobster tails, cut in half lengthwise
12 uncooked medium shrimp, shelled and deveined
1 squid, sliced
*3½ cups Chicken Broth**
24 fresh small clams, scrubbed
24 mussels, scrubbed
12 pitted olives
3 slices pimiento
½ cup green peas, cooked
1 tablespoon chopped parsley

1. In large skillet, heat the oil and sauté the chicken on both sides until brown.

2. Add the onion and simmer for 2 minutes. Stir in the rice, ham, *chorizo,* garlic, saffron, lobster, shrimp and squid. Add the Chicken Broth, cover and bake for 15 minutes in preheated 350° F. oven.

3. Remove from the oven and add clams, mussels, olives and pimiento. Return to oven and bake for 5 to 10 minutes.

4. Sprinkle with hot peas and chopped parsley. Serve.

PORK CHOPS CHARCUTIERE (4 servings)

8 pork chops, 1 inch thick
1 tablespoon melted butter
2 large onions, finely chopped
salt and pepper to taste
1½ cups beef broth (canned)
½ cup tomato purée
1 teaspoon dry mustard
½ teaspoon freshly ground black pepper
½ tablespoon butter
½ tablespoon flour
2 tablespoons finely chopped sour gherkins
1 tablespoon chopped parsley

1. Sauté the pork chops in melted butter until they are browned.

2. Add onions, cover pan and cook over medium heat until the chops are tender. Add salt and pepper. Remove chops to a hot platter.

3. Add broth to the pan and bring to a boil. Add tomato purée, mustard and black pepper.

4. Blend butter to a paste with flour. Add to the pan and beat the paste into the sauce with a wire whisk.

5. Add gherkins and parsley to sauce. Serve sauce hot over pork chops.

PORK CHOPS PADUA (6 servings)

1 tablespoon olive oil
6 loin pork chops, 1 inch thick
4 ripe tomatoes, peeled, seeded and finely chopped
3 cloves garlic, minced
1 medium green pepper, finely chopped
1 teaspoon basil
½ cup black olives

1. Heat oil in a large skillet and brown the chops lightly on both sides.

2. Add tomatoes, garlic, green pepper and basil. Cover and simmer for 25 minutes. Turn chops once during cooking.

3. Add olives and cook for 10 minutes over very low heat.

PORK CHOPS WITH MUSHROOMS (6 servings)

6 loin pork chops, 1 inch thick
1½ teaspoons Kitchen Bouquet
2 tablespoons butter
2 tablespoons finely chopped onion
1 teaspoon salt
pinch marjoram
¾ cup sliced mushrooms, cooked in butter
½ cup beef broth (*canned*)
1 lemon, unpeeled, thinly sliced
1 tablespoon cornstarch
2 tablespoons dry sherry

1. Brush chops on both sides with Kitchen Bouquet.

2. Melt butter in a heavy skillet, add chops and brown rapidly on both sides. Add onion, salt and marjoram and cook for 1 minute. Add mushrooms, broth and lemon slices. Cover and simmer over very low heat until chops are tender.

3. Discard the lemon slices. Mix cornstarch with the sherry and stir into the liquid in the pan. Cook, stirring constantly, until sauce becomes thick and clear.

ROAST LOIN OF PORK ST. CLOUD (6 servings)

4-pound pork loin roast
1 clove garlic, slivered
salt and pepper to taste
2 tablespoons melted butter
1 cup dry white wine
1 cup applesauce
1 large apple, sliced thin
brown sugar
½ cup heavy cream

1. Cut small gashes in the meat with a sharp knife and insert the garlic slivers into the gashes. Rub the meat with salt and pepper.

2. Place fat side up in a roasting pan. Roast in preheated oven at 450° F. for ½ hour. Mix the butter and wine with the fat in the pan and baste the pork with this mixture 2 or 3 times while roasting during this ½ hour. Reduce heat to 350° F. and continue roasting for 1 hour longer, basting with pan drippings.

3. Remove the pan from the oven and pour off about three-quarters

of the fat in the pan. Spread the meat with the applesauce. Sprinkle the apple slices with brown sugar and arrange around the roast. Return the pan to the oven and bake, basting the apple slices until they are tender.

4. Add cream to the pan and let it cook with the apples and pan juices for 5 minutes.

WARSAW PORK CHOPS (3 servings)

6 pork chops, 1 inch thick
1 tablespoon melted butter
salt and pepper to taste
1 tablespoon chopped onion
1 tablespoon chopped fresh dill, or 1 teaspoon dried dill seed
1½ cups sour cream

1. Sauté chops in melted butter until browned and tender. Season with salt and pepper and sprinkle with onion. Remove chops to a hot platter.

2. Add dill and sour cream to the pan and blend thoroughly. Heat thoroughly but do not boil.

3. Serve hot over the pork chops.

AGNEAU AU FOUR MONTREAL (6 servings)

Baked Lamb with Eggplant and Tomatoes

4 tablespoons olive oil or salad oil
1 large eggplant, peeled and sliced ¼ inch thick
2 tablespoons water
1 large onion, chopped
1 can (2 pounds) Italian plum tomatoes
1 tablespoon sugar
2 teaspoons salt
1 teaspoon Italian herbs
4 tablespoons dry bread crumbs
3 cups cooked lamb, cubed (leftovers may be utilized)
1 package (8 ounces) Mozzarella cheese, sliced

1. Spoon 2 tablespoons of the oil into a large pan. Arrange the eggplant, slightly overlapping, in the pan and drizzle the remaining oil and the water over them. Cover and steam for 15 minutes. Remove the eggplant.

2. Sauté the onion in the oil in which the eggplant was cooked until the onion is soft. Add the tomatoes, sugar, salt and herbs. Simmer for 10 minutes.

3. Arrange alternate layers of eggplant, bread crumbs, lamb and tomato sauce in a baking dish. Repeat the layers until all ingredients are used. Bake for 45 minutes in preheated oven at 350° F. Place slices of cheese on top and bake 15 minutes longer.

EPAULE D'AGNEAU SAN CARLO (4 to 6 servings)

Braised Shoulder of Lamb

1 3-pound shoulder of lamb, boned and rolled
salt and pepper to taste
1 clove garlic, cut in thin slivers
¼ cup olive oil
1 (1-pound, 4-ounce) can Italian plum tomatoes
½ bay leaf
½ teaspoon thyme
8 small white onions
6 very thin slices of lemon
1 large eggplant, peeled and cut into 1-inch cubes
3 tablespoons melted butter
salt and pepper to taste
¼ cup finely chopped parsley

1. Sprinkle the meat with salt and pepper. Make small gashes in the flesh with a sharp knife and insert the garlic slivers into the gashes.

2. Heat oil in a heavy kettle and brown the meat on all sides. Pour the tomatoes over and around the lamb and add the bay leaf, thyme and onions. Place the lemon slices on top of the meat. Cover and cook over moderate heat for 1¼ hours.

3. Add the eggplant cubes to the pot and pour the butter over all. Season to taste with salt and pepper. Cover and continue cooking until the eggplant and the meat are tender.

4. Remove the lamb to a hot serving platter and cook the sauce over high heat for 3 minutes. Add parsley to the sauce and serve hot over the meat.

GIGOT D'AGNEAU AU MIEL (8 to 10 servings)

Honeyed Leg of Lamb

4 cloves garlic
½ cup boiling water
⅓ cup honey
1 cup soy sauce
1 leg of lamb, about 5 pounds, boned and rolled
½ cup water
½ cup dry white wine

1. Mash garlic in a large bowl. Add the water to the honey and stir until honey dissolves. Add garlic and soy sauce. Mix well.

2. Place meat fat side down in a dish and pour half of the honey mixture over the meat. Turn the meat and add the balance of the honey mixture. Cover and refrigerate for 24 hours. Turn 2 or 3 times.

3. Put meat fat side up in a roasting pan on a rack. Add ½ cup of the marinade and ½ cup of water. Roast in preheated oven at 300° F. for 3 to 4 hours or until tender.

4. Remove lamb to a hot serving platter. Pour off almost all the pan juices into a skillet. Skim off the fat. Add the wine and heat.

LAMB KEBAB (4 servings)

- *1 pound lamb shoulder, cut into 1-inch cubes*
- *¾ cup lemon juice*
- *⅓ cup salad oil*
- *2 teaspoons salt*
- *½ teaspoon pepper*
- *1 bay leaf*
- *½ clove garlic*
- *½ teaspoon thyme*
- *½ teaspoon rosemary*
- *6 small onions, cut in half*
- *12 large mushrooms, stems removed*

1. Arrange lamb in shallow glass baking dish.

2. Put lemon juice, oil, salt, pepper, bay leaf, garlic, thyme and rosemary in blender container; cover and run on high speed just until mixed. Pour over lamb.

3. Refrigerate, covered, 24 hours, turning lamb occasionally.

4. Remove lamb from marinade and arrange on 10-inch skewers alternately with onion and mushroom. Brush skewers with marinade just before broiling. Place in broiler with top of kebabs about 3 inches from source of heat. Broil for 15 to 20 minutes or until lamb is cooked. Turn kebabs several times and brush with marinade. Serve immediately.

SAUTE D'AGNEAU AUX AUBERGINES (6 to 8 servings)
Lamb Sauté with Eggplant

¼ cup (2 ounces) butter
3 pounds lamb, cubed
1 clove garlic, chopped
1 cup chopped onion
1 to 1½ tablespoons curry powder
1 cup pared and coarsely chopped tart apple
2 tablespoons ketchup
2 cups diced pared eggplant (1½ pounds)
½ cup coarsely chopped celery
1½ teaspoons salt
¼ teaspoon pepper
¼ bay leaf
2 teaspoons grated lemon peel
2 cups water
2 tablespoons light brown sugar

1. Melt the butter in a 6-quart saucepan. Brown the lamb on all sides.

2. Add garlic, onion, curry powder and apple; cook, stirring, until the onion is tender, about 5 minutes. Add ketchup, eggplant, celery, salt, pepper, bay leaf, lemon peel and 2 cups water. Stir to mix thoroughly.

3. Bring to a boil. Reduce heat and simmer until tender, about 1½ hours. Stir in brown sugar and mix well.

RACK OF LAMB JACQUELINE (2 to 3 servings) PLATE IV

1 half rack of lamb (have butcher prepare for oven)
salt and pepper to taste
1 branch fresh rosemary, or 1 teaspoon dried rosemary
1 tablespoon chopped parsley
1 clove garlic, chopped
1 tablespoon dry bread crumbs
mint sauce or mint jelly

1. Preheat oven to 375° F.

2. Season lamb with salt and pepper and bake with the rosemary for 30 minutes or until tender.

3. Combine parsley, garlic and bread crumbs. Sprinkle on top of lamb and cook for 5 minutes more. Serve with mint sauce or mint jelly.

GIGOT D'AGNEAU A LA PIRAEUS (8 to 10 servings)

Roast Leg of Lamb, Greek Style

1 leg of lamb, about 5 pounds
1 cup yoghurt
½ teaspoon ginger
½ teaspoon powdered chili
4 cloves garlic, finely minced
⅓ cup ground almonds
½ teaspoon saffron
1 teaspoon salt
½ cup butter

1. Remove most of the fat from the leg of lamb and prick the surface with a fork.

2. Combine remaining ingredients except the butter. Rub the mixture thoroughly into the meat. Cover loosely and let stand overnight, or at least 12 hours, at room temperature.

3. Place the lamb in a roasting pan; dot with the butter. Roast, uncovered, in preheated oven at 350° F. for 15 minutes. Reduce heat to 300° F. and roast 3 to 4 hours more, or until tender. Baste the roast frequently during roasting time. Place roast on a hot serving platter. Skim fat from pan juices and discard. Serve juices hot with the lamb.

GIGOT D'AGNEAU GENIEVRE (8 servings)

Roast Leg of Lamb with Juniper Berries

½ cup dry red wine
¼ cup vinegar
2 tablespoons olive oil
2 slices of onion
2 bay leaves
1 sprig of parsley
1 clove garlic, crushed
pinch thyme
5 dried juniper berries
salt and pepper to taste
1 6-pound leg of lamb
3 tablespoons butter
2 tablespoons flour
½ cup beef broth (*canned*)
1 tablespoon red currant jelly
pinch dry mustard

1. Combine wine, vinegar, oil, onion, bay leaves, parsley, garlic, thyme, juniper berries, salt and pepper in a large bowl. Place the lamb in the marinade, cover and let stand in a cool place for 24 hours. Turn meat occasionally.

2. Drain meat and reserve the marinade. Place meat on a rack in a roasting pan; pour ½ cup of the marinade into the pan and add butter. Roast in preheated oven at 400° F. for about 2¼ hours. If a meat thermometer is used, the temperature should read 180° F. Baste frequently with the marinade.

3. Pour 2 tablespoons of the pan drippings into a saucepan. Blend in the flour and cook, stirring, until lightly browned. Gradually add remaining ½ cup of the marinade, broth, currant jelly and mustard. Cook to heat thoroughly.

4. Strain the sauce and serve hot with the meat.

NAVARIN D'AGNEAU PRINTANIER (6 servings)

Spring Lamb Stew

3 pounds shoulder of lamb, cut into 1½-inch squares
4 tablespoons oil
salt and pepper to taste
1 small onion, chopped
1 clove garlic, chopped
2 tablespoons flour
3 cups Chicken Broth, beef broth (canned) or water*
2 tablespoons tomato paste
1 bay leaf
pinch thyme
4 sprigs of parsley
6 small potatoes, peeled
1 package frozen mixed vegetables (10 ounces)
1 teaspoon chopped parsley

1. Brown meat on all sides in hot oil in skillet.

2. Transfer the meat to Dutch oven or casserole, season with salt and pepper and add onion and garlic. Simmer for a minute. Stir in the flour. Add Broth, tomato paste, bay leaf, thyme and parsley. Bring slowly to a boil, cover, reduce the heat and simmer for 45 minutes. Add potatoes and mixed vegetables and cook for 15 minutes more or until tender.

3. Sprinkle parsley over meat before serving.

VEAU BRAISE, BARBE DE CAPUCIN (10 to 12 servings)

Braised Veal with Capers

8 tablespoons butter
7- to 8-pound rump of veal, boned and rolled (bone reserved)
1 teaspoon salt
¼ teaspoon white pepper
*1 quart Chicken Broth**
⅓ cup flour
½ cup milk, hot
½ cup dry white wine
2 tablespoons cognac
⅔ cup minced mushrooms
½ bottle capers, washed and drained
½ cup sour cream
1 tablespoon flour

1. Melt 4 tablespoons of butter in Dutch oven and brown meat over high heat. Sprinkle with salt and pepper. Add Broth and the veal bone and simmer the meat, covered, for about 3 hours, or until tender.

2. Remove the meat to a warm platter, strain the Broth and discard bone.

3. Melt the remaining butter in the Dutch oven and stir in the flour. Cook, stirring, until it is golden. Add the Broth gradually, stirring constantly. Add the milk, wine, cognac, mushrooms and capers. Bring sauce to a boil, reduce heat and simmer for 10 minutes. Blend in sour cream mixed with flour.

4. Slice the veal, place in the sauce and heat for 4 minutes.

STUFFED VEAL ROLLS, SWEDISH STYLE (6 to 8 servings)

2 pounds veal cutlets, sliced thin
1½ teaspoons salt
½ teaspoon white pepper
½ cup butter
1 cup snipped parsley
2 medium carrots, cut in 1-inch chunks
2 medium onions, quartered
1 can condensed beef bouillon
¾ cup light cream
1 tablespoon flour
⅛ teaspoon white pepper
2 teaspoons sugar

1. Sprinkle veal with salt and pepper.

2. Melt ¼ cup of butter and add parsley. Spread some of the butter and parsley mixture on each slice of veal. Roll up veal and tie with string.

3. Melt remaining butter in heavy saucepan or Dutch oven and sauté carrots, onions and veal until meat is well browned.

4. Add enough water to bouillon to make 2 cups; add to meat and vegetables and simmer, covered, about 1 hour or until meat is tender.

5. Remove meat, cut off string and arrange on a heated platter. Keep warm.

6. Mash the vegetables in the liquid in the pan. Gradually stir cream into the flour, then stir briskly into the liquid in the pan. Add pepper and sugar and cook, stirring, until just heated. Strain the sauce. Serve hot with the veal rolls.

VEAL CAPRI (6 servings)

1½ pounds veal, sliced thin
½ cup grated Parmesan cheese
¼ cup butter
1 cup thinly sliced mushrooms
2 tablespoons butter
½ teaspoon salt
dash cayenne pepper
1 chicken bouillon cube
½ cup Marsala wine

1. Dip the veal in the grated cheese, coating both sides well.

2. Melt the butter in a heavy skillet. Cook the meat over low heat, turning once. When tender, remove to heated platter. Reserve meat drippings in the skillet.

3. In a saucepan cook the mushrooms in 2 tablespoons of butter and add salt and cayenne.

4. Crush the bouillon cube with a wooden spoon in the skillet with the meat drippings. Add the wine, stir and cook for 2 minutes over high heat. Pour the sauce over the veal. Arrange sautéed mushrooms around the veal.

VEAL CHOPS BAROQUE (6 servings)

6 loin veal chops
salt and pepper to taste
flour for dredging
¼ cup salad oil
1 can condensed beef bouillon
2 teaspoons grated lemon rind
1 tablespoon Worcestershire sauce
½ cup chopped pitted black olives
½ cup chopped green pepper
½ cup chopped onion
¼ cup chopped pimiento
4 tablespoons capers

1. Season veal chops with salt and pepper and dredge in flour.

2. Heat oil in large skillet and brown chops on both sides. Add all remaining ingredients, cover and simmer over low heat for about 40 to 45 minutes or until chops are tender, turning meat occasionally.

VEAL CHOPS CARMEL (6 servings)

6 veal chops
flour for dredging
2 tablespoons butter
1 avocado, peeled and pitted
¾ cup heavy cream
1 tablespoon lemon juice
salt and pepper to taste

1. Dredge chops with flour.

2. Melt butter in a large skillet. Brown chops about 7 minutes on each side. Transfer chops to a baking pan and keep warm.

3. Slice avocado thick, and brown on both sides in the skillet. Gradually stir in cream and cook until cream becomes thick. Add lemon juice and salt and pepper to taste.

4. Arrange avocado slices on chops. Pour sauce over all and broil for a few minutes until brown.

VEAL CHOPS TARRAGON (6 servings)

2 tablespoons butter
1 teaspoon chopped fresh tarragon, or ¼ teaspoon dried tarragon
flour for dredging
6 veal chops
¼ cup dry white wine
*½ cup Brown Sauce**

1. In a large skillet melt butter. Mix tarragon with flour and dredge the chops. Brown chops in melted butter about 7 minutes on each side.

2. Transfer the chops to a hot dish. Pour the wine and Brown Sauce into the skillet and cook for 1 or 2 minutes. Pour the sauce over the chops.

VEAU DE L'ETE (6 servings)

Summer Veal with Anchovy Sauce

2 tablespoons olive oil
1 3½-pound leg of veal, boned and rolled
1 large onion, sliced thin
2 carrots, finely chopped
2 stalks of celery, chopped
2 cloves garlic, finely minced
1 2-ounce can anchovy fillets
1 6-ounce can tuna fish
1 cup dry white wine
3 sprigs of parsley
1 bay leaf
pinch thyme
½ teaspoon salt
freshly ground black pepper to taste
*1 cup Blender Mayonnaise**
juice of half a lemon
3 tablespoons capers

1. Heat the oil in a large heavy kettle with tight-fitting cover, and brown meat lightly on all sides.

2. Add the chopped vegetables, garlic, anchovies, tuna fish, wine, parsley, bay leaf, thyme, salt and pepper. Cover and simmer slowly for 2 hours.

3. Remove the meat and chill.

4. Continue cooking the sauce until it is reduced by about half the original quantity.

5. Place the sauce in a blender and purée it. Chill the sauce and then blend with the Mayonnaise, lemon juice and capers.

6. Remove strings from the roast and slice thin. Spoon the sauce over the meat.

ESCALOPE DE VEAU ARLESIENNE (4 servings)

Veal Cutlet Arlésienne

2 tablespoons butter
1 tablespoon finely chopped onion
3 tablespoons diced green pepper
8 tomatoes, peeled, seeded and diced
1 clove garlic, chopped
pinch thyme
1 teaspoon chopped parsley
salt and pepper to taste
4 veal cutlets (5 ounces each), thinly sliced and breaded
4 thin slices Swiss cheese

1. In saucepan melt butter and sauté onion and pepper for 5

minutes. Add tomatoes, garlic and thyme, and cook for 5 minutes. Add parsley, salt and pepper. Remove vegetables from pan.

2. Brown cutlets on both sides in butter remaining in pan. If necessary, add more butter. Place in baking dish.

3. Spread vegetable mixture over cutlets, add Swiss cheese on top and bake in 400° F. oven until cheese melts.

COTELETTE DE VEAU RICHMOND (4 servings)

Veal Cutlet Richmond

4 veal cutlets (6 ounces each), sliced very thin
salt and pepper to taste
4 slices Virginia ham, sliced very thin
4 slices Swiss cheese, sliced very thin
flour for dredging
2 tablespoons melted butter
¼ cup dry white wine
¼ teaspoon paprika
*½ cup Brown Sauce**
2 tablespoons heavy cream

1. Season veal with salt and pepper. On each cutlet place a slice of ham and a slice of cheese. Fold the cutlets in half and secure them with toothpicks.

2. Dredge with flour and sauté in skillet with melted butter until brown on both sides.

3. Remove to a serving dish and keep warm. Add the wine and paprika to the skillet and reduce over high heat to half the original quantity. Add Brown Sauce and cream and let simmer for a few minutes. Pour over cutlets.

PAUPIETTES STROGANOFF (6 servings)

Veal Cutlets Stroganoff

½ pound mushrooms
¼ cup (2 ounces) butter
10 ounces foie gras *(goose livers)*
1 truffle, chopped
½ cup dry bread crumbs
1 egg
salt and pepper to taste
⅛ teaspoon nutmeg
6 veal cutlets, cut thin
1 medium onion, chopped
1 cup dry white wine
*¾ cup Brown Sauce**
½ cup sour cream

1. Put mushrooms through a meat grinder and cook them in 1 teaspoon melted butter until all the liquid is evaporated. Be careful not

to burn the mushrooms. Add the goose livers, truffle, bread crumbs, egg, salt, pepper and nutmeg, cooking until mixture is a paste.

2. Spread the paste on each cutlet. Roll the cutlets and tie securely.

3. Melt the remaining butter in a saucepan, add onion and cutlets and brown lightly. Add white wine and Brown Sauce. Cook slowly, covered, for 30 minutes.

4. Remove cutlets, strain the sauce and add the sour cream. Pour over the cutlets.

VEAU MENTONNAIS (4 servings)

Veal Menton Style

2 pounds leg of veal, sliced thin
flour seasoned with salt and pepper
2 tablespoons butter
2 tablespoons olive oil
1 small onion, chopped
1 clove garlic, minced
1 No. 2 can (2½ cups) tomatoes
½ teaspoon dried basil
¼ teaspoon sugar
salt and pepper to taste
chopped parsley

1. Dredge veal lightly with seasoned flour.

2. Heat butter and olive oil in a skillet. Brown meat on both sides. Transfer meat to a hot serving platter and keep warm.

3. Add onion and garlic to skillet and cook until onion becomes transparent. Add tomatoes, basil, sugar, salt and pepper and cook over low heat for 10 minutes.

4. Pour sauce over the veal and sprinkle with parsley.

VEAL SCALLOPINI VERONIQUE (4 servings)

12 very thin slices of veal, about 3 inches square
flour for dredging, seasoned with salt and pepper
2 tablespoons butter
1 teaspoon finely chopped shallots
2 tablespoons Marsala or sherry wine
*⅔ cup Brown Sauce**
4 tablespoons white seedless grapes (canned grapes may be used)

1. Dredge veal with seasoned flour.

2. Heat butter in a skillet, add the veal and brown a few minutes on both sides until meat is fork-tender.

3. Remove the veal to a serving dish and keep warm. Add the shallots to the skillet and simmer for 1 minute.

4. Add the Marsala or sherry, Brown Sauce and grapes. Bring to a boil and cook for 1 minute. Pour over the veal and serve.

VEAL STEW, INDIAN STYLE (10 to 12 servings)

¼ cup (2 ounces) butter
4 pounds cubed veal shoulder meat
3 tablespoons flour
1 onion, chopped
1 apple, chopped
1 banana, chopped
2 ounces unsweetened coconut, chopped
1 tomato, chopped
3 cloves, whole
pinch thyme
1 bay leaf
4 teaspoons curry powder
1 quart water
salt to taste
1 pint heavy cream

1. Melt butter in a deep pan, add meat and cook slowly on low fire for about 5 minutes without browning. Add flour, mixing carefully with a wooden spoon. Add chopped onion, apple, banana, coconut, tomato, cloves, thyme, bay leaf, curry powder, water and salt to taste. Stir and cook to boiling point. Cover and simmer slowly for 1 hour and 15 minutes.

2. Remove meat and place on heated platter.

3. Strain sauce, add heavy cream and simmer sauce for 15 minutes. Pour over meat and serve very hot.

BASIC FOUNDATION FOR HAUTE CUISINE (SAUCES)

IF ONE asks himself what the basic foundations for *haute cuisine* can be, the answer must inevitably be sauces. They are the major elements in changing routine meals into culinary masterpieces. As everyone knows, sauces are the supreme triumph of French cooking, and as every French chef knows, a perfect sauce is an accomplishment which will transform the prosaic to the sublime.

This has always been known to those who cook. A professional Sauce Master was employed by royal households and by rich gourmets who could afford one during the Middle Ages. Even then a special importance was attached to the art.

Sauces are common to nearly every cuisine. The French repertory alone numbers hundreds of basic recipes for sauces, both hot and cold. And what is a sauce fundamentally, one may ask? Well, it is nothing more than a liquid seasoning for food. "Nothing more," but what a difference it can make! It is generally acknowledged by chefs everywhere that the French are the masters of this art. Their sauces are without equal.

In the section which follows I shall describe the basic recipes for classic sauces, together with the several variations I believe are the most outstanding. Whatever time and effort it may take to prepare them, be encouraged by the fact that you will be well repaid by the enrichment and enhancement of the dishes for which they are intended.

Whatever sauce you make, you can be sure that it has a long history of its own, and in many cases a highly respectable pedigree. Consider, for instance, the origin of that delectable sauce we call Béchamel.* It originated during the seventeenth century, at a time when only gentlemen of high rank were eligible for the post of Lord Steward of the Royal Household in France. One of those appointed to this post under Louis XIV was the Marquis de Nointel, Louis de Bechameil. Today the Marquis gets the credit for having invented the sauce which comes to us with a slight corruption of spelling, but more likely it was the creation of some unknown court chef who named it after Bechameil as a compliment. No doubt it was not entirely original even with this chef, since it must have existed long before under some other name.

As you have gathered, perhaps, from the notes I have appended to this point, the reign of Louis XIV was notable for a variety of gastronomic creations. There was much competition among the noblemen in his court to create some new epicurean delight to please the Sun King, who was not always easy to please. One of these noblemen, the Prince de Soubise, gave his name to another sauce which has come down to us today, although probably it was his chef who invented it. A recipe for this excellent sauce was published in the *Memoires de Madame de Maintenon,* but it differs somewhat from the one we use now. It is a sauce which compliments any kind of boiled fish or meat, and you will find it is this section.

How can one tell if a sauce is correct? A skillfully prepared sauce will have a subtle bouquet, as in a good wine. Its appearance will be smooth, velvety, glossy and colorful, completely free from the taste or the sight of fatty globules. If it turns out lumpy, greasy or pasty-looking, please throw it away. It will not enhance anything at all.

I am certain that in the White House, as well as in the many fine restaurants in which I have served as chef, it was the sauces more than anything else which distinguished my creations. If what a sauce can accomplish seems like magic, it is reassuring to know that all of us who cook can be magicians. By carefully following the recipes I have given you here, you can perform the same magic, to the enchantment of those you serve.

BLENDER HOLLANDAISE SAUCE PLATE V

(Approximately 2½ cups)

1 pound butter
4 egg yolks
3 tablespoons boiling water
2 tablespoons fresh lemon juice
¼ teaspoon white pepper

1. Melt butter in top of double boiler. Skim off clarified butter by slowly pouring off top portion, leaving remaining milk solids on the bottom of the pan.

2. Place egg yolks in blender container; cover and run on low speed for about 1 minute. Continuing on low speed, slowly add boiling water, clarified butter, lemon juice and white pepper. Turn to high speed as more power is required. Blend just until mixed. Serve immediately.

VARIATIONS

MUSTARD HOLLANDAISE

Add 2 tablespoons hot dry mustard to Blender Hollandaise* recipe.

MALTAISE SAUCE PLATE V

2 large oranges
2 tablespoons sugar

1. Remove the orange portion from the skin of the oranges with a vegetable peeler. Set aside.

2. Cut oranges in half and squeeze juice (about ¼ cup). Cook orange juice, orange peeling and sugar in small saucepan over medium heat until thick (about 15 minutes).

3. Add to Blender Hollandaise Sauce* in blender container. Run on high speed until completely blended.

MOUSSELINE SAUCE

Fold ½ cup heavy cream, whipped with portable mixer, into Blender Hollandaise Sauce* just before serving.

WHITE WINE SAUCE

Prepare Blender Hollandaise Sauce,* substituting for the 3 tablespoons boiling water ¼ cup each of Fish Stock* and white wine. (The total volume of this should be ½ cup boiled down to ¼ cup.) Serve over poached fish.

BEARNAISE SAUCE (Approximately 1½ cups)

Serve with meat or fish.

1 teaspoon dried tarragon
1 to 2 shallots, chopped
1 teaspoon chopped chervil, dry or fresh
1 black peppercorn
3 tablespoons tarragon vinegar
1 pound butter
4 egg yolks
4 sprigs parsley, finely chopped

1. Put dried tarragon, shallots, chervil and peppercorn in blender container and add tarragon vinegar. Run on high speed until chopped.

2. Empty contents into small saucepan and cook rapidly over high heat until most of the liquid is gone.

3. Melt butter in the top of a double boiler. When butter is melted, skim off impurities. Slowly pour off top portion and leave remaining milk solids on the bottom of the pan.

4. Place egg yolks in blender container; cover and run on low speed for about 1 minute. Turn blender to slightly higher speed and add butter slowly. Add heated tarragon mixture to sauce in blender container; cover and run on high speed for about 6 seconds or until mixed. Keep warm in top of double boiler until serving time. Before serving, stir in chopped parsley.

BECHAMEL SAUCE (1½ cups)

Cream Sauce

1 tablespoon butter
2 tablespoons flour
1 cup milk
¼ cup cream
salt and pepper to taste
dash nutmeg, freshly grated

1. Melt the butter in a small, heavy-bottomed saucepan, stir in the

flour and cook the *roux,* stirring, for a few minutes without allowing it to color.

2. Scald the milk and pour it into the *roux,* stirring briskly with a sauce whisk. Bring the sauce to a boil, reduce heat and cook it slowly for a few minutes. If the sauce seems too thick, add a little more milk.

3. Add the cream, bring the sauce to the boil again and season it with salt, pepper and nutmeg.

BORDELAISE SAUCE (2 cups)

Serve with beef.

2 tablespoons butter
2 tablespoons finely minced shallots
¾ cup dry red wine
1½ cups Brown Sauce, or 1½ cups canned beef gravy*
salt and pepper to taste

1. Melt the butter in saucepan and cook the shallots until they are transparent.

2. Add wine and simmer until reduced to one-half original quantity. Add the Brown Sauce and heat thoroughly. Season with salt and pepper.

BREAD CREAM SAUCE (Approximately 1¼ cups)

*¾ cup Chicken Broth**
1 small onion, stuck with 2 cloves
½ cup heavy cream
⅛ teaspoon white pepper
2 to 3 slices white bread, with crusts removed

1. Boil Broth with onion for 5 minutes. Discard onion and cloves.

2. Put all ingredients except bread in blender container; cover and run on high speed. While blender is running, break each slice of bread into 6 pieces and add slowly. (Bread varies in composition and size of slice, so stop blender at intervals, as bread is added, to check consistency. This should be a thin white sauce.) Serve immediately or keep warm over hot water.

VARIATION

QUICK CHEESE SAUCE (Approximately 1½ cups)
Serve with quail.

Add ½ cup cubed Cheddar cheese to Bread Cream Sauce after bread is added. Blend until smooth.

BROWN SAUCE (2 quarts)

5 pounds veal bones
1 large onion, quartered
5 small carrots, peeled and quartered
2 stalks of celery with leaves, coarsely chopped
½ teaspoon thyme
1 teaspoon crushed peppercorns
3 bay leaves
1 tablespoon salt
½ cup flour
2 quarts water
1 bottle dry white wine (⅘ quart)
1¼ cups tomato paste
3 sprigs of parsley

1. Preheat oven to 475° F.
2. Combine bones, onion, carrots, celery, thyme, peppercorns, bay leaves and salt in roasting pan. Place in oven and bake for 45 minutes. Reduce heat if necessary to prevent bones from burning. Sprinkle with flour and bake 15 minutes longer.
3. Transfer the ingredients to a large kettle and add 2 cups of water to the roasting pan. Cook over low heat, stirring to dissolve brown particles that cling to the bottom of the pan. Pour liquid from pan into the kettle and add remaining water, wine, tomato paste and parsley. Bring to a rapid boil, reduce heat and simmer for 2 hours. Add more liquid if necessary and skim off fat and foam as it rises to the surface. Cool and strain.

VARIATION

SAUCE ROBERT (1 cup)

Add 1 tablespoon French mustard to 1 cup Brown Sauce.*

SAUCE CHORON (Approximately 1¾ cups)

This is a superb sauce with beef or veal. To serve with Filet Mignon,* broil according to taste as usual, add salt and/or ground pepper to taste, and serve Sauce Choron either poured over steak at the last minute or on the side in a gravy bowl. Some prefer their filet mignon served on a round of toast.

1. Peel, seed and dice 2 medium tomatoes.
2. Place in small saucepan and cook over medium heat, stirring constantly, until all of the liquid is gone and a thick, dark red paste is left.
3. Add this mixture to Bearnaise Sauce* and blend on high speed just until mixed.

CHEESE SAUCE (3 cups)

3 tablespoons butter
3 tablespoons flour
1½ cups milk
1½ cups grated sharp Cheddar cheese
salt and cayenne pepper to taste

1. Melt butter in the top part of a double boiler over direct heat. Stir in the flour until it is well blended.
2. Scald the milk and add to the butter-flour mixture in the double boiler, stirring vigorously.
3. Add the cheese to the sauce, place over boiling water and cook, stirring often, until the cheese melts. Add salt and cayenne.

COURT BOUILLON POUR POISSONS (About 2 quarts)

Court Bouillon for Fish or Shellfish

2 quarts water
1 cup white wine or cider vinegar
8 peppercorns
3 sprigs of parsley
½ bay leaf
1 carrot
1 teaspoon salt
½ sprig of thyme, or ¼ teaspoon dried thyme
1 whole onion, medium size
1 stalk of celery

1. Combine all ingredients in a kettle, bring them to a boil and simmer for 20 minutes. Shellfish should be plunged into boiling Court Bouillon.

2. Strain the cooked Court Bouillon before using for fish.

FISH STOCK (Approximately 3 quarts)

3 pounds fishbones
2 tablespoons butter
4 quarts water
1 teaspoon thyme
3 bay leaves
3 cloves garlic, unpeeled
2 onions, coarsely chopped
10 peppercorns
2 large carrots, coarsely chopped
1 cup chopped leeks
2 stalks of celery with leaves
2 teaspoons salt

1. Wash fishbones, changing water several times.

2. Melt butter in a large kettle and add fishbones and water. Cook about 5 minutes, stirring.

3. Add remaining ingredients and bring to a boil. Simmer about 30 minutes and strain.

SAUCE CHAUD-FROID (Approximately 4½ cups)
Jellied White Sauce

Sauce Chaud-Froid is used to coat cold chicken. It jells with a handsome shine, and makes an excellent background for truffles and other garnishes.

1 envelope unflavored gelatin
*4 cups Chicken Broth**
2 tablespoons butter
3 tablespoons flour
½ cup cream

1. Add gelatin to the Broth.

2. Make a *roux* of the butter and flour as described in Sauce Velouté.* Stir in the Broth and cook, stirring, for 5 minutes. Add cream.

3. Strain the sauce through a fine cloth and stir it.

MADEIRA SAUCE (1¼ cups)

Use with meats.

2 tablespoons butter	*1½ cups Brown Sauce**
2 tablespoons finely minced shallots	*2 tablespoons lemon juice*
	¼ cup Madeira wine

1. Melt butter in a saucepan and sauté the shallots for 5 minutes, taking care not to brown the butter.

2. Add the Brown Sauce and lemon juice. When the liquid comes to a boil, add the wine and simmer gently for 5 minutes.

SAUCE PIQUANTE (1 cup)

This sauce may be served with any leftover meat.

1 teaspoon butter	*1 tablespoon wine vinegar*
1 teaspoon finely chopped shallots or onions	*1 cup Brown Sauce**
	salt and pepper to taste
1 tablespoon white wine	*½ teaspoon chopped parsley*

1. Melt butter and cook shallots for a few minutes, stirring occasionally.

2. Add wine and vinegar and simmer until the liquid is reduced to one-half its original quantity.

3. Add the Brown Sauce and boil for 1 minute. Salt and pepper to taste. Add parsley.

SOUBISE SAUCE (1¼ cups)

Serve with meats.

1½ cups milk	*salt to taste*
2 onions, sliced	*white pepper*
2 tablespoons butter	*dash nutmeg*
2 tablespoons flour	*2 tablespoons heavy cream*

1. Combine milk and onions and bring to a boil.

2. Melt butter and stir in the flour. Strain the hot milk into the butter-flour mixture, stirring vigorously. Cook until mixture is thick

and smooth, then simmer for 5 minutes, stirring occasionally. If the sauce is too thick, add a little more milk.

3. Add seasonings and cream.

SAUCE VELOUTE (1½ cups)

1 tablespoon butter
2 tablespoons flour
*1 cup Chicken Broth**
¼ cup cream
salt and white pepper to taste

1. Melt the butter in a small, heavy-bottomed saucepan and stir in the flour. Cook, stirring constantly, for about 2 minutes without letting the *roux* discolor.

2. Add the Broth gradually, stirring with a sauce whisk. Cook, stirring, until the sauce thickens and becomes smooth. If the sauce seems too thin, cook it a little longer; if it is too thick, add a little more Broth.

3. Add the cream, salt and pepper and blend.

COCKTAIL SAUCE (1½ cups)

Serve with sea food or Avocado Cocktails.*

1 cup chili sauce
¼ cup lime juice
¼ cup sherry

Combine ingredients and mix thoroughly.

COCKTAIL SAUCE CORDEAU (Approximately 1 cup)

Serve with sea food.

*½ cup Blender Mayonnaise**
¼ cup whipped heavy cream
½ teaspoon lemon juice
1 teaspoon onion juice
1 tablespoon chopped chives
½ tablespoon finely chopped celery
salt and pepper to taste
dash Tabasco sauce

Combine all ingredients and mix well.

COCKTAIL SAUCE TENTE (1⅓ cups)

Serve with sea food cocktails.

1 cup ketchup
¼ cup chili sauce
juice 1 lemon
⅛ teaspoon Tabasco sauce
1 tablespoon chopped parsley
1 tablespoon horseradish
1 teaspoon Worcestershire sauce
1 teaspoon prepared mustard

Combine all ingredients and mix thoroughly.

COCKTAIL SAUCE WITH CELERY HEARTS (2½ cups)

Serve with sea food cocktails.

1 cup chili sauce
1 can (8 ounces) tomato sauce
½ cup finely chopped celery hearts with leaves
1 teaspoon sugar
2 tablespoons horseradish
2 tablespoons lemon juice
½ teaspoon Worcestershire sauce

Combine all ingredients and mix thoroughly.

BLENDER MAYONNAISE (Approximately 1 cup)

1 tablespoon hot vinegar
1 egg
1 teaspoon salt
1 teaspoon prepared mustard
⅛ teaspoon white pepper
1 cup salad oil

1. Have all ingredients at room temperature.
2. Put vinegar in small saucepan and bring to a boil.
3. Put egg, salt, mustard and pepper in blender container; cover and run on low speed. While blender is running, slowly add the salad oil. Increase the speed when more power is necessary. Add vinegar and blend on high speed just until mixed.

CAPITAL HILL SALAD DRESSING (1 cup)

½ cup sour cream
*½ cup Blender Mayonnaise**
1 teaspoon Worcestershire sauce
½ teaspoon anchovy paste
½ teaspoon mustard
1 tablespoon chopped chives
1 tablespoon chopped parsley

Combine all ingredients and blend well. Chill.

GREEN GODDESS SALAD DRESSING (Approximately 1½ cups)

1 clove garlic
⅛ cup chopped green spring onions
1 tablespoon anchovy paste
½ cup sour cream
*1 cup Blender Mayonnaise**
⅛ cup tarragon vinegar
¾ teaspoon salt
⅛ teaspoon black pepper
¾ teaspoon sugar
1½ teaspoons lemon juice

Place all ingredients in blender container; cover and run on high speed until finely chopped and smooth in texture. If more color is desired, add 2 to 3 drops green food coloring. Serve cold.

LORENZO SALAD DRESSING (1½ cups)

*½ cup Blender Mayonnaise**
½ cup tomato ketchup
*½ cup Mustard French Dressing**
¼ cup chopped watercress

Mix all ingredients together.

SAUCE VINAIGRETTE AVEC MOUTARDE (6 servings)

Mustard French Dressing

The dressing may be made in advance and stored in the refrigerator. Shake well before using.

1 teaspoon dry hot mustard
1 tablespoon wine vinegar
½ teaspoon salt
pinch white pepper
3 tablespoons olive oil

1. Combine the mustard, vinegar and seasoning in a small bowl.
2. Stir in the oil.

RIMINI SALAD DRESSING (Approximately ¾ cup)

1 egg yolk, hard-cooked
¼ teaspoon prepared mustard
½ teaspoon Worcestershire sauce
3 tablespoons wine vinegar
½ cup salad oil
2 tablespoons grated Parmesan cheese
2 tablespoons chopped parsley
1 tablespoon grated onion
¾ teaspoon salt
¼ teaspoon garlic salt
freshly ground black pepper to taste
dash paprika

1. Mash the egg yolk with the mustard and Worcestershire sauce.
2. Blend in vinegar. Add remaining ingredients.
3. Pour into a jar with a tight-fitting cover and shake well. Refrigerate.

RUSSIAN SALAD DRESSING (1½ cups)

*1 cup Blender Mayonnaise**
¼ cup chili sauce
1 teaspoon minced pimiento
1 teaspoon chopped chives
1 teaspoon vodka
1 tablespoon caviar

1. Combine all the ingredients except caviar and mix well.
2. Sprinkle caviar on top.

SOUR CREAM-AND-ANCHOVY SALAD DRESSING (Approximately 1 cup)

½ clove garlic, crushed
*½ cup Blender Mayonnaise**
¼ cup sour cream
1 tablespoon anchovy paste
1½ tablespoons vinegar
4 tablespoons chopped parsley

1. Combine garlic, Mayonnaise, sour cream and anchovy paste.
2. Add vinegar slowly, stirring well. Add parsley. Chill.

THOUSAND ISLAND DRESSING (Approximately 1½ cups)

Serve with green salads.

*1 cup Blender Mayonnaise**
¼ cup chili sauce or ketchup
1 tablespoon chives
3 sprigs parsley
2 tablespoons sweet pickle relish
1 hard-cooked egg, shelled and quartered

Put Mayonnaise, chili sauce, chives, parsley and relish in blender container; cover and run on high speed. While blender is running, add hard-cooked egg and blend on high speed until ingredients are combined.

VINEGAR AND OIL SALAD DRESSING
(Approximately 1 quart)

1 cup red wine vinegar
8 teaspoons prepared mustard
2 teaspoons salt
1 teaspoon white pepper
3 cups olive oil

1. Put wine vinegar, mustard, salt and pepper into blender container and blend on high speed until salt is dissolved (about 1 to 1½ minutes).

2. Stop blender, add olive oil and run on high speed just until oil is mixed (about 20 seconds). Serve dressing over salad greens or store in Mason jar in refrigerator. (If dressing separates upon storage, place in blender and run on high speed just until combined.)

PISA TOMATO SAUCE (9 cups)

3 cups chopped onion
½ cup diced carrot
⅓ cup olive oil
3 large cloves garlic
2 cups canned Italian tomatoes
2 6-ounce cans tomato paste
*6 cups water or Chicken Broth**
2 bay leaves
1 teaspoon sugar
1½ teaspoons salt
freshly ground black pepper to taste

1. Sauté the onion and carrot in oil until the onion is lightly browned. Add remaining ingredients.

2. Simmer for about 1 hour, stirring often, until the sauce thickens. Strain sauce through a fine strainer.

RED CLAM SAUCE (Approximately 6 cups)

Can be served with freshly cooked linguini or green noodles.

2 tablespoons olive oil
2 cloves garlic, finely chopped
1 onion, chopped
3 stalks of celery, chopped
¼ teaspoon dried basil
¼ teaspoon thyme
½ teaspoon oregano
salt and freshly ground black pepper to taste
1 cup fresh tomatoes, peeled, seeded and diced
1 can tomato paste
1 cup water
2 cups fresh or bottled clam juice
2 cups minced clams, fresh or canned
¼ cup butter
½ cup chopped parsley

1. Heat the oil in a heavy kettle and add the garlic, onion and celery. Cook until the onion is transparent.

2. Add the basil, thyme, oregano, salt, pepper, tomatoes, tomato paste and water. Bring to a boil, reduce heat and simmer gently, uncovered, for ½ hour. Add clam juice and simmer ½ hour longer.

3. Approximately 5 minutes before serving, add the clams and cook gently. Stir in butter and parsley and simmer until the butter melts.

WHITE CLAM SAUCE (Approximately 4 cups)

Can be served over spaghetti or linguini.

¼ cup butter
1 small onion, finely chopped
4 mushrooms, sliced
1 large clove garlic, finely chopped
2 tablespoons flour
2 cups clam juice, fresh or canned
¼ cup chopped parsley
salt and freshly ground black pepper to taste
½ teaspoon dried thyme
½ teaspoon oregano
2 cups minced clams, fresh or canned

1. In a saucepan heat the butter, add onion, mushrooms and garlic and cook for 1 minute over moderate heat.

2. Stir in the flour with a wire whisk. While stirring, add the clam juice. Add parsley, salt, pepper, thyme and oregano and simmer gently for 10 minutes.

3. Add minced clams and heat.

BARBECUE SAUCE (½ cup)

Use as a marinade or basting sauce for broiling and roasting meats.

¼ cup salad oil
¼ cup bourbon
2 tablespoons soy sauce
1 teaspoon Worcestershire sauce
1 large clove garlic, finely chopped
freshly ground black pepper to taste

1. Blend all ingredients thoroughly.

2. Pour over meat and refrigerate, turning occasionally. Roast should marinate for 24 to 48 hours. Steaks should marinate for 4 hours.

COATING FOR ROAST LAMB (Approximately 1 cup)

½ teaspoon ground rosemary
1 clove garlic, minced
1 tablespoon soy sauce
½ cup Dijon prepared mustard
4 tablespoons cooking oil

Mix first 4 ingredients, then beat in oil by droplets to make a thick sauce. Coat lamb with this mixture before roasting.

CREAMY MUSTARD SAUCE (6 servings)

Serve over cold lobster and garnish with capers.

1 cup sour cream
1 tablespoon Dijon mustard
1 teaspoon prepared mustard
2 dashes Tabasco sauce

Combine all ingredients and beat lightly.

CUCUMBER SAUCE (2 cups)

Serve with fish.

1 cup whipping cream, chilled
¼ teaspoon salt
2 tablespoons lemon juice
¼ teaspoon paprika
1 large cucumber, pared, seeded and quartered

1. Put cream in blender container; cover and run on low speed until stiff.

2. Add salt, lemon juice, paprika and cucumber to the cream; cover and run on high speed just until the cucumber is chopped.

CUMBERLAND SAUCE (2 cups)

Serve cold with cold duckling.

1 jar (12 ounces) red currant jelly
1 orange
1 lemon
2 tablespoons orange juice
1 tablespoon lemon juice
2 tablespoons port wine
½ teaspoon dry mustard
¼ teaspoon ground ginger
dash of cayenne

1. Squeeze the currant jelly through a fine cheesecloth.

2. Peel the orange and lemon very thinly, cut the skins into small shreds and parboil the shreds for 10 minutes in water to cover. Drain.

3. Add the peel to the jelly. Add the orange and lemon juices. Stir in the wine and seasonings to taste.

CURRY SAUCE (3 cups)

Serve with chicken.

1 medium onion, chopped
1 clove garlic, chopped
½ bay leaf
sprig of parsley
1 tart apple, diced
½ cup butter
2 tablespoons flour
½ teaspoon mace
1½ teaspoons curry powder
*2 cups Chicken Broth**
½ cup heavy cream

1. In a medium-sized saucepan combine onion, garlic, bay leaf, parsley, apple and butter. Cook for 8 minutes, stirring occasionally.

2. Stir in flour, mace and curry powder and cook 4 minutes longer.

3. Add the Broth and simmer for 1 hour. Strain into another saucepan, rubbing the solids through a sieve. Add cream.

HOT MUSTARD SAUCE (1 cup)

Serve hot with ham, cabbage wedges and boiled potatoes.

½ teaspoon dry mustard
½ teaspoon flour
¼ teaspoon salt
2 beaten egg yolks
¾ cup milk, scalded
2 tablespoons lemon juice

1. In the top of a double boiler mix mustard, flour and salt. Add egg yolks and beat well. Gradually add the milk. Cook until thick.

2. Stir in lemon juice. Serve hot.

MUSHROOM SAUCE (2 cups)

Serve over rice and meats.

2 tablespoons butter
1 small onion, finely chopped
1 stalk celery, finely chopped
3 sprigs parsley, finely chopped
½ pound mushrooms, sliced
2 teaspoons salt
½ teaspoon dried basil
dash pepper
1 tablespoon flour
1 cup water
1 tablespoon lemon juice

1. Melt butter in a skillet, add onion, celery and parsley and cook until the vegetables become limp.

2. Add mushrooms and cook for 7 minutes. Sprinkle with salt, basil, pepper and flour. Mix well.

3. Add water and lemon juice and cook slowly for about 5 minutes or until sauce is thick and bubbly.

MUSTARD SAUCE (Approximately ½ cup)

Serve with hot or cold smoked meats.

¼ cup Bahama-type prepared mustard
1 teaspoon dry mustard
*¼ cup Blender Mayonnaise**
2 tablespoons sour cream

Combine all ingredients and mix well.

ORIENTAL SAUCE (1 cup)

Serve with chicken or pork.

¾ cup soy sauce
3 ounces honey
¾ teaspoon ground ginger
⅛ teaspoon garlic powder

Combine all ingredients and mix well.

SAUCE AUX RAISINS (1 cup)

Raisin Sauce for Roast Duck

¾ cup raisins
1½ cups hot water
1½ tablespoons vinegar
1½ tablespoons lemon juice
¾ teaspoon grated lemon rind
3 tablespoons drippings from roast duckling
3 tablespoons flour

1. Combine raisins, water, vinegar, lemon juice and rind in a saucepan. Bring to boiling point and simmer for 10 minutes.

2. Remove duckling from roasting pan and pour off excess fat, leaving 3 tablespoons brown drippings. Add flour and stir until smooth.

3. Pour in raisin mixture and cook until smooth and thickened, stirring constantly. Serve hot with roast duckling.

REMOULADE SAUCE (1 cup)

Serve with sea food.

*1 cup Blender Mayonnaise**
1 teaspoon French mustard
½ teaspoon fresh chopped tarragon, or ¼ teaspoon dried tarragon

Blend all the ingredients well.

SAUCE CHARCUTIERE (Approximately 1 cup)

Sauce is to be served with pork chops.

1 teaspoon butter
1 teaspoon finely chopped shallot or onion
1 tablespoon white wine
1 tablespoon wine vinegar
*1 cup Brown Sauce**
salt and pepper to taste
½ teaspoon chopped parsley
2 tablespoons finely chopped sour pickles

1. Melt butter and cook shallot for a few minutes, stirring occasionally.

2. Add wine and vinegar and simmer until the liquid is reduced to half its original quantity.

3. Add Brown Sauce and boil for 1 minute. Salt and pepper to taste. Add parsley and pickles.

SAUCE FOR COLD SHRIMP (About 2⅓ cups)

Serve with shrimp cocktail and shrimp salad.

*1½ cups Blender Mayonnaise**
*¼ cup Mustard French Dressing**
¼ cup chili sauce
2 tablespoons minced chives or scallion
2 tablespoons chopped green olives
1 teaspoon horseradish
1 teaspoon Worcestershire sauce
salt and pepper to taste

Combine all ingredients. Chill.

SAUCE FOR ROAST LAMB (Approximately ¾ cup)

1 tablespoon fat from roast lamb juices
¼ cup dry vermouth
1 cup beef broth (canned)
1 teaspoon tomato paste

Pour off all but 1 tablespoon fat from the roasting pan juices. Scrape the bottom of the pan with a wooden spoon to release particles. Add the vermouth, broth and tomato paste to the pan. Boil rapidly to reduce the liquid by half its original quantity.

SAUCE GRIBICHE (1½ cups)

This sauce is served cold with fish, poultry and veal.

2 hard-boiled eggs
2 tablespoons wine vinegar
1 teaspoon French mustard
salt and pepper to taste
1 cup vegetable oil
1 teaspoon chopped chives
½ teaspoon dried tarragon
½ teaspoon chopped parsley
½ teaspoon chopped shallot or onion
½ tablespoon chopped capers
½ tablespoon chopped sour pickle

1. Place egg yolks in bowl and add vinegar, mustard, salt and pepper. Mix well with wire whisk, mashing yolks.

2. Add the oil drop by drop, and then in a gradually increasing amount as the mixture thickens.

3. Slowly add chives, tarragon, parsley, shallot, capers, pickle and chopped egg whites. (Don't be concerned if sauce separates; merely mix and serve.)

SAUCE REMICK (2 cups)

This sauce can be used with any shellfish.

½ teaspoon English mustard
¼ teaspoon paprika
pinch celery salt
dash Tabasco sauce
dash Worcestershire sauce
*1 cup Blender Mayonnaise**
1 cup chili sauce
½ teaspoon tarragon vinegar
salt and pepper to taste

Combine all the ingredients.

TARTARE SAUCE (Approximately 1½ cups)

Serve with fish.

*1 cup Blender Mayonnaise**
2 sprigs parsley
1 tablespoon chopped chives
1 tablespoon chervil
1 tablespoon capers
2 sweet pickles

Put all ingredients in blender container and cover. Run on high speed just until chopped.

VINAIGRETTE SAUCE PLATE V

2 tablespoons wine vinegar
½ teaspoon salt
1 pinch white pepper
6 tablespoons olive oil

Combine vinegar and the seasonings in a small bowl and stir in the oil.

WINE AND DILL SAUCE FOR STEAK (4 servings)

Use as marinade and serve hot over broiled sliced steaks.

1 clove garlic, crushed
1½ teaspoons salt
1 teaspoon pepper
¼ teaspoon dried dill
1 cup dry red wine
1 tablespoon butter

1. Stir seasonings into the wine and pour over steaks in a shallow dish. Cover and refrigerate for 4 hours. Turn once every hour.

2. Remove steaks from marinade and pat dry.

3. Pour marinade into a saucepan, add butter and simmer until sauce is reduced by one-half.

DESSERT SAUCES

CHOCOLATE FUDGE SAUCE (Approximately 1 cup)

Serve warm with coffee ice cream, top with whipped cream and decorate with chocolate-covered coffee beans (a candy).

3 squares unsweetened chocolate
¾ cup milk
¼ teaspoon salt
1½ cups sugar
3 tablespoons light corn syrup
1 tablespoon butter
¾ teaspoon vanilla extract

1. Melt the chocolate in the milk in a saucepan, stirring constantly. Beat until smooth.
2. Add salt, sugar and corn syrup. Cook, stirring, for 5 minutes.
3. Add butter and vanilla extract. Serve warm.

CHOCOLATE SAUCE (1½ cups)

Serve warm over ice cream.

½ cup cream
¼ cup water
6 ounces semi-sweet chocolate morsels

1. Heat cream and water just to boiling point in a small saucepan. Pour over chocolate pieces in a blender.
2. Blend at high speed for 1 minute or until smooth. Serve warm.

HOT CHOCOLATE SAUCE (Approximately 2 cups)

Serve over Délice Du Roi.*

¾ cup hot milk or hot coffee
1 cup sugar
2 teaspoons vanilla extract
4 squares unsweetened chocolate, cut up

Put all ingredients in blender container, cover and run on high speed until chocolate is liquefied. Serve immediately.

HOT RUM AND CHOCOLATE SAUCE (Approximately 1 cup)

Serve hot over ice cream.

1 6-ounce package semi-sweet chocolate morsels
6 tablespoons water
1 teaspoon instant coffee
1 tablespoon dark rum

1. Combine the chocolate, water and coffee in top of double boiler and cook over simmering water, stirring occasionally, until chocolate melts and sauce is smooth.
2. Stir in rum. Serve hot.

SAUCE AUX FRAMBOISES (Approximately 2 quarts)

Raspberry Sauce

Use sauce over ice cream or as cake filling.

2 quarts raspberries
½ cup raspberry cordial

1. Mix raspberries and cordial together.
2. Place mixture in a blender, adding 2 cups at a time, until all ingredients are puréed.
3. Strain the purée through a sieve to remove the seeds.

RICH CHOCOLATE SAUCE (6 servings)

This sauce is delicious with vanilla ice cream. It can be stored in the refrigerator in a tightly covered container.

8 ounces sweet chocolate
2 squares unsweetened chocolate
½ cup sugar
½ cup water
1 teaspoon butter
3 tablespoons heavy cream

1. Place first 4 ingredients in top of double boiler over simmering water until melted.
2. Add butter and cream and mix well.

RUM RAISIN SAUCE (Approximately 1 cup)

Serve warm over ice cream.

¼ cup raisins
⅔ cup water
¼ cup currant jelly
1 tablespoon butter
1 teaspoon cornstarch
1 tablespoon water
¼ cup rum

1. Simmer raisins in water until raisins become soft and fluffy. Add currant jelly and butter and mix well.

2. Blend cornstarch with water. Add to raisins and stir until boiling. Boil 1 minute. Add rum. Serve warm.

RUM RAISIN SAUCE WITH PECANS (Approximately 1 cup)

Serve warm over ice cream.

½ cup rum
½ cup raisins
½ cup sugar
¼ cup water
1 stick of cinnamon
¼ teaspoon vanilla extract
1 tablespoon grated lemon peel
1 tablespoon grated orange peel
½ cup pecan pieces

1. Pour rum over the raisins and let stand until raisins become soft and fluffy.

2. Mix sugar, water and cinnamon stick. Bring to a boil and continue boiling for 2 minutes. Discard cinnamon stick. Add the rum and raisins and cook for 5 minutes over medium heat. Add vanilla extract.

3. Remove from heat and add lemon and orange peels and nuts. Serve warm.

SAUCE SABAYON AU MARSALA (2 to 3 servings)

Serve warm in sherbet glasses or as a sauce for cake.

2 egg yolks
3 tablespoons sugar
⅔ cup Marsala wine

1. Beat the yolks with a wire whisk. Add the sugar and Marsala.

2. Place the mixture in the top of a double boiler and cook over hot water, stirring constantly, until the mixture thickens. Do not overcook.

TAFFY NUT SAUCE (Approximately 1 cup)

Serve warm over ice cream.

1 tablespoon cornstarch
1 cup brown sugar
¼ cup butter
½ cup water
¼ cup chopped nuts

1. Place first 4 ingredients in a saucepan. Blend well and bring to a boil. Boil for 1 minute.

2. Remove pan from heat, add nuts and stir to mix well. Serve warm.

VANILLA SAUCE (Approximately 1½ cups)

Chill mixture before serving over Arlequin Soufflé.*

1 cup milk
3 egg yolks
¼ cup sugar
1 teaspoon vanilla extract

1. Heat milk to boiling on high heat in small saucepan.

2. Put yolks, sugar and vanilla in blender container; cover and run on high speed. While blender is running, add hot milk slowly. Serve chilled.

WHIPPED CREAM AND COFFEE ICE CREAM SAUCE (Approximately 1 cup)

Serve over ice cream.

¼ cup sugar
¼ cup hot water
1 tablespoon instant coffee
1 cup whipped cream

1. In a small skillet stir sugar over low heat until golden brown and syrupy. Gradually stir in the hot water and coffee. Boil, stirring constantly, until smooth. Cook slightly.

2. Fold in the whipped cream.

VEGETABLES, RICE AND NOODLES

ONE of the souvenirs of my White House days which I treasure is a note written to me in French by Mrs. Kennedy which says, in part, "The dinner was fantastic this evening." Of course she was always most generous with her compliments when she was pleased with my cooking, but this seemed to me a very special reward. I have looked again at the menu I served that night, and here it is so that you may judge for yourself, at least in imagination, how "fantastic" it may have been.

It began with a rockfish soufflé, accompanied by one of the great French wines, a Chateau Margaux 1957. This was followed by breast of pheasant St. Hubert, with wild rice and Green Beans with Almonds,* and with this another memorable wine, Chateau Haut-Brion 1955. After the Mimosa Salad* with Brie cheese came the dessert, biscuit glacée with peaches and petits fours, served with one of the superior champagnes, Piper Heidsieck 1955.

Without meaning to disparage the soufflé or the pheasant, not to mention the formidable wine list, it is possible that one of the details of this menu which especially pleased Mrs. Kennedy was the Green Beans with Almonds.* Adding almonds to green beans is one of those small touches that makes a routine dish into something a little out of the ordinary.

I have a repertory of such small hints which have to do with vegetables. Here are just a few of them:

If you want cauliflower to retain its whiteness, cook it with ¾ cup of milk, and if you are disturbed by its odor, which may linger in the air when the guests arrive, put two or three slices of bread on top while you are cooking it. That will absorb the smell. I have been asked whether this trick also works with cabbage. It seems logical, but I must confess I don't know; I've never tried.

To have Brussels sprouts retain their green color, don't put a cover on top of the pan. You may let them cool off, if you like, and then reheat them before serving.

The fresh green color of string beans can be retained by dipping them in hot water just a few minutes before you serve, with a little butter and herbs added upon serving.

Green peas will retain their fresh appearance, too, if you cook them in a pot without a cover. After you drain them, let them cool off, then reheat them and dip them under hot water. Add a little butter when serving.

A small trick with purée of carrots is to cook them with a tablespoon of rice added to the five or six carrots you are using. These, of course, are cooked with the cover on.

There are many such touches available to every cook. Consider monosodium glutamate, which does so much to enhance the flavor of vegetables, and is equally effective with soups, salads or meats. Most housewives know about this additive, but perhaps not so many know that it originated in the Far East, where seaweed had long been used as a foodstuff and its nutritional value well known. In time it was learned that dried seaweed, ground into powder, had a delightful effect when it was sprinkled over meat or vegetables, serving to sharpen the natural flavors. This is monosodium glutamate, known more familiarly today by its best-known brand name, Ac'cent. It is, of course, made from sources other than seaweed, which would not be so accessible in this country.

Another touch that requires a great deal more of delicacy in its use is garlic. We use it discreetly today in a wide variety of dishes, but there was a time when the temple priests of the ancient world declared it "an unclean abomination" and forbade anyone with the smell of garlic on his breath to enter a temple. In spite of this condemnation, working people continued to eat it—a testimonial to its powerful attraction. In fact, Aristotle, Pliny and many oriental physicians praised its medicinal properties. I have told you how cautious we had to be in using garlic at the White House, but it is true, nevertheless, that its wise application is indispensable to *haute cuisine*. Yet always remember—use it with discretion. It *can* be a disaster.

With or without garlic, it is not always easy to make vegetables interesting, especially for children, many of whom seem to dislike them intensely. Mrs. Kennedy appeared to be aware of this problem, but was intent on seeing that Caroline got her vegetables. She always made sure that her daughter had a good, nutritious lunch, with not too many sweets, and very often she included in it a stalk of celery or a carrot.

Caroline's lunches could have been a problem if it had not been for her mother's calm insistence that she should eat with the other White House school children, although it was her own home, and, as they did, have a box lunch and a bottle of milk. Mrs. Kennedy believed that if the other pupils could not lunch at home with their families, neither should Caroline. As for Caroline herself, she did not seem to regard herself as a "special case" in the least.

There was, as I have said, an unpretentious relationship in the Kennedy family which often made them seem no different from millions of others, in spite of their extraordinary position. I remember, for example, that the President and Mrs. Kennedy came into my kitchen one summer evening with young John and Caroline, the President in his Bermuda shorts with a white shirt and slippers. It appeared that John's hair needed trimming and I was asked for a pair of sharp scissors, which were applied on the spot to John's bangs by Mr. Kennedy while Mrs. Kennedy looked on and made suggestions. Caroline, who didn't want John's hair cut at all, cried through the whole barbering.

Such charming, warm and unaffected moments were not at all unusual in the White House. Nothing could have been more unpretentious than the spectacle of the first family at luncheon on the occasional days when there was no state function. They had it in their quarters, often from trays. Typically, the luncheon might consist of cups of consommé, and cold beef or grilled cheese sandwiches. The President usually had milk or tea; he preferred coffee only at breakfast.

In the recipes that I have set down here for vegetables, rice and noodles, you will find something of the Kennedy simplicity, but also many of the touches that transform a family dinner into a gourmet meal for entertaining.

ASPARAGUS VINAIGRETTE (2 to 3 servings) PLATE V

1 pound asparagus
2 cups boiling water
½ teaspoon salt
*Vinaigrette Sauce**

1. Wash asparagus thoroughly. Cut off and discard the tough ends of the stalks. Peel the stalks up 2 to 3 inches.

2. Place the asparagus flat in a shallow skillet; add enough boiling salted water to cover. Cook uncovered until the tips are tender, about 10 to 12 minutes. Drain at once. Cool.

3. Marinate the asparagus in the Vinaigrette Sauce for about two hours, turning frequently, then drain. If desired, serve with additional Vinaigrette Sauce.

NOTE: Boiled asparagus, while delicious with Vinaigrette Sauce,* is also excellent served hot with either Hollandaise Sauce,* Maltaise Sauce* or melted butter (PLATE V). In haute cuisine, melted butter is usually called clarified butter. It is prepared by placing the desired amount of butter in the top of a double boiler over hot water and allowing the butter to melt by itself, without stirring. The clear butter will rise to the surface, while the impurities will remain on the bottom. The clear butter should be poured over the asparagus gently and slowly; the residue on the bottom should be discarded.

FONDS D'ARTICHAUTS AU FOIE GRAS TRUFFE (6 servings)

Artichoke Hearts with Goose Liver and Truffles

1 cup wine vinegar
2 cloves garlic
1 onion stuck with 4 cloves
1 bay leaf
1 teaspoon salt
3 cups water
6 artichokes, with tough outer leaves removed
1 small can foie gras
1 small can truffles, sliced

1. Combine the vinegar, garlic, onion, bay leaf, salt and water. Bring to a boil and simmer for 10 minutes. Add the artichokes, cover and simmer until leaves are tender, approximately 20 minutes.

2. When the artichokes are cool enough to handle, cut off the top two-thirds with sharp scissors. Remove the center leaves and the choke. Chill the artichoke bottoms.

3. Fill the cavity of the artichoke with *foie gras* and garnish each with a slice of truffle.

ARTICHOKES PROVENCALE (6 to 8 servings)

2 tablespoons oil
1 can artichoke bottoms, quartered
1 package frozen peas
½ cup shredded lettuce
salt and pepper to taste

Heat oil in a saucepan; add remaining ingredients and simmer for 10 minutes.

CHOU-FLEUR A LA POLONAISE (6 servings)

Cauliflower with Eggs and Watercress

1 medium-sized cauliflower
4 tablespoons butter
2 tablespoons dry bread crumbs
1 teaspoon lemon juice
2 tablespoons minced watercress
salt and pepper to taste
2 hard-cooked eggs, chopped

1. Cook whole head of cauliflower in water to cover about a third of the head. Cover pan and test at the end of 10 minutes. Cooking time will vary according to size of cauliflower.

2. Melt butter in a saucepan over low heat; when butter begins to brown, add crumbs and cook, stirring, until brown.

3. Add lemon juice, watercress, salt and pepper to taste.

4. Pour mixture over cauliflower. Sprinkle with eggs.

ENDIVES AU GRATIN (4 to 6 servings)

1 pound mushrooms
2 shallots, chopped
2 tablespoons melted butter
salt and pepper to taste
3 cans endives
*1 cup Béchamel Sauce**
2 tablespoons grated Swiss cheese
2 tablespoons grated Parmesan cheese

1. Wash mushrooms and put them through a grinder.

2. Brown shallots in 1 tablespoon melted butter, add mushrooms and cook until liquid evaporates. Add salt and pepper to taste.

3. Brown endives in remaining tablespoon of melted butter in a frying pan.

4. Lay the mushrooms and shallots in a baking dish and place the endives on top. Cover with Béchamel Sauce, sprinkle with cheese and brown in preheated 450° F. oven.

CARI D'AUBERGINE (6 to 8 servings)

Curried Eggplant

1 medium eggplant (1¼ pounds)
¼ cup salad oil
1 cup chopped onion
¼ clove garlic, chopped
2 to 3 teaspoons curry powder
1 teaspoon salt
¼ teaspoon dry mustard
dash cayenne pepper
1 large green pepper, seeded and chopped
1 cup water

1. Wash eggplant but do not peel. Cut into 1-inch cubes.

2. In hot oil in a medium skillet sauté onion, garlic and curry powder, stirring until golden, about 5 minutes. Add eggplant, salt, mustard and cayenne. Mix thoroughly and simmer for 10 minutes.

3. Add green pepper and water. Bring to a boil. Reduce heat and simmer for 15 minutes.

AUBERGINES EN CASSEROLE (3 servings)

Eggplant Casserole

3 tablespoons olive oil
½ large onion, chopped
¼ cup chopped celery
½ medium green pepper, chopped
¾ pound ground beef
¾ cup canned tomatoes
¼ teaspoon basil
¼ teaspoon thyme
¾ teaspoon salt
pepper to taste
1 small eggplant (¾ pound), cut in ¾-inch slices
¼ cup dry bread crumbs
¼ cup grated sharp Cheddar cheese

1. Heat half of the olive oil in a large skillet, add the vegetables and cook over low heat for 10 minutes.

2. Add the beef and cook over medium heat until lightly browned. Pour off excess fat. Stir in tomatoes and seasonings.

3. Heat remaining olive oil and cook eggplant until lightly browned on both sides.

4. In a casserole make 2 layers each of eggplant and meat mixture.

5. Mix bread crumbs with Cheddar cheese and sprinkle on top of casserole.

6. Bake in preheated oven at 350° F. for 45 minutes.

AUBERGINE DE BAGHDAD (8 servings)

Eggplant Casserole, Baghdad Style

1 large eggplant
salt and pepper to taste
⅓ cup olive or salad oil
2 tablespoons lemon juice
1 clove garlic, minced fine
4 eggs, separated
2 tablespoons butter
1 tablespoon sesame seeds
½ cup yoghurt

1. Peel and slice the eggplant and season with salt and pepper.

2. Sauté eggplant slices in hot oil until soft and golden.

3. Mash the eggplant with a fork and add additional salt and pepper if desired. Add lemon juice and garlic and stir in egg yolks.

4. Fold in stiffly beaten egg whites.

5. Melt the butter in a 2-quart casserole. Add the eggplant mixture and stir. Bake for 30 minutes in preheated oven at 350° F.

6. During the last 10 minutes of baking, toast the sesame seeds on a sheet of aluminum foil.

7. Top with sesame seeds and serve with yoghurt. May be served hot or cold.

AUBERGINES DE CALABRIA (6 servings)

Eggplant with Cheese and Tomatoes

1 medium eggplant (1¼ pounds), pared and cut in ½-inch-thick slices
½ cup olive or salad oil
*¼ cup Pisa Tomato Sauce**
¼ cup grated Parmesan cheese
1 teaspoon salt
1 teaspoon oregano
⅛ teaspoon pepper
3 large tomatoes, peeled and cut in ½-inch-thick slices
3 slices Mozzarella cheese, quartered

1. Brown eggplant slices in hot oil and drain on paper towels.

2. Mix together Tomato Sauce, Parmesan cheese, salt, oregano and pepper.

3. In a casserole make 2 layers each of eggplant and tomato

slices, with Tomato Sauce mixture divided evenly between each layer.

4. Bake, uncovered, in preheated oven at 350° F. for 30 minutes. Arrange Mozzarella slices on top and bake 15 minutes longer.

AUBERGINES D'AMIENS (6 servings)

Eggplant with Chicken and Ham

¼ cup salad oil
3 medium eggplants
1 cup cubed cooked chicken
¼ cup chopped celery
½ cup cubed cooked ham
1 tablespoon sautéed chopped onion
1 tablespoon butter
1 tablespoon flour
1 cup milk
¼ teaspoon salt
½ cup grated Cheddar cheese

1. Heat oil in a large skillet.
2. Halve the eggplants and remove some of the pulp, leaving about ¼ inch of pulp in the shells. Mince pulp that has been removed and reserve.
3. Sauté eggplant shells in hot oil until tender.
4. Combine minced eggplant pulp with chicken, celery, ham and onion. Heat and fill the eggplant shells with this mixture.
5. Melt the butter in a saucepan, add the flour and blend well. Stir in milk and salt, heat to boiling, stir in cheese and cook, stirring, until cheese is melted. Pour over eggplants.

AUBERGINES AUX CHAMPIGNONS ET TOMATES (4 to 6 servings)

Eggplant with Mushrooms and Tomatoes

1½ cups olive or salad oil
3 small eggplants, pared and cut in ½-inch-thick slices
½ cup chopped onion
¼ pound mushrooms, sliced
2 cloves garlic, chopped
salt and pepper to taste
1 tablespoon prepared mustard
½ cup chopped parsley
6 tomatoes, peeled and quartered
¼ cup melted butter
1 cup fine dry bread crumbs

1. Heat ½ cup oil in a saucepan, add eggplant and cook until tender.

2. Add remaining oil, onions, mushrooms, garlic, salt, pepper and mustard. Cook for 5 minutes and add parsley.

3. Remove eggplant and arrange on a heatproof platter. Place tomatoes over the eggplant.

4. Add melted butter to the saucepan mixture and pour the mixture over the ingredients on the platter. Sprinkle with crumbs and bake in preheated oven at 400° F. for 10 minutes.

AUBERGINES FARCIS (4 servings)

Stuffed Eggplant

¼ cup olive oil
3 large onions, minced
1 large green pepper, minced
1 cup tomatoes (canned), drained and chopped
⅓ cup minced parsley
2 small eggplants, cut in half lengthwise with pulp scooped out, leaving ½-inch wall
3 tablespoons grated Parmesan cheese
1 teaspoon salt
pepper to taste
Mozzarella cheese, sliced
paprika

1. Heat oil in a large skillet. Sauté onions and green pepper. When vegetables are soft, add tomatoes, parsley, eggplant pulp that has been minced, Parmesan cheese, salt and pepper. Mix all ingredients thoroughly.

2. Fill eggplant shells with vegetable mixture. Place in a baking dish set in a pan with 1 inch of hot water and bake in preheated oven at 350° F. for 50 minutes.

3. Cover with slices of Mozzarella, dust with paprika and bake until cheese melts.

HARICOTS VERTS AUX AMANDES (5 to 6 servings)

Green Beans with Almonds

1½ pounds string beans, cooked until barely tender
2 tablespoons butter
3 tablespoons slivered almonds, toasted

1. Drain the cooked string beans.

2. Heat the butter until it sizzles and becomes lightly browned. Add the beans and cook over medium heat for 2 minutes to coat the beans with the browned butter. Add almonds and toss lightly.

PUREE FAVORITE (6 servings) PLATE IV

1 pound string beans
1 bunch broccoli
1 tablespoon butter
½ cup heavy cream, hot
salt and pepper to taste
dash nutmeg

1. In separate saucepans cook vegetables in small amount of salted boiling water until barely tender. Drain.

2. Put vegetables through a meat grinder, using the finest blade, to get a purée.

3. Heat butter, add cream and seasonings and add to puréed vegetables.

HEART OF PALM AU GRATIN (4 to 6 servings)

Serve with veal or chicken.

1 teaspoon butter
6 hearts of palm (canned)
*1 cup Béchamel Sauce**
3 tablespoons grated Swiss cheese

1. Butter the bottom of a baking dish.

2. Split hearts of palm lengthwise and place them in the baking dish.

3. Pour the Béchamel Sauce over the hearts of palm and sprinkle with the cheese.

4. Bake for 10 minutes in preheated 400° F. oven.

SAUTEED MUSHROOMS AND ARTICHOKES (4 servings)

8 large mushrooms, sliced
¼ cup butter
1 tablespoon flour
½ cup milk
½ cup light cream
1½ teaspoons prepared mustard
1½ cups hearts of artichokes
4 Pastry Shells, baked (small size)*
1 tablespoon chopped chives

1. In a skillet sauté mushrooms in butter until tender. Remove mushrooms, add flour to skillet, cook until bubbly and add milk,

cream and mustard. Cook until thick. Return the mushrooms, add the artichoke hearts and heat through.

2. Pour into Pastry Shells and top with chives.

PETITE POIS A LA FRANCAISE (3 to 4 servings)
French-Style Peas

1 package frozen peas with tiny onions
1 teaspoon butter
½ cup shredded Boston lettuce
1 teaspoon sugar
¼ teaspoon salt
2 tablespoons water

Mix all ingredients together in a covered saucepan and simmer for 8 to 10 minutes.

PIMENTS DE MONTDIDIER (6 to 8 servings)
Pickled Peppers

4 large red or green sweet peppers
1 clove garlic, cut in half
½ cup olive oil
¼ cup vinegar
½ teaspoon salt
pepper to taste

1. Place whole peppers on broiler 5 inches from the heat and broil, turning often, until peppers are blistered all over.

2. Remove from oven and quickly place peppers in a large paper bag and close tightly. Let steam in bag for 20 minutes.

3. Halve and seed peppers and cut into thin strips. Place in a small bowl that has been rubbed with cut clove of garlic.

4. Mix the olive oil, vinegar, salt and pepper and pour over peppers.

5. Chill for several hours.

ALGERIENNE POTATOES (4 to 6 servings)

½ cup puréed sweet potatoes
½ cup puréed chestnuts (canned)
2 egg yolks
salt and sugar to taste
1 egg, whole
½ cup dry bread crumbs
2 tablespoons butter

1. Combine potatoes and chestnuts in a saucepan and heat over low heat. Add egg yolks and seasoning and mix. Cool.

2. Shape into ¼-inch-thick patties about the size of a silver dollar.
3. Beat whole egg. Dip patties into egg and then into bread crumbs.
4. Melt butter in a frying pan and fry slices until golden brown.

BAKED POTATOES STUFFED WITH AVOCADOS (6 servings)

3 Idaho potatoes
1 cup sour cream
½ cup diced avocado
2 teaspoons salt
freshly ground black pepper to taste
butter

1. Bake the potatoes until done. Halve the potatoes lengthwise and scoop out the insides with care.

2. Whip the potato pulp together with sour cream, avocado, salt and pepper.

3. Fill the potato shells, dot with butter and bake in a preheated 375° F. oven for about 10 minutes until lightly browned.

POMMES DE TERRE CHANTILLY (6 servings)

Chantilly Potatoes

3 cups mashed potatoes
salt and pepper to taste
½ cup heavy cream
⅓ cup grated cheese

1. Season potatoes with salt and pepper. Pile into a greased baking dish.

2. Whip cream until stiff and spread over mashed potatoes.

3. Sprinkle grated cheese over all and bake in preheated oven at 450° F. until the cheese melts and browns slightly.

POMMES DAUPHINE (8 to 10 servings) PLATE IV

Dauphine Potatoes

2 medium Idaho potatoes, peeled and quartered
2 egg yolks
1 tablespoon butter
dash nutmeg
salt to taste
*Cream Puff Paste**

1. Cook potatoes in salted boiling water until tender. Drain and mash the potatoes.

2. Over medium heat stir the potatoes with a wooden spoon for 2 minutes.

3. Remove from heat and add yolks, butter and seasoning. Mix thoroughly.

4. Mix potato mixture with Cream Puff Paste. Using a teaspoon, drop mixture by spoonful into hot deep fat.* The potatoes will automatically turn by themselves. When they turn golden brown, remove them. Cooking time: about 6 minutes.

* Cooking oil, about 4 inches deep in pan, may be used.

VARIATIONS

CHAMONIX POTATOES

Add ½ cup grated Swiss cheese to the potato-cream puff mixture.

IDEALE POTATOES

Add 2 tablespoons diced truffles to the potato-cream puff mixture.

LYONNAISE POTATOES (4 servings)

2 cups diced boiled potatoes, slightly underdone
salt and pepper to taste
1 teaspoon minced onion
2 tablespoons fat
1 tablespoon chopped parsley

1. Season potatoes with salt and pepper.

2. Sauté the onion in fat until lightly browned. Add potatoes and stir with a fork until all sides are brown. Sprinkle with parsley.

CASSEROLE DE POMMES DE TERRE ET CAROTTES (4 servings)

Casserole of Potatoes and Carrots

3 medium potatoes
3 medium carrots
1 cup warm milk
2 tablespoons butter
½ teaspoon salt
⅛ teaspoon pepper

1. Pare potatoes and carrots and cook together in boiling salted water until tender.

2. Mash vegetables together.

3. Add milk, butter, salt and pepper to mashed vegetables and beat until very fluffy.

4. Pile into a greased casserole and bake in a preheated 350° F. oven for 20 minutes until browned.

POTATOES ARLIE (6 servings)

3 Idaho potatoes
1 tablespoon butter
1 tablespoon chopped chives
½ cup sour cream
salt and pepper to taste
dash of nutmeg
2 tablespoons grated Swiss cheese

1. Bake potatoes for 45 minutes to 1 hour in a preheated 350° F. oven, or until soft.

2. Split potatoes in half and scoop the insides into a bowl. With a fork, mash the potatoes and add butter, chives, sour cream and seasonings.

3. Refill the shells of the potatoes with the mixture and sprinkle with the Swiss cheese.

4. Bake at 350° F. for 10 minutes or until golden brown.

GRATIN SAVOYARD (6 to 8 servings)

Potatoes with Cheese

2 pounds potatoes
1 tablespoon butter, room temperature
1 clove garlic, cut in half
1 cup grated Swiss cheese
salt and pepper to taste
3 cups milk
1 cup heavy cream

1. Peel the potatoes and cut into thin round slices.

2. Spread butter over bottom of a baking pan. Rub the bottom of the pan with cut garlic.

3. Arrange potatoes and cheese in layers, seasoning with salt and pepper between each layer. Pour milk over the top and bake for 45 minutes in preheated oven at 350° F.

4. Pour cream over all and bake 15 minutes longer.

POMMES DE TERRE CHAVIGNOL (4 servings)

Potato Puffs Chavignol

2 cups mashed potatoes, hot
2 tablespoons butter
2 eggs, separated
1 cup milk
salt and pepper to taste

1. To mashed potatoes add butter, well-beaten egg yolks, milk, salt and pepper. Beat until very light and fluffy.
2. Beat egg whites until stiff and fold into potato mixture.
3. Pile into a greased baking dish and bake in preheated oven at 350° F. for 10 minutes.

WHIPPED POTATO CASSEROLE (4 servings)

4 medium potatoes
5 tablespoons butter
¼ cup cream
1 large onion, chopped
salt and pepper to taste
2 eggs, separated
grated Parmesan cheese

1. Cook potatoes in boiling salted water until tender. Drain and pare.
2. Mash potatoes with electric mixer or potato masher. Gradually beat in 3 tablespoons of butter and the cream to make potatoes light and fluffy.
3. Melt remaining butter in a skillet. Add onion and sauté until tender. Add to whipped potatoes. Season with salt and pepper to taste. Cool.
4. Beat egg yolks into cooled potatoes.
5. Beat egg whites until stiff but not dry. Fold into potatoes.
6. Generously grease a casserole, and spoon in potato mixture. Sprinkle top with cheese. Bake, uncovered, for 15 or 20 minutes in preheated oven at 350° F. Place under broiler for a few minutes to crisp the top.

PATATES ET BANANES AU FOUR (6 to 8 servings)

Baked Sweet Potatoes and Bananas

5 medium sweet potatoes
2 medium bananas, peeled
salt to taste
dash nutmeg
hot milk (approximately ¼ cup)
2 egg yolks
1 egg white

1. Boil sweet potatoes until tender; peel and rice.
2. Mash bananas and add to riced potatoes. Season with salt and nutmeg. Add enough hot milk to moisten; add egg yolks and beat until very fluffy and light.
3. Fold in egg white that has been beaten until stiff.
4. Pile into a greased baking dish and bake in preheated oven at 475° F. for 10 minutes or until lightly browned.

GRATIN OF CHOPPED SPINACH WASHINGTON
(6 to 8 servings)

2 cups fresh corn, cooked and drained
*1 cup thin White Sauce**
1½ cups chopped, cooked and seasoned spinach
½ cup grated Swiss cheese
2 tablespoons grated Parmesan cheese

1. Butter the bottom of a 3-quart casserole.
2. Add the corn to the White Sauce.
3. Spread a thin layer of spinach on the bottom of the casserole. Pour part of the creamed corn over the spinach. Repeat layering process with spinach and corn, ending with corn on top.
4. Sprinkle top of casserole evenly with grated cheeses.
5. Place casserole in a shallow pan containing boiling water. Bake for about 20 minutes in preheated oven at 350° F. or until heated through. If desired, brown the top by placing under the broiler.

SPINACH SOUFFLE (6 servings)

grated Parmesan cheese or flour
1 10-ounce package frozen spinach
4 tablespoons butter
4 tablespoons flour
1 cup milk, boiling
6 eggs, separated
pinch of salt
1 teaspoon salt
⅛ teaspoon nutmeg
¼ teaspoon black pepper

1. Grease 6½×3-inch soufflé dish with shortening and refrigerate. When chilled, spread again with shortening. Sprinkle dish with Parmesan cheese or flour and shake off excess.

2. Cook spinach following the instructions on the package. Cool immediately by running cold water over the spinach or by placing ice cubes in the pan. Pour spinach into a strainer and press out all moisture. Spinach must be dry. Place in a bowl and set aside.

3. Melt butter in a small pan over medium heat; add flour slowly, stirring constantly, until flour is cooked. Remove from heat and let cool slightly. Add one-third of the boiling milk, stirring vigorously. Add remaining milk and replace on heat. Keep stirring mixture with wire whisk until smooth and thick.

4. Place white sauce and spinach in blender container; cover and run on high speed until spinach is chopped. Add egg yolks and blend on high speed just until mixed (about 5 seconds).

5. Beat egg whites with pinch of salt in a medium bowl with food mixer until soft peaks form. Fold one-third of egg whites into spinach mixture, then add remaining egg whites. Fold until mixed. While folding, season with salt, nutmeg and pepper.

6. Pour into prepared soufflé dish and set on sheet pan with boiling water in oven. Bake in preheated oven at 350° F. for 30 to 35 minutes, or until firm. Serve immediately, plain or with Bread Cream Sauce.*

AMERICAN STUFFED SQUASH (6 servings)

3 medium acorn squash
2 cups chopped onion
3 tablespoons butter
1 6-ounce can sliced mushrooms, drained
2 tablespoons chopped parsley
salt and pepper to taste
1 cup shredded American cheese
1 tablespoon buttered corn flakes crumbs

1. Cut squash in half lengthwise and remove fibers and seeds. Bake, cut side down, in shallow pan in preheated oven at 350° F. for 35 to 40 minutes or until almost tender.

2. Cook onion in butter until tender. Add mushrooms and parsley.

3. Season squash with salt and pepper. Fill squash with mushroom mixture. Bake 15 to 20 minutes.

4. Sprinkle with cheese, top with crumbs and bake until cheese melts.

BONNET DE PRETRE GLACE (8 servings)

Candied Squash

2 medium butternut or acorn squash
½ cup butter
½ cup brown sugar
½ cup water
2 tablespoons light corn syrup
¼ teaspoon cinnamon

1. Cook whole squash in a large amount of boiling water for about 15 minutes or until tender. Drain, pare, halve, remove seeds and cut into chunks.

2. Melt butter and brown sugar in a large frying pan and stir in remaining ingredients until blended. Add squash and toss until well coated. Cover pan and cook over low heat for 10 minutes. Uncover and cook 5 minutes longer.

PANACHE (6 to 8 servings)

Spanish Vegetable Pâté

½ pound green beans
2 large sweet onions, thinly sliced
¼ cup olive oil
½ pound canned artichoke hearts, drained and liquid reserved
3 eggs, beaten until frothy
½ green pepper, chopped
1 teaspoon salt
freshly ground pepper to taste
1 small can pimientos, cut in strips
parsley

1. Cook green beans until tender and drain.

2. Cook onions in oil over low heat until tender.

3. Place beans, onions with oil in which cooked and artichoke

hearts in a blender. Blend until smooth. If necessary, add 1 tablespoon of artichoke liquid.

4. Mix blender contents with eggs and add green pepper, salt and pepper.

5. Pour into a well-buttered 1-quart mold. Set in a pan of water. Bake in preheated oven at 450° F. for 5 minutes; reduce oven temperature to 300° F. and bake for about 55 minutes until set.

6. Turn out on a serving platter. Decorate with lattice of pimientos and garnish with parsley. Serve chilled.

RATATOUILLE NICOISE (6 servings)

Vegetable Stew, Nice Style

1 onion, chopped fine
4 tablespoons olive oil
1 eggplant, peeled and cubed
1 zucchini, peeled and cubed
6 tomatoes, peeled and cubed
1 clove garlic, crushed
1 tablespoon chopped parsley
½ bay leaf
pinch thyme
salt and pepper
½ cup grated Swiss cheese

1. Sauté onion in oil until brown. Add vegetables, garlic and parsley. Add remaining seasonings. Cook until the vegetables are tender, about 20 minutes.

2. Place in a shallow baking dish and sprinkle with Swiss cheese. Brown under the broiler.

SAFFRON RICE WITH WINE (4 servings)

1 cup rice
1 tablespoon butter
1 tablespoon olive oil
*2 cups boiling Chicken Broth**
¼ teaspoon saffron
¼ cup dry white wine
salt and pepper to taste

1. Brown the rice in the butter and olive oil in a saucepan.

2. Add the Broth, saffron and wine. Cover and cook over low heat until the liquid is absorbed (about 20 minutes). Season with salt and pepper.

NOUILLES EN CASSEROLE AUX FROMAGES (4 servings)

Casserole of Noodles with Cheeses

8 ounces noodles
1 cup cream-style cottage cheese
½ cup blue cheese, room temperature
¼ cup melted butter
¼ cup chopped parsley
¼ cup minced onion
3 eggs, well beaten
1 small clove garlic, crushed
salt and pepper to taste

1. Cook noodles until tender and drain.
2. Combine the remaining ingredients, add noodles and toss well.
3. Grease a 1½-quart casserole, add noodle mixture and bake in preheated oven at 350° F. for 30 minutes.

FETTUCINI RENE (3 to 4 servings)

½ pound noodles
1 tablespoon butter
2 shallots, chopped (optional)
*1 cup Chicken Broth**
½ cup heavy cream
1 cup sour cream
2 tablespoons chopped chives
¼ cup grated Parmesan cheese

1. Cook noodles until tender and drain.
2. In a saucepan melt butter, add shallots and simmer for a few minutes. Add Broth and cook for 3 minutes over high heat. Remove from heat and add the cream.
3. Add the cooked noodles to the pan and the sour cream, chives and cheese. Toss well.

NOUILLES A L'ITALIENNE (3 servings)

Noodles Italian Style

4 ounces medium noodles
2 ounces cream cheese
¼ cup light cream
¼ cup milk
⅛ cup grated Parmesan cheese
⅛ teaspoon salt
pepper to taste
chopped parsley

1. Cook noodles.
2. Soften cream cheese in a medium-size bowl and blend in cream, milk, cheese, salt and pepper.

3. When noodles are tender, drain. Pour cheese sauce over noodles and toss lightly to coat well. Spoon into serving dish. Garnish with parsley.

NOUILLES CHINOIS (8 servings)

Noodles with Chestnuts

4 cups medium noodles
3 tablespoons butter
1 cup milk
salt and pepper to taste
1 can water chestnuts, drained
chopped almonds

1. Cook noodles until tender and drain.

2. Place in a casserole with butter, milk, salt, pepper and chestnuts. Mix ingredients together. Cover and refrigerate overnight.

3. Bake in preheated oven at 350° F. for 1 hour, stirring occasionally. Sprinkle with almonds.

NOUILLES A L'EPINARDS ET JAMBON (6 servings)

Noodles with Spinach and Ham

1½ pounds fresh spinach, cooked until just barely tender and drained
1 tablespoon lemon juice
3 tablespoons butter
1 tablespoon finely chopped onion
1 clove garlic, finely chopped
3 tablespoons flour
1 cup light cream
salt and freshly ground black pepper to taste
⅛ teaspoon nutmeg
½ cup finely chopped prosciutto or cooked ham
1 pound noodles cooked until barely tender, drained
½ cup buttered bread crumbs

1. Chop spinach and add lemon juice.

2. Melt the butter and cook the onion and garlic in it until tender. Blend in the flour. Gradually stir in the cream and bring to a boil, stirring. Season with salt, pepper and nutmeg.

3. Add the spinach to the sauce and mix thoroughly. Toss the ham, noodles and spinach mixture together and place in a buttered casserole. Top with crumbs and bake in preheated oven at 350° F. for 20 minutes.

SALADS

A GOOD SALAD properly made serves to freshen and fortify a gourmet meal. In some cases it can be made the main dish in a luncheon or even a dinner, especially in spring and summer. As has been said so truly, "Salad makes the stomach glad," which makes it all the more astonishing that cookbooks of a half-century ago did not even list recipes for them.

For the most part, salads are made up of vegetables, herbs, eggs, meat and fish. They are usually seasoned with salt, pepper, oil and vinegar. Some cooks substitute lemon juice for wine vinegar, but I do not especially recommend it. A wine vinegar of good quality will give a more piquant flavor to any salad. I also prefer olive oil, although any good nut or vegetable oil may be used, depending on taste.

A truly well-made salad must have vegetables of the best quality that are dry, crisp, cold and fresh. Flavor combinations must be appetizing, and enjoyment is enhanced if the color combinations are attractive to the eye. Finally, the salad dressing must be appropriate.

There is, alas, a drawback in salads. As those who are fond of wine know, aroma and bouquet are destroyed by eating salads. Most gourmets wait for the cheese before they resume drinking wine after the salad. If the salad has been prepared as it should be, the short wait will seem worthwhile.

I have a few suggestions about creating salads—extra touches that will make even wine lovers happy. Try sprinkling garlic powder on them instead of using bits of a clove of garlic. Be delicate, always. Some people merely rub garlic on the salad bowl, but that is a matter of taste. Garlic powder permits an even distribution of flavor. Those who prefer a more zesty French dressing may add a bit of horseradish or a suggestion of Tabasco sauce.

Edges of lettuce leaves or pineapple rings will be gayer if they are dipped in paprika. You can add an extra quality to pineapple by rolling the edges in nut meats, chives or finely chopped parsley. Grated walnuts added to the dressing or sprinkled on the salad will also be enthusiastically received.

Easily prepared fruit salad toppings include shredded cherries, chopped raisins or peanuts, and shredded coconut.

The order of things is important. When you dress salad greens with oil and vinegar, do not add the vinegar before the oil or you will discover that the oil does not cling to the wet greens and instead settles to the bottom of the bowl. First, season your salad with salt and pepper, add the oil, *then* the vinegar.

A touch of Roquefort cheese crumbled into French dressing adds flavor sophistication and gives a better tone to fruit salads. Salad greens can be enhanced by adding the tender inside leaves of raw spinach. Raw cauliflower flowerets and diced avocado which has been sprinkled with lemon juice to prevent discoloration also make a nice extra touch.

If you like your celery crisp and crackly, place it in cold water with several slices of lemon for at least an hour.

Contrast in salad color can be obtained by accenting light greens with dark parsley or watercress.

MAITRE JEAN'S CAESAR SALAD (6 servings) PLATE VI

salt to taste
freshly ground black pepper to taste
1 clove garlic, crushed
1 teaspoon Dijon mustard
1½ tablespoons lemon juice or wine vinegar
3½ tablespoons olive oil
2 bunches of romaine lettuce, washed and dried
2 tablespoons grated Parmesan cheese
1 can of anchovies, drained
2 eggs boiled for 1 minute
1 cup croutons (bread cubes toasted lightly in olive oil and pinch of oregano)

1. Sprinkle the salt and black pepper at the bottom of a wooden salad bowl. Add the garlic and mix. Add the mustard and lemon juice or wine vinegar and mix until the salt dissolves. Add the olive oil and stir until the liquid is blended.

2. Wash the romaine well and dry the leaves. Tear the leaves into bite-sized pieces and add this to the salad bowl. Sprinkle the Parmesan cheese and anchovies and break the eggs over the salad. Sprinkle with the croutons and mix gently but thoroughly.

SALAD MIMOSA (6 servings)

¼ cup olive oil
1 tablespoon wine vinegar
½ teaspoon salt
dash pepper
½ clove garlic, finely minced
2 quarts crisp salad greens
2 hard-cooked eggs, finely chopped

1. Combine, oil, vinegar, salt, pepper and garlic in a jar with a tight lid and shake vigorously.

2. Arrange greens in a salad bowl, add dressing and toss well. Sprinkle with chopped egg.

GARDEN SALAD (6 to 8 servings)

1 cup julienne of turkey
1 cup julienne of Virginia ham
1 head lettuce, torn into bite-size pieces
1 head escarole or chicory, torn into bite-size pieces
*1 cup Lorenzo Salad Dressing**

Mix turkey, Virginia ham, lettuce and escarole, then add Lorenzo Salad Dressing and serve at once.

SALADE DE JAMBON ET POULET (4 servings)
Ham and Chicken Salad

½ cup baked ham that has been cut in thin strips
½ cup diced cooked chicken or turkey
1 cup thinly sliced celery
½ cup Swiss cheese that has been cut in thin strips
*¾ cup Thousand Island Dressing**
salt and pepper to taste
lettuce

1. Combine ham, chicken, celery and cheese.

2. Add Dressing and toss lightly. Season to taste with salt and pepper. Serve on lettuce.

HAM AND POTATO SALAD (6 servings)

2 cups diced cooked ham
2 cups diced cooked potatoes
1 tablespoon minced onion
6 small sweet pickles, diced
3 hard-cooked eggs, sliced
*1 cup Blender Mayonnaise**
salt and pepper to taste

1. Combine ham, potatoes, onion, pickles and eggs.
2. Add Mayonnaise and salt and pepper. Toss lightly.

SALADE D'ARTICHAUT AU CRABE FROID (6 servings)

Chilled Artichoke and Crab Meat Salad

1 cup diced cooked artichoke hearts
1 cup crab meat
½ cup heavy cream, whipped
*1 cup Blender Mayonnaise**
½ cup ketchup
½ teaspoon Worcestershire sauce
salt and pepper to taste

1. Combine artichokes and crab meat and chill.
2. Mix whipped cream with Mayonnaise, ketchup, Worcestershire sauce, salt and pepper. Chill.
3. At serving time, combine the sauce with crab mixture.

SALADE D'HOMARDS ESSEX (6 to 8 servings)

Lobster Salad

1 cup diced freshly cooked lobster meat
*1 tablespoon Mustard French Dressing**
1 cup thinly sliced celery
1 tablespoon chopped capers
1 tablespoon chopped anchovies
1 tablespoon chopped chives
lettuce
½ cup Blender Mayonnaise (optional)*

1. Season the lobster with the Mustard French Dressing and chill.
2. Soak the celery in ice water for 1 hour, drain, dry thoroughly and slice.
3. Combine the celery, capers, anchovies and chives.
4. Serve on lettuce leaves on individual salad plates. May be garnished with stuffed olives, capers, slices of pimiento and quar-

tered hard-cooked eggs. The salad may be coated lightly with Mayonnaise thinned with tarragon vinegar.

KASHMIR CHICKEN SALAD (6 servings)

2 cups thinly sliced cooked chicken
1 can thinly sliced water chestnuts
½ pound seedless green grapes
*1 cup Blender Mayonnaise**
½ teaspoon curry powder
1 tablespoon lemon juice
¼ teaspoon salt
freshly ground black pepper to taste
1 teaspoon soy sauce
1 cup honeydew balls
1 cup cantaloupe balls

1. Combine chicken, water chestnuts and grapes.
2. Mix Mayonnaise with curry powder, lemon juice, salt, pepper and soy sauce.
3. Mix the chicken with the dressing, add honeydew and cantaloupe balls and toss lightly to coat.

SALADE D'AVOCAT ET POULET (6 servings)

Salad with Avocado and Chicken

4 tablespoons salad oil
2 tablespoons fresh lime juice
¼ teaspoon ground ginger
4 cups thinly sliced cooked chicken
1 large head lettuce, washed and dried
1 cup sliced celery
1 large ripe avocado, peeled, seeded and brushed with lemon juice

1. Combine oil, lime juice and ginger. Sprinkle over chicken, toss to coat, cover and chill.
2. Place 1 large lettuce leaf on each serving plate; shred the remaining lettuce; toss with celery and arrange around large lettuce leaves. Mound the marinated chicken on top of the large lettuce leaves.
3. Cut avocado into lengthwise slices and arrange 3 slices on top of each mound of chicken.

JELLIED WALDORF LUNCHEON SALAD (6 servings)

1 (3-ounce) package apple gelatin
1 cup hot water
¾ cup apple cider or apple juice
3 tablespoons lemon juice plus additional small amount
1 large red apple
⅓ cup toasted chopped or ready-diced almonds plus additional small amount
¼ cup minced celery
salad greens
1½ cups creamed cottage cheese

1. Dissolve gelatin in hot water. Add cider and 3 tablespoons lemon juice. Chill until slightly thickened.

2. Core apple. Cut part of apple into small wedges to make 1 cup, leaving remainder in thin slices.

3. Soak apple slices only in small amount of lemon juice to prevent fruit from darkening, and set aside for garnish.

4. Fold apple wedges, almonds and celery into thickened gelatin. Pour into 8-inch ring mold and chill until firm.

5. Unmold on salad greens. Fill center of ring with cottage cheese. Garnish with apple slices and additional almonds.

MOLDED GRAPEFRUIT SALAD (6 servings)

2 medium grapefruits
2 envelopes unflavored gelatin
½ cup cold water
¾ cup boiling water
½ cup honey
½ teaspoon salt
¼ cup lemon juice
1 medium grapefruit, peeled and sectioned for garnish

1. With a sharp knife cut off grapefruit peel, including white membranes. Remove all sections, working over a bowl to catch the juices. Cut each section into 3 pieces and drain in a strainer.

2. Soften gelatin in cold water; add boiling water and stir until gelatin is dissolved. Stir in honey, salt and lemon juice.

3. To grapefruit juices in the bowl add enough additional fresh grapefruit juice to make 1 cup. Add juice to the gelatin and chill until mixture becomes thick and syrupy.

4. Stir in the grapefruit pieces. Pour into a 6-cup mold and chill until set.

5. Unmold on a serving plate and garnish with fresh grapefruit slices.

MOULE D'AVOCAT (6 servings)

Avocado Mold

1 envelope unflavored gelatin
¼ cup cold water
1 cup boiling water
2 teaspoons sugar
1½ teaspoons salt
½ teaspoon white pepper
2 avocados, peeled and seeded
2 tablespoons lemon juice
¾ cup sour cream
*¼ cup Blender Mayonnaise**
black olives

1. Soften gelatin in cold water for 5 minutes; add boiling water, sugar, salt and pepper and stir until dissolved. Chill until it begins to set.
2. Purée avocados in a blender with lemon juice.
3. Stir sour cream and Mayonnaise into avocado purée. Add gelatin mixture and adjust seasoning.
4. Turn mixture into an oiled 8-inch ring mold. Chill until set. Unmold on serving platter; fill center with black olives.

TOMATO ASPIC LOAF (8 to 10 servings)

1 package (6 ounces) lemon-flavored gelatin
1 teaspoon salt
2 cups boiling tomato juice
1½ cups cold tomato juice
2 teaspoons prepared horseradish
1 tablespoon grated onion
⅛ teaspoon cayenne pepper
cauliflower flowerets and carrot sticks
hard-cooked eggs

1. Dissolve gelatin and salt in boiling tomato juice. Add cold tomato juice, horseradish, onion and cayenne.
2. Pour into a 9×5×3-inch loaf pan. Chill until firm—at least 3 hours or overnight.
3. Unmold. Garnish with cauliflower flowerets and carrot sticks around loaf. Arrange hard-cooked egg slices on top of loaf.

BANGALORE POTATO SALAD (10 servings)

7 cups diced cooked potatoes (about 8 medium-sized raw)
½ cup diced green pepper
1 cup diced celery
2 hard-cooked eggs, diced
*1 cup Blender Mayonnaise**
1 to 1½ tablespoons curry powder
2 tablespoons grated onion
3 tablespoons lemon juice
salt and pepper to taste

1. Combine potatoes, green pepper, celery and eggs.
2. Mix remaining ingredients until well blended and pour over potato mixture. Toss well. Chill before serving.

CHICK-PEAS SALAD GRENOBLE (6 servings)

2 cups canned chick-peas, rinsed and drained
2 anchovy fillets, chopped
1 clove garlic, finely minced
1 tablespoon capers
1 teaspoon finely chopped shallots or green onions
2 tablespoons finely chopped parsley
salt and pepper to taste
lemon juice
*¼ to ½ cup Blender Mayonnaise**

Combine all ingredients except Mayonnaise and blend well. Use Mayonnaise to bind ingredients. Chill before serving.

DUTCH POTATO SALAD (6 servings)

6 medium potatoes
⅓ cup sliced scallions
½ cup diced, peeled cucumbers
*⅓ cup Blender Mayonnaise**
⅓ cup sour cream
2 teaspoons horseradish
4 teaspoons vinegar
1 teaspoon salt
¼ teaspoon sugar
⅛ teaspoon pepper
1 teaspoon caraway seeds

1. Boil potatoes in their jackets until soft. Peel and cube them.
2. Combine potatoes with scallions and cucumbers.
3. Mix all remaining ingredients, pour over potato mixture and toss lightly. Chill before serving.

HOT PICKLED CAULIFLOWER (6 servings)

1 medium-size head cauliflower (1½ pounds)
3 tablespoons wine vinegar
2 tablespoons butter
2 tablespoons diced pimiento
2 tablespoons chopped green pepper
1 teaspoon sugar
¼ teaspoon salt

1. Break cauliflower into flowerets; cook in small amount of boiling salted water for about 10 minutes; drain.

2. While cauliflower cooks, combine remaining ingredients in a small saucepan; cook over low heat for about 5 minutes.

3. Pour over hot cauliflower.

ITALIAN WHITE BEAN SALAD (6 servings)

2 cans cannellini (white beans)
⅔ cup chopped red onion
½ cup olive oil
1 teaspoon salt
1 teaspoon basil
2 tablespoons wine vinegar

Combine all ingredients and toss well. Refrigerate for several hours before serving.

JAIPUR RICE SALAD (6 servings)

1 cup raw rice
2 tomatoes, cored, peeled and cut into small cubes
6 radishes, trimmed and sliced thin
½ cup finely chopped onion
½ cup finely chopped heart of celery
4 small beets, cooked, peeled and cut into thin strips
¼ cup sliced green olives
salt to taste
freshly ground black pepper to taste
½ teaspoon curry powder
1 teaspoon mustard, Dijon type
2 tablespoons wine vinegar
6 tablespoons olive oil

1. Cook the rice according to package directions. Chill.

2. Combine the cold rice with the tomatoes, radishes, onion, celery, beets, olives, salt and pepper.

3. Combine the curry powder, mustard and vinegar; sprinkle over the salad.

4. Toss salad lightly and sprinkle with the oil. Toss again.

MARINATED CUCUMBER SALAD (4 servings)

2 medium cucumbers, sliced thin
½ cup vinegar
¼ cup cold water
½ teaspoon sugar
dash of salt and pepper

Combine all ingredients and chill for 24 hours.

ONION SALAD (6 servings)

4 sweet onions (Spanish or red Italian)
6 tablespoons olive oil
3 tablespoons wine vinegar
anchovy fillets
pitted ripe black olives

1. Slice the onions very thin. Soak them for 30 minutes in salted water with ice cubes. Dry thoroughly with a towel.

2. Arrange onions in a large salad bowl, add oil and vinegar and garnish with anchovies and olives.

TOMATE RIVIERA (8 servings)

Tomatoes Riviera

4 tomatoes
4 hearts of palm, canned
*2 tablespoons Blender Mayonnaise**
1 teaspoon lemon juice
salt and pepper to taste
1 red pimiento
1 tablespoon chopped parsley
1 hard-cooked egg, chopped
lettuce

1. Peel tomatoes, cut in half for stuffing and remove the cores.

2. Slice the hearts of palm and mix with the Mayonnaise, lemon juice, salt and pepper.

3. Add the hearts of palm mixture to fill one-half of each tomato half. Lay pimientos on top of the mixture, then finish the tomatoes by sprinkling with the parsley and egg. Serve on top of lettuce leaf.

DESSERTS

IN THESE comments, it appears, I must always return to Louis XIV, and that is surprising because he was not considered a real gourmet by the French epicures of his day. However, as I have noted, he did encourage keen competition in his court to create something that might tempt his royal appetite. Consequently, many creations which are commonplace today originated during his reign.

I have noted them in most of this book's sections, and as we come to the last course, dessert, it seems there is again no escape from him. That staple of the dessert menu, the petit four, did indubitably appear for the first time one day when the King was being given a dinner at the country estate of a wealthy friend. The sophisticated nobles of the court who surrounded Louis had not expected much from the efforts of the country chef, who had nevertheless surprised them. When it came to the moment preceding dessert, however, there was some laughter and sneering among the nobles, who could not believe that this rural master of the kitchen could produce anything to excite the interest of those who were daily served the most fabulous creations the great chefs of Paris could produce.

At last a servant carried into the dining hall a single tiny cake, a petit four, on a silver platter and presented it to the King. The courtiers were shocked, and apprehensive as well, expecting the King to explode in one of his noteworthy fits of anger. Louis could not conceal his surprise, but he popped the cake into his mouth and gulped it in one bite. A look of rapture spread over his face and he called for more. The petit four was born.

A literal translation of this confection would be "small oven," although we are told that it refers more properly to a "slow oven," or the baking process in an oven which has cooled considerably. In any case, as I am sure you know, these little cakes come in a variety of delightful forms, and they end the meal on a note of high good humor.

I served them, of course, at the White House, where it may surprise you to know there is a tradition of sweet things dating back to that always amazing third President, Thomas Jefferson, who was himself a gourmet with a keen appreciation for gracious living. He personally selected the finest meat, fruit and vegetables at the markets in Georgetown, which he visited with his chef, Monsieur Lemaire, after he became President. Jefferson also made up the daily menus for the White House. As the nation's first Ambassador to France, Jefferson had spent a good deal of his free time in Paris visiting the finest restaurants, and so had become an epicure of formidable stature in America.

It is fairly well known that Jefferson brought spaghetti to the United States, but perhaps his contributions to American dessert menus are less familiar. While he was in France he learned to make ice cream, and was among the first diplomats to have it served at a state dinner. Of more historic significance, however, is Jefferson's introduction to America of what is now called baked Alaska, which he caused to be served at a White House function. The guests had never seen anything like it. In the Jeffersonian version, it was a hot pastry shell with a center of frozen ice cream. The guests greatly enjoyed it, as they did the many other excellencies of the White House cuisine in those days.

I must confess that I did not serve much baked Alaska at the White House. It has always seemed to me a peculiarly American dish, one inconsistent with the cuisine I was called upon to provide.

The eaters of sweets at the White House were, quite naturally, the children. There was always a plate of chunks of milk chocolate on a small table near Mrs. Lincoln's desk. It was primarily for visitors, but the children grabbed a piece whenever they could and ran off gleefully under the watchful eye of their nurse, Maud Shaw. The President never touched the chocolate himself. He never took between-meals snacks of any kind.

Like all children, Caroline and John were exceedingly fond of cookies. Caroline often came into the kitchen to ask for them, pleading the needs not only of herself but of several attendant friends. These dispensations were always subject to Miss Shaw's approval. If she nodded her consent, the cookies would be distributed. If it was too near mealtime, she would say no. Caroline was always very good about it if she was turned down. There were no tantrums. Both children were very well behaved, and always said "please" and "thank you."

The desserts that follow should provide a proper finishing touch to a good meal. I have tried to make them glamorous and dramatic, yet simple to prepare. I do hope you will enjoy them.

BATTER FOR BASIC CREPES (30 to 34 pancakes)

3 eggs
pinch of salt
⅛ cup sugar
½ teaspoon vanilla extract
1½ cups milk
1 cup flour
2 tablespoons butter

1. Place eggs, salt, sugar and vanilla extract in blender container; cover and run on low speed for 5 seconds.

2. Add milk slowly while running on low speed. Funnel in flour, using paper towel or wax paper, still running on low speed.

3. Melt butter in crepe pan[1] and add slowly to mixture while running on low speed.

4. After baking each crepe, wipe pan with lightly buttered cheesecloth. Tip pan and slowly pour in crepe batter, just coating bottom of pan (about 2 tablespoons). Tilt the pan immediately so that the batter will completely spread over the entire bottom of the pan. Cook quickly on medium heat until both sides are brown.

5. Carefully stack crepes on a platter with second browned side up.

6. If the crepes are to be sauced later, cover with plastic wrap and refrigerate.

[1] A crepe pan is a 6-inch cast iron pan large enough for making one crepe at a time.

NOTE: Batter for crepes may be stored in refrigerator, or crepes may be cooked ahead and either stored in plastic wrap or wrapped for freezing.

SUZETTE BUTTER FOR CREPES (Sufficient for 12 crepes)

2 oranges
2 strips lemon peel (1×½ inch)
⅔ cup sugar
⅔ cup butter, room temperature
6 tablespoons orange curaçao liqueur
brandy

1. Peel oranges with vegetable peeler, removing outer portion of peel only. Set aside peel.

2. Cut oranges in half and squeeze juice (½ cup). Place orange juice, orange peel and lemon peel in blender container; cover and run on low speed until peel is chopped. Add sugar, butter and 4 tablespoons of orange curaçao liqueur. Cover and blend until mixed on high speed.

3. Spoon about ½ cup of the Suzette Butter into a chafing dish or shallow skillet to melt.

4. Heat one crepe at a time in sauce; heat both sides. (Place crepe with second side cooked down, so first side cooked is on the top. This provides better color when folded). Fold crepe into quarters with a fork and spoon; add more sauce as needed. Set folded crepes around side of pan with all folded corners facing the same direction. When ready to serve, spoon 2 tablespoons brandy and 2 tablespoons orange curaçao liqueur over 12 crepes. Immediately touch with flame and baste with sauce to keep flame burning. Tip pan if necessary, to obtain sauce. For dramatic effect, flame crepes in front of guests. Serve as a dessert.

APPLES NORMANDY (Stuffing for 8 to 10 crepes)
Stuffing for Crepes

2 tablespoons butter
2 large apples, peeled, cored and diced into ¼-inch cubes
⅛ teaspoon cinnamon
2 tablespoons light brown sugar
8 to 10 crepes
¼ cup corn syrup
¼ cup Calvados (applejack brandy)

1. Melt butter in a large frying pan or chafing dish until brown.

2. Add apples and cook until tender and brown. Stir occasionally so that they will not burn. Sprinkle cinnamon and brown sugar over apples and continue to cook for 3 minutes.

3. Heat one crepe at a time in a frying pan or chafing dish.

4. Place a tablespoon of apple mixture in the center of each crepe. Roll crepe and set around side of the pan.

5. When ready to serve, add syrup and brandy to crepes. Immediately touch with a flame and baste with a spoon to keep flame burning. For dramatic effect, flame crepes in front of guests.

PECHES GLACES AMANDINE (6 servings)

Baked Peaches with Almonds

6 peach halves (canned), drained and syrup reserved
½ cup slivered almonds
2 tablespoons honey or brown sugar
2 tablespoons lemon juice
½ teaspoon grated lemon rind
1 tablespoon butter

1. Place peaches in a casserole, cavity side up. Sprinkle with almonds and honey or sugar.

2. Boil peach syrup over high heat until reduced to 1 cup. Remove from heat and add lemon juice and rind.

3. Pour syrup mixture over peaches and dot with butter. Bake in preheated oven at 325° F. for 30 minutes. Serve hot or cold.

RHUM FRAISES CHANTILLY AU CHOCOLAT (6 servings)

Creamed Strawberries with Chocolate and Rum

1 quart whole strawberries
½ cup granulated sugar
1 cup heavy cream
½ cup grated sweet chocolate
1 tablespoon confectioners' sugar
1 tablespoon light rum

1. Place berries in a serving bowl and sprinkle with granulated sugar. Chill.

2. When ready to serve, whip the cream, fold in the chocolate and confectioners' sugar, then fold in the rum. Serve over chilled strawberries.

FRUITED BREAD PUDDING (8 to 10 servings)

¼ cup diced assorted candied fruit
¼ cup raisins
1 tablespoon kirschwasser
¼ cup butter
French bread, cut in ¼-inch-thick slices
1 cup sugar
1 teaspoon vanilla extract
1 quart milk
5 whole eggs

1. Soak fruit and raisins in kirschwasser.

2. Melt butter and butter enough sliced French bread to cover the bottom of an 8×5-inch oven-proof dish.

3. Butter the baking dish and sprinkle with the candied fruit and then the raisins. Place the buttered bread on top.

4. Mix the sugar, vanilla and milk together and bring to the boiling point.

5. In a bowl, beat the eggs and gradually add the milk mixture while stirring.

6. Pour over the bread slices and bake in preheated oven at 375° F. for 25 minutes.

HONEY-BAKED APPLES (4 servings)

4 large baking apples
1 tablespoon chopped walnuts
1 tablespoon raisins
¾ cup light brown sugar
½ cup honey
1 cup water
1 cinnamon stick

1. Core apples almost through to the stem. Remove about a quarter of top of apple.

2. Mix walnuts, raisins and ¼ cup sugar. Fill apple cavities and place in a baking dish.

3. Combine honey, water, cinnamon stick and remaining sugar and boil for 4 minutes. Pour over the apples in the baking dish. Bake in preheated oven at 350° F. for 45 minutes or until apples are tender.

MACEDOINE DE FRUITS CHANTILLY (8 servings)
Mixed Fruits with Kirschwasser and Whipped Cream

1 ripe pineapple
4 tablespoons kirschwasser or cognac
sugar
3 cups strawberries
½ cup pitted canned apricots with syrup
1 cup heavy cream, whipped and sweetened to taste

1. Peel the pineapple and slice. Cut 4 of the slices in half. Add 2 tablespoons kirschwasser and 2 tablespoons sugar to the half slices and chill. Dice the rest of the pineapple slices.

2. Reserve 1 cup of berries for garnishing. Cut the remaining berries into quarters and combine with the diced pineapple. Sweeten to taste and chill.

3. Purée the apricots and syrup in a blender, add ¼ cup sugar and cook in a saucepan over medium heat, stirring, until the mixture becomes clear. Add the remaining kirschwasser and chill.

4. Place the diced pineapple and strawberries in the center of a serving dish and arrange the half slices of pineapple around them. Cover the center with the whipped cream and garnish with the reserved strawberries. Coat the pineapple slices with the apricot purée.

PEACHES STUFFED WITH ALMONDS (12 servings)

Serve hot or cold with a dollop of sour cream flavored with sugar and dark rum.

1 cup confectioners' sugar
1 cup finely ground blanched almonds
½ cup dark rum
12 peaches, peeled, pitted and cut into halves
1 cup butter (½ pound)
½ cup sugar

1. Combine 1 cup confectioners' sugar, almonds and rum. Mix to form a paste.

2. Fill peach halves with paste and put the halves together to form whole peaches.

3. Melt the butter in a baking dish, add peaches and sprinkle with ½ cup sugar. Cover and bake in preheated oven at 350° F. for 15 minutes or until peaches are soft.

PECHES AU VIN BLANC (8 servings)

Peaches with Wine

8 firm, ripe peaches
2 cups cold water
2 cups dry white wine
1 tablespoon lemon juice
1 cup sugar

1. Wash and dry peaches.

2. Combine remaining ingredients and bring to a boil. Simmer until sugar dissolves.

3. Drop peaches into simmering syrup. Return to a boil, lower heat and simmer until peaches are tender.

4. Chill syrup. To serve, peel peaches and serve in the syrup.

POIRES KARACHI (6 servings)

Pears Karachi Style

½ cup butter
½ cup brown sugar
1 tablespoon curry powder
½ teaspoon salt
12 pear halves (canned), drained

1. Mix butter, brown sugar, curry powder and salt and spoon into pear halves.
2. Place under broiler until bubbly.

ANANAS ET FRAISES CHANTILLY (6 servings)

Pineapple and Strawberries with Cream

1 ripe pineapple, cubed
2 pints strawberries, hulled
2 tablespoons sugar
¼ cup Cointreau
whipped cream or vanilla ice cream

1. Toss together the pineapple cubes and the strawberries.
2. Sprinkle them with the sugar and Cointreau. Refrigerate.
3. Serve cold with sweetened whipped cream or vanilla ice cream.

STRAWBERRIES AND CREAM CHEESE DESSERT (6 servings)

1 pound cream cheese, room temperature
½ cup sugar
16-ounce package (1 pound) frozen strawberries, sliced, thawed and drained
1 cup heavy cream, whipped

1. Beat the cream cheese until fluffy; add sugar and beat to blend well.
2. Fold in strawberries and whipped cream.
3. Spoon into a 1-quart mold and freeze for at least 4 hours.

FRAISES AU GRAND MARNIER (6 to 8 servings)

Strawberries with Liqueur and Whipped Cream

1 egg white
⅛ teaspoon cream of tartar
4 tablespoons sugar
½ cup heavy cream, whipped, and additional whipped cream
½ teaspoon vanilla extract
1 quart strawberries, hulled
6 tablespoons wild strawberry preserves
3 tablespoons kirschwasser
3 tablespoons Grand Marnier

1. Beat the egg white with the cream of tartar until frothy. Gradually beat in the sugar and beat until the mixture stands in firm peaks.
2. Fold in the ½ cup whipped cream and vanilla extract.
3. Spread mixture over the bottom and sides of a shallow serving dish.
4. Arrange the strawberries, pointed side up, over the meringue.
5. Thin the strawberry preserves with the kirschwasser and Grand Marnier. Spread the glaze over the whole strawberries. Serve with whipped cream.

FRAISES AUX FRAMBOISES CHANTILLY (6 servings)

Strawberries with Raspberry Sauce and Whipped Cream

1 pint strawberries
1 10-ounce package frozen raspberries, partly thawed
1 tablespoon lemon juice
whipped cream

1. Wash and hull strawberries and place in a serving dish.
2. Place raspberries in a blender with lemon juice and blend until smooth.
3. Pour raspberries over the strawberries and chill. Garnish with whipped cream.

BISCUITS BRABANT (32 cookies)

Brabant Cookies

1 cup butter
½ cup sugar
3 egg yolks
¼ teaspoon salt
2½ cups flour
jelly
3 egg whites
1 cup sugar

1. Preheat oven to 325° F.

2. Combine butter, sugar, egg yolks, salt and flour and mix thoroughly.

3. Pat into 2 ungreased 8-inch square pans. Spread tops with jelly.

4. Beat egg whites with sugar until stiff but not dry. Spread over jelly.

5. Bake for 30 to 35 minutes. Cool in pans. Cut into squares.

MOQUES HOLLANDAISES (*SABLES*) (80 cookies)
Dutch Cookies

½ pound (1 cup) butter, room temperature
1 cup confectioners' sugar
2½ cups flour
½ teaspoon salt
¼ teaspoon vanilla
granulated sugar

1. Cream the butter and combine it with sugar, flour, salt and vanilla. Chill for 1 hour.

2. On a lightly floured pastry board roll the dough and arrange it in a sausage shape. Then roll dough in granulated sugar.

3. Cut slices ¼ inch thick. Bake on greased and floured cookie sheets in preheated oven at 450° F. for 8 minutes.

MADELEINES (Approximately 24 madeleines) PLATE VII

5 eggs
1¼ cups sugar
1¼ cups flour
¾ cup melted butter
1 teaspoon vanilla extract

1. Preheat oven to 370° F.

2. Beat the eggs, adding sugar gradually, over low heat until lukewarm.

3. Remove from heat and blend in the flour. Add melted butter and vanilla extract.

4. Lay in a madeleines mold and bake in oven for about 18 minutes.

ORANGE TILE COOKIES (30 cookies)

½ cup butter, room temperature
½ cup sugar
3 ounces almonds, sliced
juice of 1 orange
peel of 1 orange, chopped very fine
2 drops red food coloring

1. Preheat oven to 400° F.

2. Mix all ingredients thoroughly.

3. Drop by rounded teaspoonful on a well-greased cookie sheet and flatten with a fork to the size of a half dollar. Bake 7 or 8 minutes, or until edges turn brown.

4. While hot, place on a rack or fancy roof tile and form into "U" shapes.

PALAIS AU RAISIN (Approximately 75 cookies)

Sugar Cookies with Raisins, or Chocolate Chip Cookies

½ pound raisins
½ cup dark rum
1 cup (½ pound) butter, room temperature
1 cup (½ pound) sugar
4 whole eggs
1½ cups flour

1. Preheat oven to 400° F.

2. Put the raisins into a saucepan and add the rum. Place over heat for 1 minute just to flame the rum and raisins, and stir with a spoon. Remove from stove and cool.

3. Cream together butter and sugar and mix in the eggs, one by one. Add the flour and the cooled raisins.

4. Force the dough through a pastry bag onto a greased and floured cookie sheet. Make each cookie the size of a walnut. Bake for about 7 minutes.

NOTE: You can replace raisins with chocolate chips.

BISCUITS TULLES (3 dozen cookies)

Tulle Cookies

½ cup shortening
½ cup sugar
1 teaspoon vanilla extract
1 egg yolk
1 cup sifted flour
1 teaspoon baking powder
¼ teaspoon salt
red jelly

1. Preheat oven to 350° F.

2. Cream shortening and sugar until fluffy.

3. Add remaining ingredients except jelly and blend well.

4. Drop by rounded teaspoonful on greased cookie sheets. Make an indentation in the center of each cookie and fill with a dab of red jelly. Bake for 10 to 12 minutes.

DELICE DU ROI (KING'S DELIGHT) (2 dozen puffs)

Cream Puffs

SHELLS

½ cup water	*½ cup flour*
¼ teaspoon salt	*2 eggs*
¼ cup butter	

1. Preheat oven to 400° F.

2. Put water and salt in a small saucepan and bring to a boil. Add butter to saucepan and melt. Add flour and stir with wire whisk until mixture forms ball in center of pan. Remove from heat and spoon into small mixing bowl of food mixer. Mix at medium speed and add eggs one at a time. Continue mixing until stiff.

3. Place mixture in pastry tube and squeeze out walnut-sized balls onto a greased and floured sheet pan. Bake at 400° F. for 25 minutes, then at 350° F. for 5 minutes. Cool and fill.

FILLING

½ pint whipping cream
1 tablespoon sugar
4 drops almond extract

1. Make small opening in the bottom of the puffs with the point of a knife. Opening should be large enough to insert tube point for filling.

2. Whip cream in blender container on low speed until stiff. Add sugar and almond extract to blender container and run until mixed. Insert mixture into the puff with a pastry tube. Serve immediately or refrigerate.

NOTE: Filling could be vanilla ice cream with Hot Chocolate Sauce.*

BAKED BLACKBERRY DESSERT (6 servings)

2 cups blackberries	*½ cup butter*
1¼ cups sugar	*1 egg*
1¾ cups sifted flour	*1 teaspoon vanilla extract*
2¼ teaspoons baking powder	*½ cup milk*
⅓ teaspoon salt	*sweet cream*

1. Wash and pick over blackberries. Drain thoroughly. Mix with ½ cup sugar.

2. Sift together flour, baking powder and salt.

3. Cream the butter until fluffy, gradually add remaining sugar and beat in the egg and vanilla. Add the flour mixture alternately with the milk, mixing thoroughly.

4. Place the blackberries in the bottom of a buttered baking dish. Pour the batter over the fruit and bake in preheated oven at 350° F. for 50 minutes. Serve with sweet cream.

BLUEBERRY AND CHEESE CAKE (6 servings)

⅓ cup butter
⅓ cup sugar
2 eggs
¾ cup milk
1½ cups flour
1 tablespoon baking powder
2 cups blueberries, fresh
1 3-ounce package cream cheese, room temperature
2 tablespoons sugar
1 tablespoon lemon juice
1 cup flour
¼ cup sugar
¼ cup butter
¼ teaspoon cinnamon

1. Preheat oven to 375° F.

2. Cream butter and sugar until fluffy. Add eggs and beat well. Add milk and flour mixed with baking powder.

3. Add 1 cup of blueberries to the batter and mix thoroughly.

4. Pour into buttered 9-inch cake pan and sprinkle remaining blueberries on top.

5. Combine cream cheese, sugar and lemon juice and spread over the top of the berries.

6. Combine flour, sugar, butter and cinnamon and mix together until crumbly. Sprinkle the crumb mixture over the top of the cake. Bake for 30 minutes.

DEVIL'S FOOD CAKE WITH HONEY (8 to 10 servings)

2½ cups sifted flour
2 teaspoons baking powder
½ teaspoon baking soda
½ teaspoon salt
½ cup shortening
½ cup sugar
¾ cup honey
1 egg, separated
4 ounces (squares) unsweetened chocolate, melted
¾ cup milk
1 teaspoon vanilla extract

1. Preheat oven to 350° F.
2. Sift flour, baking powder, soda and salt together.
3. Cream shortening with sugar and honey until thoroughly mixed. Add egg yolk and melted chocolate and beat thoroughly.
4. To chocolate mixture add dry ingredients and milk and vanilla alternately in small amounts, beating well after each addition.
5. Beat egg white until stiff and fold into batter.
6. Pour into 2 greased 8-inch-square cake pans and bake 30 minutes. Cool, fill and frost as desired. Whipped cream is suggested.

FRENCH FRUITCAKE (15 to 20 servings)

1¼ cups candied fruits
¾ cup raisins
1 ounce dark rum
1¼ cups butter, room temperature
1½ cups sugar
3 whole eggs
2 egg yolks
1½ cups sifted flour
4 egg whites

1. Mix fruits and raisins with the rum and allow to soak overnight.
2. Preheat oven to 325° F.
3. Soften the butter in a large mixing bowl and gradually blend in the sugar. One by one, mix in the 3 eggs and 2 yolks.
4. Mix the flour with the rum-soaked fruits and add this to the butter mixture.
5. Whip the egg whites very stiff and fold in.
6. Line 2 9×5×3-inch loaf pans with parchment paper. Divide the batter evenly. Bake until toothpick comes out clean, about 45 minutes. Halfway through the baking, use a knife to make a slit in the middle of the cake.

GATEAU D'ABRICOT A L'ORANGE (6 servings) PLATE VIII

Orange-flavored Cheesecake with Apricots

8 ounces cream cheese, softened
1 can (15 ounces) sweetened condensed milk
⅓ cup lemon juice
½ teaspoon orange extract
1 9-inch Graham Cracker Crumb Crust, baked and cooled*
6 to 8 canned whole, pitted apricots, drained and syrup reserved
¼ cup sugar
1½ tablespoons cornstarch
dash of salt
½ cup apricot syrup
½ cup strained orange juice

1. Beat cream cheese until fluffy. Gradually add milk, beating until well blended. Beat in lemon juice and orange extract.
2. Pour into baked crust and chill for 3 hours.
3. Arrange apricots on top of cake.
4. In a small saucepan mix sugar, cornstarch and salt. Stir in apricot syrup and orange juice; mix until smooth. Cook, stirring, until thick and clear. Cool.
5. Cover apricots with cooled glaze and chill for 2 hours.

SPICECAKE WITH BANANAS (8 servings)

¾ cup shortening
2¼ cups cake flour
1 cup sugar
1 teaspoon baking powder
¾ teaspoon baking soda
1 teaspoon salt
½ teaspoon ground cloves
¾ teaspoon cinnamon
¾ cup brown sugar
1 cup buttermilk
3 eggs
2 cups cream, whipped
2 medium bananas, sliced thin and brushed with lemon juice

1. Preheat oven to 350° F.
2. Stir shortening to soften. Add dry ingredients, brown sugar and buttermilk. Beat vigorously for 2 minutes.
3. Add eggs to batter and beat vigorously for 2 more minutes.
4. Pour into 2 greased 9-inch layer cake pans and bake for 30 to 35 minutes. Cool.
5. Fill layers and top with whipped cream and sliced bananas.

GENOISE (8 servings)

Spongecake

4 eggs, room temperature
¾ cup sugar
¾ cup flour
¼ cup melted butter, cooled

1. Preheat oven to 325° F. Lightly grease and flour the bottom of 2 9-inch layer pans.

2. Break the eggs into bowl of an electric mixer. Beat at highest speed until soft peaks can be formed. (Do not underbeat the eggs. It may take as long as 30 minutes, depending upon the power of the mixer.) While beating the eggs, pour the sugar in a fine stream over them, taking a few minutes to add all the sugar.

3. Lower the speed and sift the flour over the surface of the mixture as the bowl turns. Add the butter. Scrape the sides of the bowl and beat at lowest speed for 1 minute.

4. Pour the batter into the prepared pans and bake for 40 minutes or until a toothpick inserted in the center comes out clean. Let the cake cool at room temperature before removing it from the pans.

GATEAU DES FRAISES AU DOUBLE CREME (6 servings)

Strawberry Cake with Almonds and Cream Cheese

11 ounces cream cheese (1 8-ounce package and 1 3-ounce package)
2 eggs
½ cup sugar
½ teaspoon vanilla extract
*1 Graham Cracker Crumb Crust**
2 cups sour cream
¼ cup sugar
¼ cup toasted whole almonds
whole strawberries
4 tablespoons currant jelly
1 tablespoon water

1. Preheat oven to 350° F.

2. Place cream cheese in a large mixing bowl and blend slowly with an electric mixer. When quite smooth, add eggs, one at a time, beating well after each addition. Gradually add the ½ cup sugar and vanilla extract.

3. Pour into prepared Crust and bake for 20 minutes.

4. Blend the sour cream with the ¼ cup sugar and almonds. Spread over the top of the cake.

5. Turn off oven heat. Return cake to the oven for 4 minutes. Cool cake slightly; chill until set.

6. Before serving, garnish top of cake with whole strawberries.

7. Mix currant jelly and water and heat until jelly melts. Pour over the strawberries to glaze.

SUE'S CHEESECAKE (6 to 8 servings)

*Graham Cracker Crumb Crust**
2 8-ounce packages cream cheese
1 teaspoon vanilla extract
1 teaspoon lemon extract
¾ cup sugar
3 eggs
1 pint sour cream

1. Preheat oven to 375° F.

2. Butter a 9-inch spring form pan. Press crumbs on bottom.

3. Blend cheese until smooth and fluffy in an electric mixer. Add ½ teaspoon each of vanilla and lemon extracts. Add ½ cup of sugar and the eggs and blend well.

4. Pour into prepared pan and bake for 20 minutes. Remove and let stand for 20 minutes.

5. Raise oven temperature to 475° F.

6. Mix sour cream with remaining ½ teaspoon each of vanilla and lemon extracts and ¼ cup sugar. Spread evenly over cheesecake. Bake 10 minutes longer. Cool.

WALNUT CAKE AUGUSTA (16 squares)

½ cup shortening
1 cup sugar
2 eggs, 1 of them separated
1½ cups flour
½ teaspoon salt
1½ teaspoons baking powder
½ cup milk
1 teaspoon vanilla extract
½ cup chopped walnuts
1 cup brown sugar
½ teaspoon baking powder

1. Preheat oven to 350° F.

2. Cream shortening and sugar. Beat in whole egg and additional yolk.

3. Sift together the flour, salt and 1½ teaspoons baking powder. Add to the egg mixture alternately with the milk. Add vanilla extract.

4. Pour the batter into a greased 8-inch square baking pan. Cover the top with the nuts. Bake for 30 minutes. Remove from oven.

5. While cake is baking, beat remaining egg white until stiff but not dry. Gradually beat in brown sugar mixed with ½ teaspoon baking powder until white is very stiff. Spread over baked cake and bake 10 minutes longer. Cool. Cut in squares to serve.

GRAHAM CRACKER CRUMB CRUST (for 1 9-inch pie plate or spring-form pan)

15 graham crackers
1 tablespoon sugar
½ teaspoon cinnamon
¼ cup melted butter

1. Break 5 crackers at a time into quarters and place in a blender container. Run on low speed until crackers are finely crumbed. Empty crumbs into a bowl and continue the process until all crackers are crumbed.

2. Stir in sugar and cinnamon. Add melted butter and mix until all crumbs are moistened.

3. Press crumbs against sides and bottom of a buttered baking pan. Chill before adding fillings or bake in a moderate oven (375° F.) for 8 minutes.

PASTRY SHELL (2 crusts)

2 cups sifted flour
¾ teaspoon salt
⅔ cup shortening
4 to 6 tablespoons cold water

1. Sift flour and salt together.

2. Cut in shortening with 2 knives or pastry blender.

3. Add water, using a small portion at a time, until mixture will hold together.

4. Divide dough into 2 parts. Roll out on floured board.

5. Line a pie pan with 1 piece of dough. After filling is placed in pastry, dampen edges of lower crust with cold water and cover with remaining dough which has been rolled out and slashed in several places to allow steam to escape.

6. Press edges of dough together and bake.

7. To bake unfilled place in preheated oven at 450° F. for 15 minutes or until delicately browned.

PATE BRISEE (3 9-inch pie shells)

Pie Shell

4 cups flour	*1 teaspoon salt*
1¼ cups butter, room temperature	*2 eggs*
	½ cup cold water

1. Place flour, butter and salt into a large bowl and work together with hands until smooth. Add eggs and water and work with hands until of rolling consistency.

2. Roll pastry out on floured board to within ¼- to ⅛-inch thick.

3. Place pastry in 9-inch pie tin and crimp edges. Chill for 1 hour.

4. To bake unfilled, place in a preheated oven at 425° F. for about 12 minutes.

PUFF PASTE

1 pound unsalted butter	*4 cups flour*
1½ cups ice water	*½ teaspoon salt*

1. Knead the butter in ice water until smooth and waxy. Squeeze out pockets of water and shape the butter into a rectangular flat cake. Wrap in wax paper and refrigerate.

2. Sift flour and salt onto marble slab or pastry board. Gradually add ice water, pouring with the left hand and working it into the flour with the right hand. The dough should be very firm. The butter should be of the same consistency as the dough. Chill for ½ hour.

3. Roll dough into a square and put the cake of butter in the center. Fold the 4 sides of the dough over the butter to enclose it completely. Chill for 15 minutes. Roll the dough into a rectangle 3 times as long as it is wide. Fold the left-hand third over the middle and the right-hand third over the left, making 3 layers. This process of rolling and folding is called a "turn." Make another turn and chill the dough for 20 minutes. Make 4 more turns, 2 at a time, chilling between sets and moving the dough a quarter turn to the right before each, so that the dough will be rolled out in a different direction each time. Chill for ½ hour after the last turn.

4. To bake unfilled, place in a preheated oven at 400° F. for about 25 minutes.

(Approximately 1 dozen patty shells)

NOTE: If used for pastry, add 1 teaspoon sugar to this recipe.

TOURTE DES ANGES (8 servings)

Angels' Pie

1 egg, separated
2 tablespoons sugar
2 tablespoons lemon juice
8 ounces cream cheese
½ cup cream for whipping
1 tablespoon confectioners' sugar
1 teaspoon vanilla extract
1 baked 9-inch Pastry Shell, cooled*
2 pints strawberries, washed and hulled
⅔ cup sugar for frosting
¼ teaspoon cream of tartar
¼ cup water
⅛ teaspoon salt

1. Blend the egg yolk, 2 tablespoons sugar and lemon juice in the top of a double boiler. Cook, stirring, for 5 minutes until thick.

2. Remove from heat and slice in cream cheese, beating until no streaks of white remain.

3. Beat cream with confectioners' sugar and ½ teaspoon vanilla extract until cream is stiff. Fold into cheese mixture.

4. Spread on Pastry Shell. Chill for 30 minutes until set. Arrange whole strawberries, points up, in a single layer to cover top. Chill.

5. Combine ⅔ cup sugar, cream of tartar and water in a small pan, covered. Heat to boiling, uncover and cook rapidly until a teaspoon of the syrup will form a soft ball in cold water. Note: Step 5, with beaten egg white, is known as "Divinity Icing."

6. Beat egg white with salt until it forms peaks. Pour in the hot syrup in a fine stream, beating constantly until it stands in firm peaks. Beat in ½ teaspoon vanilla extract.

7. Pile egg white mixture in the center of the pie and chill for 2 hours. Remove from refrigerator 1 hour before serving.

TARTE TATIN (6 servings)

Apple Tart

1 tablespoon butter
½ cup granulated sugar
4 or 5 tart apples, peeled, cored and quartered
Puff Paste (10 inches in diameter and ¼ inch thick), or frozen commercial puff paste, thawed*

1. Preheat oven to 400° F.

2. Melt the butter in an 8½-inch wide ovenproof frying pan. Stir

in the sugar. Over low heat stir constantly until the sugar melts, is free from lumps and turns a light caramel in color. Arrange the apples to cover entire bottom of pan in circular fashion.

3. Cover the mixture with the Puff Paste and tuck the rim of the paste under the mixture. Prick the top for the escape of steam.

4. Bake for about 10 minutes or until brown.

5. Place a flat lid on top of the crust and turn over fast. Remove to a flat cake server or any serving dish.

TOURTE AUX CERISES ET DOUBLE CREME (6 servings)

Cheese Pie with Cherries

1 (8-ounce) package cream cheese, room temperature
⅓ cup sugar
1 tablespoon flour
2 eggs, beaten
¼ teaspoon vanilla extract
½ teaspoon almond extract
¼ cup sour cream
*1 unbaked 9-inch Pastry Shell**
3 tablespoons sugar
2 tablespoons cornstarch
¼ teaspoon cinnamon
1 can (1 pound, 4 ounces) pitted sour cherries, drained
1 cup juice from canned cherries

1. Preheat oven to 450° F.

2. Combine cream cheese, ⅓ cup sugar and flour. Add eggs, vanilla and almond extracts and sour cream and blend thoroughly.

3. Pour into unbaked Pastry Shell and bake for 10 minutes at 450° F. Lower oven temperature to 200° F. and bake 10 minutes longer or until set. Cool at room temperature.

4. Make glaze by combining 3 tablespoons sugar, cornstarch and cinnamon. Measure cherry juice, adding water, if necessary, to make 1 cup. Slowly stir cherry juice into sugar mixture. Cook over low heat, stirring often, until mixture becomes clear and thick.

5. Remove from heat and stir in cherries.

6. Spread glaze over top of pie. Chill before serving.

CHERRIES FLAN TART (6 servings)

½ cup sugar
2 eggs, well beaten
⅔ cup sifted flour
2 cups milk
½ teaspoon vanilla or ¼ cup chartreuse liqueur
1 can (1 pound) pitted black cherries, drained
whipped cream

1. Mix sugar, eggs, flour, milk and vanilla or chartreuse.
2. Place the cherries in a well-greased pan (8 inches square and 2 inches deep) and pour the batter over them.
3. Bake in a 400° F. oven for about 45 minutes.
4. Serve hot with whipped cream.

CHOCOLATE CHEESE PIE (8 servings)

1 9-inch Graham Cracker Crumb Crust prepared with 1 tablespoon light brown sugar and ⅛ teaspoon nutmeg.*
1 cup semi-sweet chocolate morsels
8 ounces cream cheese
¾ cup brown sugar
⅛ teaspoon salt
2 eggs, separated
1 cup whipped cream
1 teaspoon vanilla extract

1. Chill Crust while preparing filling.
2. Melt chocolate over hot water in a double boiler. Cool for about 10 minutes.
3. Blend cream cheese with ½ cup brown sugar and salt. Beat in egg yolks. Stir in melted chocolate.
4. Beat egg whites until stiff and gradually beat in remaining ¼ cup brown sugar. Fold into chocolate mixture.
5. Fold in whipped cream and vanilla.
6. Pour into Graham Cracker Crust. Chill overnight.

TOURTE AU FOUR MAINE (6 servings)

Chocolate Pie with Ice Cream

½ cup butter
1 cup sugar
2 eggs, separated
2 squares unsweetened chocolate, melted and cooled
1 teaspoon vanilla extract
⅓ cup flour
⅛ teaspoon salt
1 quart vanilla, butterscotch or coffee ice cream
*Chocolate Sauce**

1. Preheat oven to 325° F.
2. Cream butter and sugar and add egg yolks one at a time, beating well after each addition. Blend in chocolate, vanilla extract and flour.
3. Beat egg whites and salt until stiff but not dry. Fold into batter.
4. Pour into a greased 8-inch pie pan. Bake for about 40 minutes or until a cake tester comes out dry.
5. Top with ice cream and Chocolate Sauce. Serve hot.

TOURTE DE BANANE AU DOUBLE CREME (6 servings)

Graham Banana-Cheese Pie

1 envelope unflavored gelatin
½ cup water
3 eggs, separated
¼ cup sugar
4 3-ounce packages cream cheese
1 tablespoon lemon juice
⅛ teaspoon salt
1 cup sour cream
3 ripe bananas, sliced
1 Graham Cracker Crumb Crust (no sugar added) in a 9-inch pie pan*

1. Soften gelatin in ¼ cup water. Set aside.
2. Combine yolks, slightly beaten, with sugar and ¼ cup water in the top part of a double boiler. Cook over simmering water until thick, stirring constantly. Remove from heat and stir in gelatin mixture.
3. In a large bowl, beat cheese until soft. Add the gelatin mixture, lemon juice and salt. Beat until blended. Fold in sour cream, then fold in stiffly beaten egg whites. Let stand until partly set.
4. Alternate thin layers of cheese mixture with sliced bananas in the

pie Crust, reserving some of sliced banana for garnish. Start and end with cheese mixture. Chill for about 3 hours.

5. Garnish with slices of banana dipped in lemon juice.

TOURTE DES POMMES AU MIEL (6 servings)

Honeyed Apple Pie

½ cup sour cream
¾ cup honey
¼ teaspoon salt
1 teaspoon cinnamon
½ teaspoon nutmeg
6 large tart apples, thinly sliced
Pastry Shells for a 2-crust 9-inch pie, unbaked*

1. Preheat the oven to 450° F.

2. Combine the sour cream, honey, salt and spices. Add apples and mix thoroughly.

3. Spoon apple mixture into pie crust, heaping it in the middle. Place top crust over apples, seal, and flute the edge or otherwise decorate. Prick the top crust with a fork. Bake for 40 to 45 minutes until apples are tender.

PEACH PECAN PIE (6 servings)

2 pounds sliced fresh peaches
¾ cup sugar
2 tablespoons quick-cooking tapioca
½ cup flour
¼ cup brown sugar
½ stick (¼ cup) butter
½ cup chopped pecans
1 9-inch Pastry Shell, unbaked*

1. Preheat oven to 450° F.

2. Mix peaches, sugar and tapioca in a large bowl.

3. Combine flour and brown sugar. Cut in butter until mixture becomes crumbly. Stir in nuts.

4. Sprinkle a third of flour mixture over the bottom of the Pastry Shell; top with peaches and sprinkle remaining flour mixture over peaches.

5. Bake at 450° F. for 10 minutes; reduce oven temperature to 350° F. and bake 20 minutes longer.

RALEIGH PECAN PIE (6 to 8 servings)

½ cup melted butter, cooled
1 cup brown sugar
1 cup white corn syrup
pinch of salt
4 eggs, lightly beaten
½ cup coarsely chopped pecans
1 9-inch Pastry Shell, unbaked*

1. Preheat oven to 400° F.

2. Combine butter, sugar, corn syrup and salt. Stir in eggs and pecans.

3. Pour the custard into Pastry Shell and bake for 10 minutes. Reduce oven temperature to 350° F. and bake 35 minutes longer, until the crust is browned. Test by inserting a knife near the center of the pie. If it comes out clean, it is done.

STRAWBERRY TART (6 to 8 servings)

3 pints fresh strawberries
¾ cup sugar
2½ tablespoons cornstarch
½ cup water
2 drops red food coloring
1 baked 9-inch Pastry Shell or Tart Shell**

1. Wash and hull the strawberries.

2. Crush 1 pint of the strawberries.

3. In a saucepan blend together sugar, cornstarch and water. Add the crushed berries and food coloring. Bring to a boil and cook until mixture is clear, about 2 minutes. Strain.

4. Arrange remaining whole berries in baked Pastry Shell. Spoon glaze over berries, carefully coating each berry. Cool.

FLOATING ISLAND (8 to 10 servings) PLATE VII

8 eggs, separated
1½ cups sugar
1 quart milk
2 teaspoons vanilla

1. Beat the egg whites until foamy. Gradually add ½ cup of the sugar, continuing to beat until the egg whites are stiff.

2. In large skillet bring milk to a boil; add remaining sugar and vanilla.

3. Remove the skillet from the heat and drop the beaten egg whites on the milk in very large rounded spoonfuls.

4. Return the skillet to very low heat. Cook the mounds of egg whites for 2 minutes. Turn with skimmer and cook for 2 minutes on the other side, or until the meringues are firm to the touch.

5. Remove the meringues to a pastry sheet. Reserve the milk.

6. In a bowl beat the egg yolks and add the hot milk gradually, stirring constantly. Return this mixture to skillet and cook for a few seconds; do not boil. Strain through a fine sieve or cheesecloth. (This is called "Crème Anglaise"—English Cream.)

7. Sprinkle sugar on top of the meringues and brown under the broiler. Keep broiler door open because they brown very fast.

8. Fill serving dishes with the Crème Anglaise and place the meringues on top. Cool. Serve with petits fours.

MERINGUE SHELLS (6 individual shells)

4 egg whites
1 cup plus 1 tablespoon sugar
pinch of salt
¾ teaspoon vanilla extract

1. Preheat oven to 225° F.

2. Beat egg whites with an electric mixer or egg beater until stiff enough to hold a peak. Gradually beat in the sugar, salt and vanilla extract.

3. Cover baking sheets with wax paper. Shape meringues into desired forms by using a pastry bag or spoon.

4. Meringue has to bake slowly until firm and dry but still white, about an hour and perhaps a bit longer.

SOUFFLE DE CHOCOLAT AU CREME DE CACAO
(12 to 14 servings)
Chocolate Soufflé with Crème de Cacao

2 envelopes unflavored gelatin
½ cup water
⅔ cup crème de cacao
1¼ cups brown sugar
1 12-ounce package semi-sweet chocolate morsels
8 eggs, separated
½ teaspoon salt
2 cups heavy cream, whipped
½ cup chopped pistachio nuts

1. Mix the gelatin, water, crème de cacao and ½ cup of the sugar in a saucepan and place over low heat. Stir constantly until the gelatin and sugar dissolve.

2. Add the chocolate morsels and stir until melted. Remove from heat. Beat in the egg yolks, one at a time. Cool.

3. Add the salt to the egg whites and beat until stiff but not dry. Gradually beat in the remaining sugar and continue beating until very stiff.

4. Fold the beaten egg whites into the gelatin mixture. Fold in the whipped cream. Turn into a 2-quart soufflé dish with a 2-inch collar, or into a 2-quart serving bowl. Chill for several hours or overnight.

5. Sprinkle with pistachio nuts.

ARLEQUIN SOUFFLE (6 servings)

Dessert Soufflé

1 cup milk
8 egg whites
1 tablespoon sugar
6 egg yolks
¼ cup sugar
¼ cup flour
2 teaspoons vanilla extract
½ ounce (half of 1 square) unsweetened chocolate

1. Preheat oven to 350° F.

2. Grease 6½×3-inch soufflé dish with shortening and refrigerate. When chilled, spread again with shortening and coat dish with sugar. Divide the prepared soufflé dish in half with folded aluminum foil.

3. Pour milk into saucepan and bring to a boil.

4. Put egg whites in large bowl and beat with food mixer until very light and stands in soft peaks. Gradually add sugar and mix until combined. Set aside.

5. Beat 2 egg yolks in small bowl of food mixer until light. Add ¼ cup sugar and flour and mix until it reaches thickened paste consistency. Add paste to hot milk in saucepan and beat with wire whisk over high heat until thick and smooth. Add vanilla and blend until combined.

6. Divide mixture into 2 saucepans. Add chocolate and 2 egg yolks to 1 pan and stir until chocolate is melted and combined over medium heat. Set aside. Add 2 egg yolks to other saucepan and stir constantly over medium heat until mixed.

7. Fold two-thirds of beaten egg whites into the chocolate mixture and the other third into the vanilla mixture.

8. Pour chocolate mixture into half of prepared dish and vanilla mixture into other half of dish. Remove aluminum foil carefully.

9. Set soufflé dish on sheet pan and bake at 350° F. for 30 to 35 minutes or until firm. Serve immediately with Vanilla Sauce.*

CHOCOLATE MOUSSE (10 to 12 servings)

6 ounces sweet chocolate
1 ounce (1 square) unsweetened chocolate
½ cup coffee
4 egg yolks
1 cup sugar
1 quart whipping cream

1. Place chocolates and coffee in top of double boiler over simmering water and heat until chocolate is melted and well blended.

2. Beat yolks and sugar. Add chocolate mixture and beat well.

3. Whip the cream. Mix it well with chocolate mixture. Put in a 2-quart mold and place in freezer or refrigerator to harden. Serve with whipped cream sprinkled with grated chocolate.

MOUSSE AFRICAINE (8 servings)
Mocha Mousse

3 ounces (3 squares) unsweetened chocolate
⅓ cup water
¾ cup sugar
pinch of salt
3 egg yolks
1 tablespoon instant coffee
½ teaspoon vanilla extract
2 cups whipped cream

1. Combine chocolate and water in a saucepan and heat slowly, stirring constantly.

2. When chocolate is melted, add sugar and salt and cook over low heat for 2 minutes, stirring constantly.

3. Beat egg yolks well in a bowl. Pour in the chocolate mixture, beating constantly. Add the coffee and cool.

4. Fold in vanilla extract and whipped cream. Pour into refrigerator trays and freeze.

STRAWBERRY MOUSSE (8 to 10 servings)

1 quart strawberries, washed and hulled
½ cup sugar
½ cup dry white wine
2 envelopes unflavored gelatin
½ cup cold water
½ cup boiling water
2 cups whipped cream

1. Reserve several strawberries for garnish.
2. Run remaining berries through a blender until liquefied. Combine berries, sugar and wine; stir well. Chill.
3. Soften gelatin in the cold water. Add boiling water; stir to dissolve. Cool.
4. Combine gelatin and chilled strawberry mixture. Beat until fluffy and slightly thickened. Fold in whipped cream.
5. Turn into a 2-quart mold. Chill for 3 hours or longer.
6. Unmold onto a chilled serving platter. Garnish with reserved whole strawberries.

POMMES CHANTILLY AU FRAISES (6 servings)
Apple Strips with Whipped Cream and Strawberries

3 eggs, separated
1¼ cups milk
½ cup plus 1½ tablespoons sugar
1 envelope unflavored gelatin
1 apple, peeled and cut into thin strips
½ pint whipped cream
1 pint whole strawberries

1. Beat the egg yolks until they are foamy. Add the milk, sugar and gelatin and mix thoroughly.
2. Cook in a small saucepan over low heat, stirring constantly. When thickened and custard-like, remove from heat and cool.
3. Beat the egg whites until they form soft peaks. Fold the beaten egg whites and the apple into the milk mixture. Pour into an oiled 1-quart mold and refrigerate until set.
4. Unmold and garnish with whipped cream and strawberries.

PARFAIT AUX FRAMBOISES NOYAU (4 servings) PLATE VIII

Champagne Parfait with Raspberries

1 cup frozen raspberries
2 tablespoons unflavored gelatin
⅓ cup cold water
1 cup champagne
¾ cup sugar
½ cup Noyaux liqueur (fruit-nut kernel liqueur)
2 cups whipped cream

1. Thaw and heat the raspberries and put through a sieve.
2. Soften gelatin in cold water and add to the raspberry pulp, heating until the gelatin dissolves.
3. Add champagne, sugar and Noyaux liqueur. Stir the mixture over cracked ice until it begins to thicken, then fold in whipped cream.
4. Fill parfait glasses with the raspberry cream and chill for several hours.

MANDARIN ORANGE MOLD (4 servings)

1 package (3 ounces) orange-flavored gelatin
1 cup hot water
1 pint orange sherbet
1 can (11 ounces) mandarin oranges, drained
fresh orange for garnish
fresh strawberries for garnish

1. Dissolve gelatin in hot water in a medium-sized bowl.
2. Stir in the sherbet, stirring until melted.
3. Fold in the mandarin oranges.
4. Pour into a mold and chill at least 3 hours. Unmold on serving platter and garnish with slices of fresh orange and whole fresh strawberries.

RASPBERRY CREAM (6 servings)

1 package raspberry-flavored gelatin
1 cup hot water
1 package unthawed frozen raspberries
½ pint vanilla ice cream

1. Dissolve gelatin in 1 cup hot water.
2. Stir in frozen raspberries and add ice cream, stirring until it melts.
3. Refrigerate until set, about 20 minutes. Spoon into serving dishes.

MOULE VICTORIA (5 servings)

Victoria Cream Cheese Mold

2 3-ounce packages cream cheese, room temperature
2 tablespoons confectioners' sugar
1 teaspoon vanilla extract
1 tablespoon unflavored gelatin
1½ cups milk, warm
½ cup whipped cream
frozen raspberries
frozen peaches

1. Mix cheese with sugar and vanilla extract.

2. Dissolve gelatin in ½ cup milk. Add balance of milk. Add to cheese and mix thoroughly. Refrigerate for 15 minutes.

3. Fold whipped cream into cheese mixture. Pour into custard cups. Chill.

4. Unmold and serve with thawed frozen raspberries and peaches.

CREAM CUSTARD FLAMBE GEORGIA (6 to 8 servings)

½ cup sugar
1 tablespoon water
1 pint (2 cups) milk
3 eggs
1 teaspoon vanilla
6 peach halves, canned
3 tablespoons Grand Marnier
3 tablespoons brandy

1. Preheat oven to 375° F.

2. Place 3 tablespoons of the sugar in a heavy saucepan with the water. Caramelize at high heat. Pour caramelized sugar into a 1-quart mold, dish or bowl, making sure that it coats the bottom of the bowl.

3. Pour the milk into saucepan and bring to a boil.

4. Put eggs, vanilla and remaining sugar into blender container; cover and run on low speed. While blender is running, slowly add hot milk and blend just until mixed. Pour mixture into mold.[1] Bake mold in shallow pan containing 1 inch water. For best results, place one layer of paper (i.e., paper toweling) in the bottom of the pan; place mold on paper. The paper will prevent the custard from splitting

[1] If foam forms when blending the mixture, remove by skimming.

or cracking. Bake at 375° F. for about 1 hour. Chill mold for 24 hours.

5. Serve unmolded in the center of a large platter. Surround the mold with peach halves, cut side up. Flame Grand Marnier and brandy in a pan and, in front of guests, pour into center of peach halves.

CHERRIES JUBILEE (6 servings)

1 tablespoon cornstarch
1 tablespoon sugar
1 can (1 pound) pitted black cherries
3 or 4 strips of orange peel
dash of lemon juice
½ cup warm brandy
vanilla ice cream

1. Mix cornstarch and sugar together. Add liquid from canned cherries and the orange peel. Cook until thick. Discard orange peel. Add cherries and lemon juice.

2. At the table, add warm brandy and ignite. Serve over vanilla ice cream.

NUT BALLS (Approximately 24 balls)

⅔ cup butter
1 cup ground walnuts
1 cup sifted flour
3 tablespoons sugar
1 teaspoon vanilla
confectioners' sugar

1. Cream butter, add next 4 ingredients and work with fingers until well blended. Pinch off bits and roll into balls the size of large marbles.

2. Bake on lightly buttered cookie sheet in moderately hot preheated oven (375° F.) for about 10 minutes. While hot, roll in confectioners' sugar.

PECAN BALLS WITH BOURBON (4 dozen)

1 cup graham cracker crumbs
1 cup chopped pecans
1 cup confectioners' sugar, plus additional small amount
2 tablespoons cocoa
½ tablespoon white corn syrup
¼ cup bourbon

1. Place graham cracker crumbs in a large bowl and add pecans, 1 cup sugar and cocoa.

2. Mix corn syrup and bourbon together and add to crumb mixture. Mix all ingredients thoroughly and form into a ball. If not moist enough to form a ball, add a few more drops of bourbon.

3. Moisten hands with bourbon and form into balls about the size of marbles. Roll in confectioners' sugar. Keep in a cool place.

BAKED ALASKA (4 servings)

1 Spongecake 1 inch thick, shaped to size of platter, leaving 1 inch border*
4 egg whites
confectioners' sugar
1 pint ice cream

1. Place spongecake on oven-proof platter or dish.

2. Make meringue as follows: Beat white of eggs until they are as stiff as possible. Sprinkle with confectioners' sugar and mix carefully so lightness is retained.

3. Mound ice cream on cake and cover with meringue, sealing sides well. Smooth with spatula to about ½ inch thick. Decorate with more meringue, using a pastry bag.

4. Bake in preheated 500° F. oven for about 3 minutes until meringue browns. The heat should not reach the ice cream inside.

MOULE DE CREME A LA GLACE AUX FRAISES (4 servings)

Ice Cream and Strawberry Mold

1 3-ounce package strawberry-flavored gelatin
1 cup hot water
1 cup cold water
1 pint strawberry ice cream
1 pint fresh strawberries

1. Dissolve the gelatin in the hot water. Add the cold water.

2. Add the ice cream and, when it melts, add the fresh strawberries.

3. Pour into a mold or glass serving bowl and refrigerate for at least 3 hours.

CREME A LA GLACE AUX FRUITS AMANDINE (6 servings)

Ice Cream with Peaches and Almonds in Raspberry Sauce

6 ripe peaches
*1 cup Raspberry Sauce**
¾ cup toasted slivered almonds
1½ pints vanilla ice cream

1. Peel the peaches and roll them in the Raspberry Sauce and the almonds.

2. Spread the ice cream in a serving bowl. Make 6 depressions in the ice cream and fill them with raspberry sauce. Place the peaches in the sauce.

LIME ICE (4 to 5 servings)

4 cups water	*grated rind of 1 lime*
2 cups sugar	*¾ cup lime juice*

1. Boil the water with the sugar for 5 minutes.
2. Add grated lime rind and lime juice. Cool and strain into refrigerator trays. Freeze.
3. If desired, a drop of green coloring may be added.

FRAISES GRANITE (4 to 6 servings)

Strawberry Ice

2 quarts strawberries	*1 cup sugar*
juice of 1 small lemon	*1 cup water*

1. Wash and hull the strawberries. Place in a blender with half the lemon juice and purée.
2. Boil the sugar and water for 5 minutes. Combine with the strawberry purée and stir in remaining lemon juice.
3. Pour into refrigerator trays and freeze.

SUGGESTIONS FOR FOOD PREPARATION

TRY to avoid having guests arrive more than a half-hour before you expect to serve dinner. Otherwise they may eat too many canapés and drink too much, and the dinner you have so carefully prepared will not be fully appreciated. I realize this is difficult to do, but sometimes it is necessary to decide which is more important, the food or the alcoholic consumption of the guests. If they come to drink rather than eat, one need not take as much trouble with the meal.

Wine glasses should be only about two-thirds filled. Some hostesses, trying to be generous, fill them to the brim, and the result is usually spilling.

Try some chopped spinach in your next omelet mix.

For easier grating of orange rinds, put some in your freezer after you extract the juice from the oranges.

Be sure to read a recipe carefully before you start to use it. Next, assemble all the ingredients and utensils you will need. If the oven is used, center the pan in it: if the pan is placed too close to an oven wall, the results may be uneven.

Griddlecake batter can be enhanced by adding finely chopped nuts and some grated orange rind.

While you are cleaning celery, save the leaves when you cut them off. They add flavor to soups and stuffings. When you separate stalks to clean celery, remove blemishes and wash well.

Remember that cream doubles in volume when it is whipped, so whip a cup at a time if your recipe calls for more than that amount.

Any meat can be made more tender by placing it on a flat surface and pounding it repeatedly on both sides. If you have no meat hammer use the edge of a heavy plate.

An extremely tasty dish is a sautéed fillet of veal topped with anchovies and melted Gruyère cheese.

If you have a problem unmolding gelatin dishes, try running the tip of a knife around the top edge to loosen it and then invert it onto a chilled serving plate. If that does not work, wring a hot towel almost dry and wrap it around the mold. Repeat this process if necessary.

To enliven a coleslaw, add diced, unpeeled red apples to it.

If your cake is too dry, it may have too much leavening, overbeaten egg whites, too much flour, not enough shortening or sugar, or it may be simply the victim of plain overbaking. Such things happen to every chef, even on occasion to the professionals. Try again.

If you have served hors d'oeuvres or appetizers to your guests, do not repeat any of the food in the main part of the meal. Repetition, in this case, is not a virtue. Select your appetizers wisely, with an eye for complementary flavors, variety of shape and contrasting color and texture. Plan so that you will not have to prepare them at the last minute.

Softened butter is easier to spread, but avoid letting it stand at room temperature any longer than necessary. Butter's delicate flavor and its vitamin A content will be affected adversely if it is left standing too long in temperatures above 50 degrees Fahrenheit, where light and air can get at it.

All hot foods, especially vegetables, should be served as soon as possible after cooking. Try to avoid reheating. One way is to insist that people, including members of your family, be on time for meals. Reheating results in loss of vitamins.

Plan your marketing ahead of time, taking into consideration the recipes you plan to use and the foods which are seasonally available. Have a bulletin board in your kitchen, with pad and pencil attached, and jot down whatever you need. It is much too easy to forget. Try to shop at markets where the vegetable turnover is quick, and buy only the freshest items. The longer they stay, the more vitamins they lose.

A household scale is a good investment. Check all delivered goods when you receive them.

Since your butcher will charge you for the weight of meat *before* he trims it, have him send along these trimmings. You can make a fine vegetable soup by simmering the bones with soup greens, and the fat is useful for sautéeing.

It is now perfectly safe to store foods in opened cans. Just cover the top with aluminum foil and refrigerate.

An easy way to shell Brazil nuts is to heat them in a 350-degree oven for about 15 minutes. The heat will also improve the flavor.

Parsley is a good source of vitamin C. In addition to using it as a garnish, try adding it to soups, salad dressings, salads and sauces in chopped form.

Use a low decoration as a centerpiece for a formal dinner, so that guests will have no trouble seeing each other. Small flower units, ornaments of glass, silver or china, or fruit may be used.

In seating guests, it is the responsibility of the hostess to tell each one where to sit. It is customary for the host and hostess to be on opposite ends of the table. Usually the lady guest of honor sits at the immediate right of the host. The gentleman guest of honor sits to the immediate right of the hostess. To avoid confusion or embarrassment, the seating arrangement should be planned before guests arrive.

Brewing good coffee may be an eternal mystery for some people, but it need not be if they will follow these simple suggestions:

1. Be sure your coffeepot is clean. Wash it in hot water and don't skip the soapsuds. Use a thin brush for spouts and tubes. Rinse thoroughly in hot water, then in cold water, and dry carefully.

2. Your coffee must be fresh. Buy a vacuum can which is tightly sealed after use, or grind your own—just enough for your needs at that particular time.

3. Use the correct amount of coffee per cup of water, usually a tablespoonful per cup of water. If you prefer stronger coffee, add coffee to taste accordingly, but don't brew it longer.

4. Keep measurements accurate and consistent. With an automatic coffee maker, all you have to do is turn it on once the cold water and

coffee are added. Some people add a pinch of salt or cocoa to the coffee for a little more "flavor" and "body."

5. For nonautomatic percolators, if you want six or more cups, percolate the coffee for 9 minutes, counting from the time it first begins to percolate. For less than 6 cups, 7 minutes will suffice. If you percolate too long, the coffee will become bitter. When the percolating is finished, remove the coffee grounds compartment promptly, or it will absorb aroma and flavor.

When your salad greens arrive home from the market, examine them and discard the wilted portions. Wash thoroughly with cold running water, and store them promptly in your refrigerator in a covered vegetable crisper or in a refrigerator bag which can be tightly closed.

Try cooking a sprig or two of fresh mint with applesauce. It is delightful with pork, lamb or goose.

Frozen meat thaws at the rate of about 2 hours per pound when left at room temperature. If you are in a hurry for the thawing, put the meat in front of an electric fan, which will reduce the time required by more than half.

If you have prime meat of good quality, a nicely broiled steak is one of the simplest major pleasures of gastronomy. To broil it properly, first preheat the broiler rack and rub it over with fat. For a 2-inch-thick steak, place it on the rack about 3 inches from the source of heat, where the temperature at the meat surface will be about 350 degrees Fahrenheit. When the meat is browned on one side to the degree desired, salt to taste and turn it over by inserting the fork in the fat part of the meat in order to avoid losing meat juices. When the second side is browned properly, salt again and place the steak on a hot platter. If you want the steak rare to medium, broil it 8 to 10 minutes in all if it is about 1 inch thick, or 10 to 15 minutes if it is 1½ inches thick. If you start with solidly frozen meat, the broiling time is approximately doubled.

To remove the brown skin covering from nut meats, cover them with boiling water and let stand about 5 minutes in a covered dish. After draining, the skins can be rubbed off easily. For Brazil nuts, use a small sharp knife.

If you want to reheat biscuits, put them in a wet paper bag, tie it tightly and place it in a moderately hot oven for a few minutes.

To avoid cracked eggs when you're boiling them, let them stay at room temperature for a while after removal from the refrigerator. Puncture the rounded end with a needle before you put the egg in water.

If you have to beat egg whites, use a bowl, not an aluminum pan. The eggs will darken the aluminum.

When several eggs are required for a recipe, it is a good idea to break them separately in a small dish, where they can be checked for freshness. It is annoying, to say the least, if you break several eggs and find that the last one is rotten, thus spoiling the entire batch. It is cheap insurance to proceed one at a time.

In buying fish, allow about ¾ pound per person.

To make fish more flavorful, rub it with lemon juice before you bake, broil or boil it. This also helps to prevent the fish from falling apart and keeps it in good color.

Poking raw fish is a test for freshness. If a dent remains, the fish is not fresh. If the flesh springs back, it is.

If you want to lift the morning pancakes from routine, add a cup of drained, canned, crushed pineapple to a rather thick pancake batter. When they are done, serve hot with plenty of butter and a sprinkle of brown sugar.

If you have an electric knife, use it to cut angel cake, or sponge-cake of any kind. It's much easier.

For a buffet dinner, have two hot dishes, such as Lobster Newburgh* and Beef Stroganoff,* then add cold ham and roast beef and a pastry.

I could give you many more suggestions drawn from a lifetime of cooking, but now it is time for *you* to cook. Remember, it can be a great joy if you are willing to spend the time and take the care required. Don't be discouraged by an occasional setback. Find out what went wrong and try again. The effort will be well worth it.

My most cordial wishes to you, my fellow cooks, for the happiest of times in the kitchen!

EPILOGUE

The Mellon Party for Mrs. Kennedy

EARLY in July 1966, Mrs. Kennedy's secretary called to ask me if I knew a chef I could recommend to handle a special dinner party for Mrs. Kennedy, being given by Mrs. Paul Mellon early in August. I told her I would be very happy to take care of the dinner party myself.

Mrs. Mellon had been a White House guest on a number of occasions, and indeed had planned the flower gardens there. Her hobby is flower-bed design and horticulture. She had also planted herbs in Mrs. Kennedy's garden.

A month before the party, I met her at her New York apartment and we discussed the menu. I was told it was to be an informal affair, with ninety-six people in all, seated at ten tables.

Mrs. Mellon asked me what Mrs. Kennedy liked. Since it was summer, I suggested cold fresh salmon to start, but the five- to six-pound size I wanted was not available, so we settled on rock bass as a first course. The recipe is called rock bass *combaceres*. It is a striped bass garnished with tomatoes and peeled and sliced cucumbers, with sour cream and deviled eggs, all arranged decoratively around the tray. On the side, there would be green sauce St. Vincent, which is made with mayonnaise, spinach, watercress, parsley, chervil and tarragon. All the herbs would be picked from Mrs. Mellon's garden in Osterville on Cape Cod, where the party was to be held.

It was decided that the main dish should be a rack of lamb, roasted with fresh rosemary and sprinkled with parsley, bread crumbs and light garlic, to be served in its own juices, and mint jelly sauce brought on separately. Vegetables would include Champs Elysée potatoes, which are shredded like shoestrings but in short pieces, served with truffles, and sliced string beans with almonds. Salad was Bibb lettuce with French dressing, with Brie cheese on the side.

Dessert, we decided, would be glacé Alexandra, made with vanilla ice cream and crushed macaroons, and fresh peaches poached in heavy syrup, flavored with lemon rind and Grand Marnier and covered with a raspberry sauce. Petits Fours Sec and Demitasse were to end the meal.

I selected the wines with care: a Pouilly Fumé with the fish, Château Margaux for the lamb and Dom Perignon 1959 with the dessert.

My daughter had just arrived from France to visit me. She had just graduated from preparatory school and intended soon to enter the university, where she would study medicine. When I asked if she might accompany me to the party, Mrs. Mellon kindly consented, and invited her to join the guests in dancing. Kathlynn told me later, "Papa, it was the best time I ever had in my life." She also helped me prepare the dinner, peeling potatoes and cutting string beans and assisting with the salad like a veteran in the kitchen.

When I was ready to leave New York for Osterville, the Mellons sent the family plane to La Guardia to take me, thus rescuing me from an airline pilots' strike then in progress. My daughter and an assistant chef flew with me. Our host aboard the plane proved to be Mr. Paul Mellon himself.

At Osterville, preparations for the dinner went well. Discussing the meal with me, Mrs. Mellon said, "René, I'd like you to serve dessert. Mrs. Kennedy still doesn't know you're here, and it will be a nice surprise for her."

When the time came for me to play my small part in the service, I led ten waiters into the flower-decorated dining area. Each of the waiters carried a platter for his table.

My appearance could hardly have surprised Mrs. Kennedy more. "Oh, René," she exclaimed, "it's not true! I knew there was something familiar about the dinner," she went on, "but I didn't know why. And now I do know—it was your cooking! Please come to see me tomorrow morning."

I did visit her the following morning, at her home in Hyannisport, and we talked for a half hour or so. She asked me about my work and how I was getting along, and as usual was completely gracious and charming.

The Mellon party was the last occasion I had to serve Mrs. Kennedy and members of her family and friends. It was a memorable postscript to an association which has been the greatest honor and privilege of my life.

INDEX